Mythmaking
on
Madison
Avenue

How Advertisers
Apply The Power Of
Myth & Symbolism To
Create Leadership
Brands

Sal Randazzo

PROBUS PUBLISHING COMPANY
Chicago, Illinois
Cambridge, England

© 1993, Sal Randazzo

ALL RIGHTS RESERVED. No part of this publication may be reproduced, stored in a retrieval system, or transmitted by any means, electronic, mechanical, photocopying, recording, or otherwise, without the prior written permission of the publisher and the copyright holder.

This publication is designed to provide accurate and authoritative information in regard to the subject matter covered. It is sold with the understanding that the publisher is not engaged in rendering legal, accounting or other professional service.

Authorization to photocopy items for internal or personal use, or the internal or personal use of specific clients, is granted by PROBUS PUBLISHING COMPANY, provided that the US$7.00 per page fee is paid directly to Copyright Clearance Center, 27 Congress Street, Salem MA 01970, USA; Phone: 1-508-744-3350. For those organizations that have been granted a photocopy license by CCC, a separate system of payment has been arranged. The fee code for users of the Transactional Reporting Service is: 1-55738-427-4/93/$0.00 + $7.00.

ISBN 1-55738-427-4

Printed in the United States of America

BB

1 2 3 4 5 6 7 8 9 0

To Rea and our three wonderful sons, Perry, Rudy and Ally.

Contents

• • • • • • • • • • •

Foreword vii
Preface ix
Acknowledgements xiii

Introduction 1

Part I   **A New Perspective** **3**

Chapter 1   The Brand 5

Chapter 2   The Mythological Realm 28

Part II   **Mythologies** **52**

Chapter 3   Female Mythologies 55

Chapter 4   Male Mythologies 85

Chapter 5   Brand Mythologies 121

Part III   **Building and Maintaining Brand Mythologies** **159**

Chapter 6   Building Your Brand's Mythology: Information,
             Insight, and Ideas 163

Chapter 7   Building Your Brand's Mythology: Positioning,
             Message, and Execution 195

Chapter 8   Maintaining Your Brand's Mythology 232

             References 269

             Index 275

Foreword
• • • • • • • • • •

During the feeding frenzy for mergers and acquisitions that occurred in the early 1980s, the worth of brands was a subject often discussed and debated. Did Philip Morris pay too much for General Foods? After all, it was a company with assets consisting largely of brands such as Maxwell House Coffee, Jello, and Post Raisin Bran. Did Kraft, with its great brand names, sell too cheaply? How could you evaluate what a brand was worth? And who could begin to explain exactly why a brand was valuable in the first place?

In order to measure the power of a brand you have to go to the source of its strength. And that is what Sal Randazzo has done in *Mythmaking on Madison Avenue: How Advertisers Apply the Power of Myth and Symbolism to Create Leadership Brands.* He starts with the theory that brands are important to our unconscious, "not our conscious," selves. A product may sell because of its logical appeal to our conscious minds, but a brand—as opposed to an individual product—builds emotionally over time, and enters our unconscious, not via logic, but on a tide of emotions. And there it helps fill a vacuum that longs to be occupied by myths.

The author points out that myths have, since the dawn of time, come from many different sources; from medicine men, story tellers, soothsayers, and today in America from Hollywood and advertising.

Mythmaking on Madison Avenue contains several different definitions of a "myth," the simplest being "dressed up reality." As the book unfolds, one realizes that this definition, while accurate, is too narrow. Merely dressing up reality doth not a myth make. One needs to be in touch with, and understand, many of the feelings that emanate from the unconscious. Randazzo points out that the successful mythmaker *is* in touch, whether he or she be writing for MGM or GM.

For the advertising writer who, like myself, is constantly looking to "open up" his or her instincts and feelings in order to see new ideas, this book will provide a unique and exciting mind-expander. For the advertising account person who is asked to judge brand building ideas, Randazzo's insights should prove invaluable.

Finally, for the director of marketing who is tempted to put most of his or her marketing dollars into short-term solutions such as promotions and product-based, or urge-to-action, advertising. *Mythmaking on Madison Avenue* provides a fresh look at exactly why and how the umbrella of a brand can add pull to the logic of product, whether that logic be a superior product formula, convenience, or price-off "for a short time only."

Beyond the direct practitioners and users of advertising probably lies a whole other audience for this book, as well: the armchair students of advertising. Who are they? If you are involved with advertising in any way, you know them as well as I do. They are everyone everywhere. They are your wife, your brother-in-law, your dentist, and the stranger at the party who asks you what you do for a living. People just cannot be exposed to thousands of advertising impressions weekly without forming opinions about what they see and hear. *Mythmaking on Madison Avenue* will provide all of them with some fascinating new insights.

William M. Backer
Vice-Chairman and Executive Creative Director
Backer Spielvogel Bates, Worldwide
Author of *The Care and Feeding of Ideas*

Preface

●●●●●●●●●●

The idea for this book grew out of a confluence of interests and vocations: advertising, mythology, and psychology. I have worked as an advertising researcher for 14 years. From the beginning, the connection between advertising and mythology seemed fairly obvious to me. Myths are more than entertaining little stories about gods, goddesses, and heroic characters. The universality of myths, the fact that the same myths recur across time and many different cultures, suggests that they originate from somewhere inside of us. Psychoanalyst Carl Jung said that myths, like dreams, are really projections that emanate from the soul or unconscious psyche. Myths represent humanity's collective dreams, instinctive yearnings, feelings, and patterns of thinking that seem to be hard-wired in humans and that function somewhat like instincts to shape our behavior.

In a similar sense, brands functions as projection holders. Advertisers sell products by mythologizing them, by wrapping them in our dreams and fantasies. Advertising often mirrors our cultural mythologies, the same values and sensibilities that shape our lives and our culture. Advertising is a form of mythmaking—a storied form of communication. It tries to communicate information about products and at the same time tries to make the communication vehicle more entertaining. Products are more appealing when they come wrapped in mythical worlds and embodied by heroic characters.

I began presenting this idea in articles, presentations, and lectures,

X

and the response by people both inside and outside the advertising community was overwhelmingly positive and enthusiastic. People were fascinated by the connection between the images and ideas that are found throughout various world mythologies and advertising. The same universal (archetypal) images that provide the basis for many of our cultural mythologies are also the foundation for many images used in advertising. For example, the universal image of a Great Mother that occurs in all cultural mythologies and that represents the nurturing instinct in all of us also serves as the foundation embodied by advertising personae such as Betty Crocker. In the same way, political advertisers "package" and "advertise" male presidential candidates as embodiments of the Great Father.

My layperson's interest in mythology flourished through the years. Reading mythology helps to make my daily hour-long commute to and from New York City much more enjoyable. And I especially enjoy reading myths to my children. Even in a video game world, the classical myths have the power to hold children in rapt attention.

But my interest in mythology goes beyond fun and entertainment. My fascination with myths involves a deeper emotional need. Just as the storylines of ancient myths describe universal experiences (birth, sibling rivalries, rites of passage through life) which help to guide us through life's journey, I have taken comfort in the many parallels between my own life and the characters in Greek mythology. For example, in Homer's epic poem, *The Odyssey,* Telemachus conducts a father quest for his long-absent father, Odysseus. Odysseus has been away for 20 years fighting in the Trojan War. Many of the town people have given his father up for dead, and a group of unwanted suitors have begun hanging around his mother's house, trying to convince Penelope to marry. Telemachus, a teenager who has grown up without a father, watches his mother being pestered and his inheritance dwindle, but he doesn't know how to deal with the malingerers. Finally, the goddess Athena intervenes and orders Telemachus to find his father. I too, grew up without a father in New York's tough lower east side neighborhood. My mother worked hard to try to raise two sons by herself. By the time my brother and I got to be teenagers, my mother had her hands full. Unable to cope, she literally told me: Go find your father. I did, in a bar, in the Bronx. It was moment I will never forget, full of mixed emotions. I had no idea then, that in searching out my father, I was reenacting a universal mythical theme from many different world mythologies.

The other source of my fascination with mythology comes from my interest in psychology. There is an important connection between mythology and psychology. Jung revealed the connection between myth and the unconscious psyche in his work with psychiatric patients, who expressed archaic images and patterns of thinking that could not be explained by their personal histories. Jung found the same or similar images in mythology, alchemy, and other ancient, mythopoeic (soulfelt) sources. I was especially drawn to Jung's work because some of his experiences paralleled mine. Jung's work is full of his "confrontations with the unconscious psyche," which usually took the form of visions or apparitions. Jung had direct confrontations with images and entities that emanated from his unconscious psyche, just as I did.

Sigmund Freud discovered the unconscious component of the human psyche that eludes our control. Indeed, the unconscious and subconscious often control our behavior from behind the scenes. Most people have no idea that there is literally a whole other world operating inside of us. It is the world we go to in our dreams. But it is also possible to enter this strange netherworld while we are awake, as Jung did. It is a mythological realm, a strange world full of archetypal beings, demons, and all manner of strange entities. Jung was drawn to this inner world because he realized that the unconscious psyche held the key to understanding not only myths but the human soul. The unconscious psyche is both the source from which mythology springs and the wellspring of creativity—art, poetry, and music. Jung decided that the only way to really understand the unconscious psyche was to enter this world, knowing full well the dangers. The images confronted in the unconscious psyche, with its power to fascinate and compel, are the same images that fatally confused his psychiatric patients. Most western Europeans have no stomach for direct encounters with the unconscious psyche. There are ways (meditation, breathing techniques, or drugs) to initiate a direct confrontation with the unconscious psyche. Sometimes a period of intense crisis triggers a confrontation with the unconscious psyche so that it erupts in our normal waking consciousness as a vision or prescient experience.

For uninitiated people this comes as a tremendous shock. Modern Europeans and Americans do not believe in spirits or demons. But the unconscious psyche can send up all kinds of strange beings, and if the uninitiated, nonbeliever encounters one of these ghostly inhabitants of the netherworld, it can be a spooky, frightening experience that causes panic, a feeling of losing one's mind.

In my own limited confrontations with the unconscious psyche, I have found these experiences fascinating, but I indeed do not have the stomach for them. I say my prayers and sleep with a night light. And when my children come to me in the night afraid of "slimy green monsters under the bed," I tell them that I know exactly how they feel.

● ● ●
Nota Bene

My intent in writing this book is to help advertisers understand how to leverage the power of myth and symbols to build and maintain brands. Advertising is not simply in the business of "selling soap." The thesis of this book is that advertising is an important part of our culture, an enormously powerful medium that shapes our values and sensibilities, both individually and culturally. With this enormous power comes an enormous responsibility. Speaking from the agency side, it is high time that advertising agencies recognize the power they wield in our culture and take responsibility for their actions.

Helping our clients build brands and businesses is a priority for advertising agencies, as is running a profitable business. But at the same time advertisers have a responsibility that goes beyond selling and helping our, clients make money. We have a responsibility to our children, our planet, and humanity to use the power of advertising wisely.

Sal Randazzo

Acknowledgements

• •

My wife Rea and sons Perry, Rudy and Ally, whose love and support made this work possible. My mother, Antoinette Perro, whose love and hard work provided a home for my brother and me. My father, Santo Randazzo, who loved us after all. My brother, Steven Randazzo, who somehow always managed to make us laugh in spite of it all.

The Perros, my wonderful extended family who provided so much love and happiness. Dominic Perro ("Uncle Dom") who, early on, helped me to discover the joy of reading and learning. Rose Beach ("Grandma Rosie") who graciously helped out on the homefront.

Friends and colleagues, who in various ways, supported or encouraged this project: Joseph Plummer, William Backer, Theodore D'Amico, Randy Ringer, Douglas Muzzio, Rita Rochlen, Ronald Lawrence, Michael Aquilante, Maurice Eidelsberg, Phyliss Tozzi, Manuel Morales, Ursula Wolff, John Fischetti, Jonathon Thompson, Steve Fenton, Rosalyn Arnstein, Allan Baldinger, Michael Naples, the staff of the Pequannock Township Library.

Special thanks to DMB&B Worldwide Communications for its support and encouragement.

Special thanks to Jim McNeil, Kevin Thornton, Lynn Brown (Brown Editorial Services) and all the people at Probus Publishing who enthusiastically supported this project.

Introduction
● ● ● ● ● ● ● ● ● ● ● ● ● ●

Albert Lasker, one of the pioneers of advertising, defined advertising as "salesmanship in print" (Bovee and Arens, 1986). Bovee and Arens, in their excellent advertising textbook, provide a more thorough definition: "Advertising effectively blends the behavioral sciences (anthropology, sociology, psychology) with the communicating arts (writing, drama, graphics, photography, and so on.) to motivate, modify, or reinforce consumer perceptions, beliefs, attitudes, and behavior" (Bovee and Arens, 1986 p.5).

But my favorite definition of advertising is the one used by the McCann Erickson Advertising Agency: "Truth well told." I, too, believe that effective advertising is founded on truths or insights that give the advertising a strategic focus.

However, the power of advertising goes beyond its ability to sell and persuade. The unique power of advertising lies in its ability to build and maintain successful, enduring brands by creating perceptual entities that reflect the consumer's values, dreams, and fantasies. Advertising turns products into brands by mythologizing them—by humanizing them and giving them distinct identities, personalities, and sensibilities that reflect our own. In some sense, advertising brands have, in our consumption-driven society, come to serve a similar function as the ancient Greeks' pantheon of gods. They function as projection holders wherein we project our dreams, fears, and fantasies.

It has often been said that Madison Avenue is in the business of selling dreams. Advertisers have discovered a powerful truth: Dreams sell. Advertisers have learned that they can make their sales pitch more effective if they wrap their products in our dreams and fantasies. There are people in and around advertising (like myself) who spend a good deal of their time trying to understand our dreams—not our individual, idiosyncratic dreams, but our collective dreams, America's dreams, the world's dreams. And this is the realm of mythology.

Myths and dreams come from the same place (the unconscious psyche). Myths are literally the stuff of dreams—humanity's dreams. Like Hollywood, Madison Avenue is in the business of mythmaking, of creating and perpetuating the myths that reflect and shape our values, sensibilities, and lifestyles.

1

Part I
• • • • • • • • • •

A New Perspective

The objective of Part I is twofold: to introduce you to a unique way of thinking about and understanding brands, and advertising's unique role in building and maintaining brands; and to provide a basic understanding of mythology, mytho-symbolic imagery, and the unconscious psyche from which they spring. Chapters 1 (The Brand) and 2 (The Mythological Realm) will serve as foundation for Parts II, and III.

Chapter 1 (The Brand) begins by underscoring the fact that a brand is not simply a product, but also a perceptual entity that exists in psychological space — in the consumer's mind. What we see on the supermarket shelf (or wherever) is not the brand, but rather its physical aspect: the product and packaging. The product and packaging is for the most part unchanging. But a brand also has a psychic aspect, which is dynamic and malleable. Advertising is the vehicle that allows us to access the consumer's mind wherein we can establish a perceptual brand space. You can use advertising to fill this perceptual brand space, to create a unique perceptual inventory of imagery, symbolism, feelings, and associations that the consumer will ultimately come to associate with your brand. You can use advertising to create mythical worlds with mythical characters that work to engage and entertain the consumer and at the same time, to communicate important product and at the same time emotional benefits. In short, you can use advertising to create a brand mythology.

In Chapter 2, (The Mythological Realm) we shift gears and move into a subject matter that is radically different than what most advertising and marketing people might expect from a book about advertising. The purpose of Chapter 2 is to provide a basic understanding of mythology and the unconscious psyche—the instinctual, feeling aspect of human psyche from which mythologies spring. The focus is on helping the uninitiated develop a deeper understanding of the unconscious psyche with its power to compel and fascinate. An exploration of the mysterious force we called the unconscious psyche is inherently strange, and the advertising practitioner may be tempted to gloss over it "to get down to business." But in my lectures and presentations on the material covered in this book, I found that a deeper understanding of the unconscious psyche is crucial to understanding how advertising can leverage the power of mythology and mytho-symbolic imagery to create strong, enduring brands. For example, when I speak of how we can use the power of an archetypal image to build a strong brand, I find that most people don't really understand what I'm talking about. Where does this power come from? By taking the reader inside the unconscious psyche, I hope to convey a sense of the power of the unconscious psyche and of the archetypal, mytho-symbolic images that spring from it.

Chapter 1
• • • • • • • • • •

The Brand

The chapter begins by emphasizing the fact that a brand is more than a product—that a brand exists as a perceptual entity in the consumer's mind. Manufacturers who are used to thinking in terms of a physical product must begin to think in terms of a brand that has both a physical dimension and a psychic dimension. The chapter next defines *brandness* in terms of a number of core elements that together comprise what we perceive as an advertising brand.

> If a man writes a better book, preaches a better sermon, or makes a better mousetrap than his neighbor, tho' he build his house in the woods, the world will make a beaten path to his door .
>
> (Ralph Waldo Emerson,
> *The Oxford Dictionary of Quotations*)

Emerson's "build a better mousetrap" quotation has been a perennial, if overused, favorite among manufacturers and entrepreneurs. Like a lot of powerful ideas, it is simple : If we create a superior product, we won't have to go looking for customers, they will seek us out. Because manufacturers and entrepreneurs dedicate much of their time to creating, manufacturing, or improving "mousetraps," Emerson's idea has become almost an article of faith. Of course it is exactly what they would like to believe, but unfortunately, with all due respect to Mr. Emerson, in today's highly competitive, highly communicative, high-tech marketing environment, building a better mousetrap is no longer enough.

Product parity is rampant. Take the beer category, for example. No sooner did the Miller Brewing Company successfully introduce Miller Lite than every other major brewer quickly followed suit by introducing its own version of a light beer.

In a world of instant mass communications, there are no secrets. The technology needed to create a light beer, a low-fat ice cream, or a healthy grain cereal is available to all. Manufacturers cannot count solely on product improvements or product quality to guarantee greater market share. They must not let themselves fall prey to "mousetrap myopia" (a serious condition that often leads to stumbling in the marketplace). To compete successfully, manufacturers must learn to look beyond the physical product to the brand.

● ● ●
Defining the Brand

A brand is more than a product; it's both a *physical* and a *perceptual* entity. (See Figure 1.1) The physical aspect of a brand (its product and packaging) can be found sitting on the supermarket shelf (or wherever). It is mostly static and finite. However, the perceptual aspect of a brand exists in psychological space—in the consumer's mind. It is dynamic and malleable.

In order to understand the concept of branding, we need to understand both its physical and its psychic aspects.

The Product Aspect of a Brand

Unbranded, a product is a thing—a commodity, a bag of coffee, or a can of soup. For most product categories, the consumer's perceptions of a generic, unbranded product tend to be dominated by the product's thingness, its physical attributes and benefits, and/or how the product is used. For example, when consumers think of soup, they think of its attributes and benefits: something warm and nourishing. When consumers think of milk, they think of the most common usage: something for babies or children.

On the other hand, although it is true that the consumer generally perceives the generic, unbranded product as a physical entity, a thing, most products (unless they are entirely new product categories), also have a latent psychic aspect, a *latent product mythology.* Awareness of a product's existing latent mythology varies from product to product and from consumer to consumer. However, if consumers have any awareness of the product mythology, it is generally not top of mind—it is latent. It exists below the consumer's threshold of awareness.

The latent product mythology goes beyond the product's physical at-tributes/benefits and usage. This mythology includes all of the perceptions, beliefs, experiences and feelings that are associated with that product. The latent product mythology is derived from the consumer's experiences with the generic product, as well as the history, facts and folklore surrounding it —not unlike what Leo Burnett often referred to as the "inherent drama in

● ●

Figure 1.1

A Brand is More than a Product

Product
- a thing
- physical attributes and benefits

Quality ingredients
Delicious Nourishing

Brand
- perceptual entity
- physical attributes & benefits

"The halo of psychologial meanings,
the associations of feelings", etc.

Quality Ingredients
Delicious Nourishing
Campbell Soup Kids
"Mother Love"
Children
Nurturance
Goodness
Caring
Warmth
Norman Rockwell's
Americana

● ●

every product." It often provides important insights about the consumer's perceptions of the product as well their motivations for using it. The latent product mythology is important because, as we will see later on, it is often the basis for building and maintaining a strong enduring *brand mythology*.

It is worth noting that there are a few product categories where the product mythology is not latent—it is top of mind. For example, champagne and perfume are product categories that tend to be dominated by their product *mythologies*. When the consumers buy a product like perfume or champagne, they are buying an appealing fantasy as much as a product.

The Psychic Content of a Brand

A brand exists in psychological space, in the consumer's mind. It is a perceptual entity with a definite psychic content that is malleable and dynamic. Advertising is the vehicle that allows us to access the consumer;'s mind, to create a perceptual inventory of imagery, symbols, and feelings that come to define the perceptual entity we call a brand. Within this perceptual brand space we can create appealing mythical worlds and characters that, through advertising, become associated with our product, and that ultimately come to define our brand. The Marlboro Man is a great example of a mythical brand character that has come to define the Marlboro brand.

• •
"Within this perceptual brand space we can create appealing mythical worlds and characters which, through advertising become associated with our product."
• •

Advertisers can also use this perceptual brand space as a mirror which reflects the lifestyle and values of our intended consumer. A brand can function as a projection holder into which the advertiser projects the consumer's values and sensibilities, or a badge, a way of expressing and reinforcing our personal and cultural identities. Every brand has its own *brand mythology* with its own unique perceptual inventory of images, symbols, feelings and associations.

Brand Mythology

The brand mythology is what the brand stands for in the consumer's mind. It is generally a mix of imagery, symbols, feelings and values which come out of the brand's unique perceptual inventory, and which collectively define

Figure 1.2

Latent Product Mythology Vs. Brand Mythology

Product
(A Physical Entity)

(Top of Mind)
Physical product

- Attributes
- Benefits
- Packaging and label

(Not Top of Mind)
Latent Product Mythology

- Beliefs, perceptions and feelings associated with the generic product
- Derived from consumer's experiences with the generic product, as well as the history, facts, folklore surrounding it

Brand
(A Perceptual Entity)

(Top of Mind)
Brand Mythology

- What the brand stands for in the consumer's mind
- The brand's unique perceptual inventory of imagery, symbolism, feelings, and associations
- Includes the physical product at tributes and benefits
- The brand mythology is created and communicated mostly through advertising
- The brand mythology is often drawn from the latent product mythology

the brand in the consumer's mind. For example, the top-of-mind association most consumers have with Marlboro cigarettes is the Marlboro cowboy and the American west. When asked to think about it further, they may in turn associate these images with the great outdoors, the American frontier, rugged individualism, a spirit of freedom, etc.

The Marlboro brand mythology (like all brand mythologies) comes out of the brand's unique perceptual inventory. It is communicated through the combined effects of advertising, packaging, labels, logos, and the consumer's experiences with the product. However, advertising plays a key role in creating and communicating the brand mythology. Advertising functions as a storied form of communication, a narrative fiction that uses fictitious character, places, situations, and so on, to engage and entertain the consumer, communicate the brand's attributes and benefits (both physical and emotional), and perceptually position the brand in the consumer's mind. Advertising allows us to to access the consumer's mind, wherein we can create appealing mythical worlds and characters. Every image, symbol, feeling, and association created and communicated through advertising becomes part of the brand's perceptual inventory. Every commercial and advertisement should be thought of as an individual advertising mythology and should be carefully considered because it will ultimately affect the brand's overall mythology, image, and personality.

Latent Product Mythology vs. Brand Mythology

It is important to understand the distinction between the brand mythology and the latent product mythology (see Figure 1.2). The brand mythology is top of mind whereas the latent product mythology is not. The consumer's perceptions of the generic product center around the physical product (its thingness), and consumers are generally not aware of the latent mythology which underlies the product. The latent product mythology comes out of the consumer's experiences with the product, but also the history, facts, folklore and beliefs surrounding the product. The latent product mythology often plays a key role in building brand mythologies. Information, insights and ideas which come out of the latent product mythology are often used in advertising and eventually become part of the brand mythology. For example, when Dannon Yogurt was introduced into the U.S., the advertiser used advertising to create a brand mythology which focused on the health benefits of yogurt—the fact that some people (in Soviet Georgia) who eat yogurt live longer and stay healthier. The idea for this brand mythology comes right out of the latent product mythology, such as, the facts, folklore, beliefs, etc., surrounding yogurt. (Eastern European history and folklore has it that people who eat a lot of yogurt live well past one hundred years old.)

• • •
The Brand Concept

Brand concept is a term used to cover a number of disparate, core elements that collectively define the brand. The brand concept is divided into product components (product attributes and product benefits), and perceptual components (user image, emotional/psychological benefits, brand soul, brand personality, brand image, and brand positioning). Table 1.1 summarizes the components of the brand concept. Table 1.2 provides a hypothetical example of the brand concept.

Brand Concept: Product Components
Product/Service Attributes

The brand's product (or service) *attributes* are the specific product/service qualities that are usually derived from the manufacturing process: ingredients, pricing, packaging, usage, heritage, or, in the case of service attributes, faster, more efficient, and so on. Some examples of product attributes are

- "Contains Stannous Fluoride"
- "Premixed"
- "All Natural"
- "Variable Conditioning Formula"

Ideally, the product/service attributes that distinguish one brand from another should be unique to that brand, and they should lead to a direct product/service benefit that is both credible and motivating.

However, in many product categories the products and services are similar and it's difficult to find unique, differentiating product attributes.

• •

"The brand's product (or service) attributes are the specific product/service qualities that are usually derived from the manufacturing process."

• •

There are several strategies that the advertising practitioner can use to compensate for the lack of a unique product service attribute.

Using Generic Product Attributes Preemptively. Brands can adopt generic product/service attributes and use them preemptively in their advertising. Eventually, the generic product attributes come to be uniquely associated with the brand. For example, Folger's Coffee boasts that it is a richer tasting

• •

Table 1.1

Brand Concept

Product Components:

Product/Service Attributes   Qualities pertaining to the product: Ingredients, pricing, packaging, usage, heritage; or service: bigger, faster, more efficient.

Product Benefits   The tangible product/service based benefits which the consumer will derive from using the product or service.

Perceptual Components:

User Image   The type of person we wish to portray as using the brand.

Emotional Benefits   The feelings and perceptions associated with using the brand.

Brand Soul   The core value(s) that define the brand—its spiritual center.

Brand Image   What the brand stands for in the consumer's mind. The brand image is a distillation of both product and perceptual components.

Brand Personality   What brand would be like if it were a person.

Brand Positioning   How the brand is positioned, both in the marketplace and in the consumer's mind.

• •

• •

Table 1.2

Hypothetical Brand Concept: Budweiser Beer

Product Components:

Product/Service Attributes	Beechwood aging, Budweiser heritage/ commited to quality
Product Benefits	Crisp, clean taste; quality

Perceptual Components:

User Image	Male, Masculine, Everyman.
Emotional Benefits	Male Identity, Male Bonding, Patriotism.
Brand Soul	Maleness.
Brand Image	A quality beer for the all-American Male.
Brand Personality	Masculine, hard working, self-assured.
Brand Positioning	Marketplace: Premium beer; consumer's mind: A premium, manly beer for the average Joe.

• •

coffee because its coffee beans are "mountain grown." Now it may be that other brands of coffee also use beans that are mountain grown, but Folger's has preemptively used this product attribute to support its promise of a richer tasting coffee, and at the same time to differentiate the Folger's brand from the competition. Mountain grown coffee beans may not be unique to Folger's, but by using this product attribute preemptively, "mountain grown coffee beans" have become uniquely associated with the Folger's brand.

Ad Hoc Product/Service Attributes. Some product attributes sound like they were concocted on Madison Avenue rather than at the manufacturing plant. In fact, marketers often develop products or reformulate products to fill a consumer need. For example, marketers might discover that women's hair conditioning needs vary, and the marketers might therefore develop a hair conditioner with an attribute that addresses this need: "a variable conditioning formula" that can handle all of women's conditioning needs. In other words, it is possible to identify an important consumer need and then create or reformulate a product with a product attribute that can satisfy that need.

Mythologized Attributes. We can use advertising to mythologize product attributes just as advertising can be used to mythologize products. Through mythologization, a generic product attribute can be presented in a way that is unique, compelling, and memorable.

For example, Stroh's Brewery describes its beers as "fire brewed." Advertisers don't know what fire brewed means, and no one has yet found a beer drinker who knows what fire brewed means. Presumably, the term refers to the fact that Stroh's beers are pasteurized. It really doesn't matter. The point is that the idea of a "fire brewed beer" appeals to beer drinkers and seems to add to the Stroh's mystique. It's a unique, beery way of saying that Stroh's beer is pasteurized. Stroh's has taken a generic product attribute (pasteurization), and made it unique and ownable by mythologizing it, by describing it in a way that is unique, compelling, and memorable.

Product/Service Benefits

Product benefits offer the consumer a tangible, product-based reason to use the product. The benefits tell consumers how they will benefit from using the product. The product benefits should be credible and motivating. The following differentiates attributes from benefits:

Attributes	Benefits
"Beechwood Aging"	Great Taste
"Contains Stannous Fluoride"	Fewer Cavities
"Variable Conditioning Formula"	Manageable Hair

Product benefits are really promises or claimed benefits, sometimes referred to as "reasons why." Consumers are generally skeptical of advertising claims and only half believe them. Consumers need a reason to believe that there is some basis for the product benefits claimed in the advertising. Product attributes provide the necessary claim substantiation. Product attributes make the claimed benefits more credible by giving the consumer a tangible reason to believe. For example, "beechwood aging" gives the consumer a reason to believe that Budweiser is a great-tasting beer.

The product benefits together with the supporting product attributes form the *selling proposition*. Rosser Reeves developed the concept of the "unique selling proposition" (USP) at Ted Bates Advertising in the 1940s. According to Reeves, every ad has to offer a unique selling proposition that contains a product benefit that is important to the consumer (Reeves, 1961).

Brand Concept: Perceptual Components

User Image

The *user image* is the description of the type of person advertisers wish to portray as using their product. User imagery is important because it can be used to create an affiliation between the brand and the consumer. In other words, the consumer should look at the advertising and say to himself or herself, "That person is a lot like me or a lot like the kind of person I would like to be. Maybe I should be using that brand."

The user image created by advertising can be either a realized user or an idealized (mythologized) user image.

Realized User Image	An image that is consistent with the user's self-image, values, and lifestyle.
Mythologized User Image	An image that reflects the type of person the consumer would like to be. For example, diet soft drink commercials invariably depict thin, beautiful women using their product. By repeatedly showing thin, beautiful women drinking diet soft drinks, the advertiser hopes to create the perception that people who use diet soft drinks stay thin and beautiful. It may be that most people who use diet soft drinks are actually overweight and ordinary. The idealized user image presented in diet soft drink commercials represents the kind of person consumers would like to be.

The perceptions created (or myths perpetuated) by advertising may have nothing to do with behavioral reality. Advertising creates its own reality. In advertising, what is *perceived* in the consumer's mind is the most important reality.

Emotional/Psychological Benefits

In addition to benefits that are derived from the product's physical attributes, advertising can also be used to communicate important emotional and psychological benefits. The emotional/psychological benefits are the perceived feelings associated with using a product. The feelings and perceptions may come from the consumer's experiences with the product, or they may be created by advertising.

Often there is some existing, latent association between specific feelings/perceptions and product usage. Advertising is used to reinforce that association. For example, many consumers may associate soup with warm, nurturing, caring feelings, but this association may be subliminal, not top of mind. Campbell's Soup advertising brings those feelings to mind and reinforces the association between soup and feelings of caring and nurturing.

On the other hand, advertising can also work to associate feelings and perceptions with a product/brand that would not ordinarily come out of the consumer's experiences with that product/brand. For example, Miller Genuine Draft advertising associates Miller Genuine Draft with a sense of "hipness" that goes beyond the physical product. Without the advertising, the consumer would probably not associate hipness with drinking Miller Genuine Draft.

In forging this association, the advertising practitioner must carefully choose emotional benefits that are both appropriate and credible. Advertisers can usually infer from the brand's mythology or the product's existing latent mythology which emotions would most likely be appropriate and credible.

Unlike the product benefits that are derived from the product's physical attributes, the emotional/psychological benefits are created or reinforced in the consumer's mind. By repeatedly associating the brand with certain emotional/psychological benefits, advertising creates or reinforces a connection/association between brand usage and those emotional/psychological benefits.

The following are some familiar, though unspoken, examples:

"If you drive this car, you will feel successful."

"If you use this deodorant, you will feel more feminine."

"If you serve this cake mix, your family will feel loved."

Through advertising, the consumer learns to associate the product with its claimed emotional/psychological benefits. Learning theorists call this type of identification of two concepts *associative learning.* And in fact, much of what people learn is learned in this fashion, by repeatedly associating two previously unrelated stimuli.

Like the product benefits, the emotional/psychological benefits are important because they are used to motivate consumers. Such benefits provide basic human needs (the need for love, power, self-esteem, and so on), and are therefore, inherently powerful motivators. By associating these emotional/psychological benefits with product usage, the powerful drives to fulfill these basic human needs can be used to motivate consumers.

Brand Soul

The notion that a brand has a soul has been around for some time. The soul of a brand can be thought of as the *brand essence.* The brand's soul is its spiritual center, the core value(s) that defines the brand and permeates all other aspects of the brand. The brand's overall identity/image and person- ality must be consistent with the soul of the brand.

In *The Strategy of Desire,* the Viennese psychologist Ernest Dichter devotes an entire chapter to "The Soul of Things." According to Dichter, the products an individual possesses often influence the reactions of other people toward the individual in specific ways. Inanimate objects thus possess a definite psychic content, a "soul" that plays a dynamic, emotional role in the daily lives of individuals within the context of their social value system (Dichter, 1960).

Dichter touches on the powerful emotional bond between human beings and the things they possess:

> Any kind of possession really functions, in a sense, as an extension of our personal power. Therefore, it serves to make us feel stronger and compensates to a certain extent for our inferiority feeling toward the world that threatens us . . . We cling to them as tangible expressions of our anchorage, for they help give us a feeling that our basis of existence is more than the narrow scaffold of our naked self. When you watch a small child cling to a piece of cloth or a doll with all its power you may begin to understand the power of ownership (Dichter, 1960).

Brand Personality

A brand's *personality* derives from many factors: packaging, logos, and advertising are just a few. Advertising—more specifically, the user image are often the primary contributors to a brand personality. Brand personality is the personification of a product: what the product would be like if it were a person.

For example, if you ask consumers what Campbell's Soup would be like if it were a person, their response is invariably something such as

> It's a she . . . a mom with two or three children. . . . She's a den
> mother for the Scouts, involved in school functions. She drives a
> station wagon or one of those minivans . . . and the mom and kids
> are on their way to a Little League game.

In short, consumers perceive Campbell's as "the all-American Mom": warm, caring, and nurturing.

Brand personality is a concept that is often associated with, and sometimes confused with, brand identity/image. The two are related, but different. A brand's personality is only one aspect of a brand's overall identity or image. In the same way that a person's personality is only one aspect of the person's overall identity (albeit an important aspect).

The idea of personifying a product may seem a bit strange at first, but consumers can often go on to describe a brand's personality in amazing detail. The consumer's ability to readily anthropomorphize brands suggests that they generally do not simply perceive brands as products, but rather as identities with distinct personalities. Personality perceptions probably exist subliminally (below the level of awareness), but they are nonetheless very important, because they help to establish a distinct brand identity, which differentiates the brand in the consumer's mind.

The personification of a brand humanizes and personalizes the product, which makes it easier for the consumer to develop an emotional bond with the product. Consumers come to know Campbell's Soup as they would a friend. Creating an emotional bond between the consumer and the brand distinguishes the brand from other brands, establishes a stronger presence in the consumer's mind, and helps to build brand loyalty.

Brand Image

A brand's image is a distillation of many factors: advertising, packaging, labels, product experiences, logos, and so on.

David Ogilvy popularized the concept of brand image in *The Confessions of an Advertising Man*. Ogilvy emphasized the importance of the "long view" in building and maintaining a positive brand image: "Every advertisement should be thought of as a contribution to the complex symbol which is the brand image" (Ogilvy, 1966).

The brand image contains both product components and perceptual components. For example, the overall brand image of Campbell's soup might be: a quality product, a trusted brand name which I associate with feelings of wholesomeness, mom, children, and Americana. Brand image is crucial in building and maintaining strong enduring brands. (The terms "brand image" and "brand identity" are used interchangeably.) Advertising plays a critical role in helping to shape a brand's identity. Advertisers are increasingly coming to understand the importance of a brand's identity. Without an identity, a product would simply be a product rather than a distinct brand. Without a brand identity, Campbell's Soup would not be a brand, it would simply be perceived as a product: soup. The imagery, perceptions, and feelings associated with Campbell's are what give Campbell's Soup its unique "warm, fuzzy" character or identity.

The Importance of Creating an Appropriate Brand Identity and Personality.

Clearly, a well-established brand identity and personality that appeals to the target consumer (the person advertisers want to use the product) can be valuable assets. The brand identity and personality must appeal to the target consumer. The brand identity and personality should either represent its target consumers—their values, lifestyles, and sensibilities—or what they would like these factors to be. A brand identity and personality that do not appeal to our target consumer at best do nothing for the brand. At worst, they can become liabilities, and turn consumers away. For example, during the 1960s, Bill Berbach's now famous advertising campaign for the Volkswagon Beetle established the memorable Beetle as "the" counterculture car. The advertising helped to create a brand image and personality with a reverse snob appeal—a utilitarian, humble car for the masses. The Beetle's image and personality were in synch with the values and sensibilities of the counterculture, and it was a huge marketing success. Then, in the 1970s, Volkswagon introduced the Rabbit, which, in terms of engineering, was a car ahead of its time. The Rabbit was basically the same size as the Beetle, but it had more space and power as well as other handling refinements. The car was marketed as a technological marvel, but it was a dismal failure. Volkswagon offered consumers a better car, but it failed to create an appropriate, appealing image and personality.

When the projected brand identity and personality are inconsistent with the way consumers see themselves or the way they would like to view themselves, the consumers may experience cognitive dissonance. *Cognitive dissonance* is a learning concept developed by Leon Festinger (Festinger, 1957) that tries to explain cognitive functioning—how we think and learn. According to his model, when information is consistent with our existing values and beliefs, it is said to be in consonance with our existing cognitive structure, and it is therefore easily assimilated.

If information is inconsistent with our existing beliefs and values, it creates a state of cognitive dissonance. This state of mind is psychologically uncomfortable, and we therefore try to resolve the incongruity between the new information and our existing beliefs and values. According to the model, we must either reject the new information or change our existing cognitive structure (beliefs and values) to accommodate the new information.

Thus, if we have a brand identity and personality that are inconsistent with consumers' existing beliefs and values, purchasers either have to change their beliefs and values to accommodate the brand personality or else change their behavior—that is, reject the brand because they no longer identify with the brand's identity and personality.

Consumers need to feel psychologically comfortable with the brand's image and personality. Consumers therefore generally choose brands they can identify with—ones consistent with their own personality, beliefs, and values or some idealized version thereof. On some level, consumers realize that the brands they choose make a statement about who they are. Do they wear a Rolex or a Timex? Drink Budweiser or Heineken?

• •

"Generally, the more involved consumers are with a purchase, the more important brand personality becomes."

• •

Pierre Martineau, in *Motivation in Advertising,* states that "... except for mere organic species behavior, every act of human behavior is a form of self-expression; it is a symbolic representation of the inner self. I am using products that I see as symbols satisfying my motive forces and consistent with my self-conceptions" (Martineau, 1957).

Generally, the more involved consumers are with a purchase, the more important brand personality becomes. For example, it is safe to say that most consumers are more involved in the purchase of a car than of toilet tissue. Brand personality takes on more importance when consumers are buying something that matters greatly to them.

Cost is generally related to product involvement. The more something costs, the more consumers are involved in its purchase. However, there are many low-cost product categories in which consumers become very involved with the product. For example, beer is a highly emblematic category. Beer drinkers "wear" their brand of beer as if it were a badge. Beer drinkers "size each other up" by the beer they drink.

Some fashion products are equally emblematic. For example, wearing Guess Jeans sends out a different signal than wearing Wranglers. Fashion-conscious consumers know this and will take great care in choosing the brand that they feel projects the "right image."

Brand Identity as the Key to Successful Branding. Brand identity essentially defines brandness. Developing an appropriate brand identity is the key to developing successful brands. It is what turns a thing (your product) into a perceptual entity with its own unique personality and perceptual inventory of imagery, feelings, and associations. A brand identity creates a stronger presence in the consumer's mind and helps to differentiate your brand from the competition. An appropriate, appealing brand identity humanizes and personifies your product, which in turn makes it easier for the consumer to form an *emotional bond* with your brand.

The importance of creating an emotional bond between the consumer and your brand cannot be overemphasized. For many product categories in which product differences have been minimized, the really important marketing battles are being fought in psychological space: a battle for a share of the consumer's heart. Savvy marketers increasingly come to realize that in order to build and maintain market share you also have to build and maintain "share of heart" (Feig, 1986). (See Figure 1.3) Futurist Jeff Hallett (The Present-Futures Group, Washington, D.C.) says that we must literally get the consumer to "love your brand."

How Much Is a Strong Brand Identity Worth? The value and significance of something as intangible as a brand's identity is often obscured by its physical

• •

Figure 1.3

Share of Heart

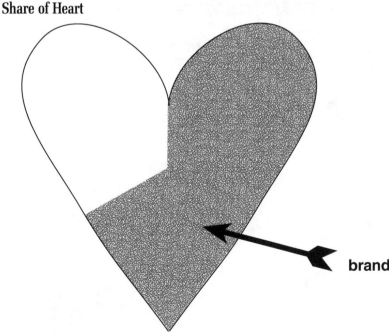

brand

attributes and tangible assets. And yet the Marlboro Man is as much an asset as any of the physical plants or real estate listed among Philip Morris's holdings. Why did Ford recently pay $2 billion for Jaguar? Was Ford buying a successful, growing business? The existing inventory? The physical plant? All of these tangible assets together could not justify the price Ford paid for Jaguar. Ford was willing to pay that $2 billion because of Jaguar's unique, enduring brand identity and the equity the brand represents.

Similarly, many of the megamergers and takeovers that characterized the 1980s were motivated by the desire to acquire established brands. Wall

• •

Figure 1.4

Brand Positioning

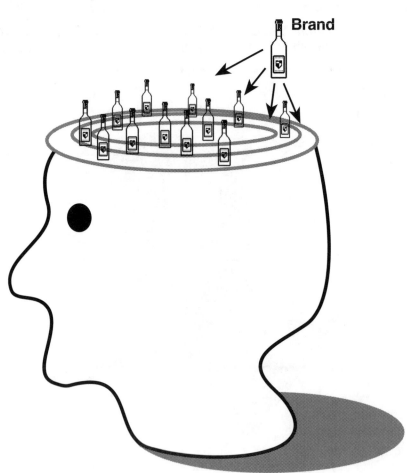

Street, too, became enamored with the real dollars-and-cents value of strong brands that have found their way into the consumer's heart.

Brand Positioning

Brand positioning is really a marketing concept, a crucial first step in developing and marketing a brand. However, because brand positioning also plays such a critical role in shaping a brand's advertising as well as its overall mythology, it must be considered as part of the overall brand concept. The brand positioning is what advertisers want the brand to stand for both in the marketplace and in the consumer's mind. The brand positioning generally captures and conveys the essence of a brand's overall mythology. The brand mythology, which is mostly created and communicated through advertising, establishes the brand's positioning, both in the marketplace and in the consumer's mind.

Sandage and Fryburger's text, *Advertising Theory and Practice,* distinguishes the brand's positioning in the marketplace from the brand's positioning in the consumer's mind: "Positioning can be viewed in different ways . . . one way is to literally position the product on the supermarket shelf" by changing the ingredients, packaging, and so on. The other way, "the ultimate positioning," is to position the product in the consumer's mind (Sandage and Fryburger, 1975, p. 195). (See Figure 1.4.)

Positioning the Brand in the Marketplace. The brand's positioning in the marketplace is generally based on the physical product—its attributes (form, size, and so on) compared to its competitors. A brand's positioning in the marketplace is generally taken against other competing brands in a particular category. For example, to position a light beer, the advertisers would most likely choose to position it against other light beers.

Positioning the Brand in the Consumer's Mind. The advertisers also need to determine how they wish to position the brand in the consumer's mind. Manufacturers who are used to thinking in terms of marketing products sometimes make the mistake of thinking only in terms of positioning the brand in the marketplace. But a brand is more than a product sitting on a supermarket shelf or wherever; a brand is a perceptual entity that exists in psychological space—in the consumer's mind. Therefore, it is equally important to consider how the brand is positioned in psychological space in the consumer's mind and heart.

For example, to differentiate the advertiser's light beer from others, he or she would need to develop a brand positioning that would differentiate our brand from other light beers. For example, the advertisers might position the brand as "the light beer with the full-bodied taste." The *perceptual positioning,* or how the brand is positioned in the consumer's mind, includes but is not limited to the marketplace positioning. In other words, because the perceptual positioning is created in psychological space (in the consumer's mind), the advertiser can go beyond the physical product attributes and benefits to create a perceptual positioning that also promises the consumer emotional and psychological benefits.

The Role of Advertising in Positioning the Brand in the Consumer's Mind. Advertising is the vehicle that grants the advertiser access to the consumer's mind to argue and establish the brand's position by communicating a compelling point of difference (product-based and/or emotional/psychological). Advertising does this by creating a brand mythology that communicates important product-based and emotional/psychological benefits, which in turn work to position the brand, both in the marketplace and in the consumer's mind.

Although brand positionings can sometimes be communicated or reinforced by packaging, pricing, promotions, and so on, advertising generally plays a dominant role in establishing brand positionings. Moreover, advertising enables advertisers to go beyond marketplace positionings, which are based on physical product attributes/benefits. By enabling advertisments to access the consumer's mind, advertising makes it possible for us to also create powerful emotional/psychological positionings that tap into the consumer's feelings and emotions.

For example, if one compares the brand positioning for the U.S. Marines

● ●

Figure 1.5

Mythology, Advertising, Brand Connection

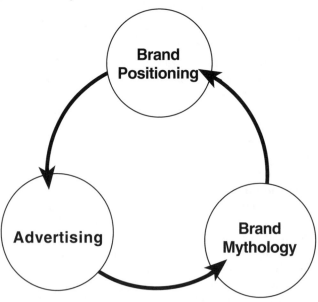

with the brand positionings for the U.S. Navy and U.S. Air Force (inferring this position from their advertising), the "Marines brand" is positioned on a more emotional/psychological level. The Marines are positioned as "an elite military/warrior organization" that tries to appeal to young men by challenging them: "We're looking for a few good men."

The compelling reason for the consumer to consider joining the Marines versus other branches of the service or college is not a rational one. It is an emotional one: to serve your country and prove you've got what it takes to become one of "the few, the proud, the brave."

It's an absolutely wonderful positioning for the Marines. Have you ever noticed that when ex-Marines meet there is an immediate, unspoken bond, no matter what their station in life? The Marines consider themselves special; they have a proud tradition and a warrior mythology based on courage and duty to their country. Advertising plays an important role in communicating and reinforcing the powerful, emotional positioning of the U.S. Marines. Advertising does this by communicating and perpetuating the U.S. Marines' brand mythology—a powerful, compelling warrior mythology.

In contrast, the brand positionings of the Navy and Air Force are much more rational. They are positioned against college as a career path. They are positioned more like career training services than a military service. The compelling reason they offer the consumer for joining the Navy or the Air Force is a rational, product-based one: It will help a young person to succeed in life by training him or her and helping the young adult finance college. There is little attempt to leverage their mythologies. This is too bad, especially for the Navy. The Navy's mythology is rooted in the lure and lore of the sea; it is an extremely rich and compelling mythology—one that has fascinated throughout recorded history.

Most of the more successful, enduring brands generally have brand positionings and brand mythologies that go beyond the physical product. They try to balance physical product attributes/benefits and emotional/psychological benefits.

• • •
Advertising—A Powerful Tool

Advertising is still the most powerful tool businesses have for building and maintaining brands. There has been a lot of press lately about the "decline of advertising" and how "advertising has lost its effectiveness." Pundits have variously pointed to media fragmentation, media proliferation, the networks' falling audience share, the high cost of advertising, product proliferation, product parity, and other likely causes.

At the same time, competition and the financial burdens assumed during the mergers and leveraged buyouts of the 1980s have put a lot of pressure on brand managers to make their brands more profitable. This has resulted in a lot of short-term, bottom-line thinking, which in turn has led to a less effective use of advertising.

Unfortunately, with everyone focusing on the bottom line, there is often no one left minding the brand. A brand is a fragile, living thing. It needs to be cultivated, nurtured, and cared for, or it will wither and die. A recent

• •

Figure 1.6

How Advertising Builds an Enduring Brand

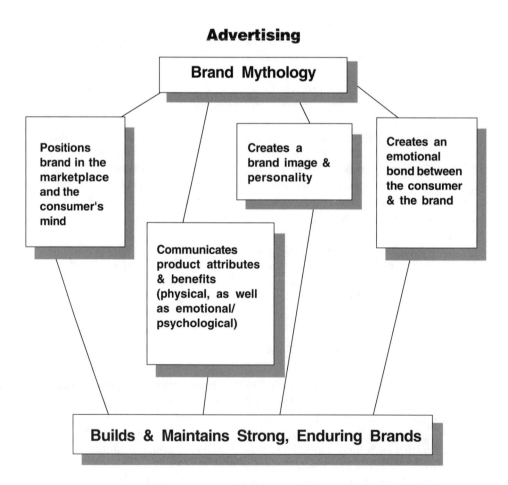

Business Week cover story makes essentially the same point with a striking picture of a group of ailing brand icons and characters.

The most powerful use of advertising is in building strong, enduring brands—not short-term, selling or bottom-line fixes. Short-term fixes are better handled through promotions, couponing, and other techniques, which indeed many brand managers have begun to do. But, brand-building advertising is still the best long-term remedy for ailing brands. Brand-building advertising often works to increase short-term sales, but the unique power of brand-building advertising lies in its ability to pay long-term dividends in the form of sustained sales and enduring brand loyalty, long after the smoke of the advertising has cleared.

Michael Miles, chairman and CEO of Philip Morris Companies, seems to concur:

> We manage more than two dozen of the world's greatest brands at Philip Morris. To maintain them, to keep these brand names fresh and polished, to present them to the consumer in the best way, we invest $2 billion annually. It's worth every penny. For we believe a strong brand gives the consumer another whole set of reasons—emotional and personal—to act. (Miles, 1992).

Brand-building advertising works to build and maintain strong, enduring brands by creating a perceptual inventory of imagery, feelings, and associations for a brand. Brand-building advertising works to humanize a brand by creating a unique brand identity and personality. Brand-building advertising works to forge an emotional bond between your brand and the consumer.

● ●

"Advertising leverages the power of myth and symbols to build and maintain successful, enduring brands."

● ●

Advertising builds and maintains strong brands by creating and perpetuating a powerful, appropriate brand mythology. Brand-building advertising builds and maintains strong, enduring brands by creating an appropriate brand identity and an emotional bond between the consumer and the brand. Advertising generates this bond by creating a powerful, appropriate brand mythology. (See Figure 1.6) Advertising leverages the power of myth and symbols to build and maintain successful, enduring brands. In order to understand how advertising leverages the power of myth in creating and maintaining strong brands, you must begin with a fuller understanding of mythology, the subject of Chapter 2.

Chapter 2
● ● ● ● ● ● ● ● ● ●

The Mythological Realm

Chapter 2 explains the mythological realm and the prescientific, mythopoeic imagination (the human intuitive, soul-felt experience of the world) that spawns mythology. The intent of the chapter is not only to provide an intellectual overview of mythology but also to convey a visceral sense of the power of the mythological experience.

This chapter reveals the "engine" that drives mythology and the mythological experience—the mysterious force we call the "unconscious." Like Dorothy's little dog Toto, this chapter pulls back the curtain and exposes the little bald-headed guy who pulls the wizard's strings.

The mythological experience is ultimately a spiritual experience that comes right out of the human soul or unconscious psyche. In order to understand the power of mythology and the power of the archetypal (universal) imagery and symbolism that compose the language of mythology, we need to gain some understanding of the "unconscious psyche." To this end, the chapter explores the source of the mythological experience— the unconscious psyche and the archetypal images that spring from the unconscious psyche. The chapter draws heavily from the work of Carl Jung, who spent most of his life trying to understand the unconscious, and from the research of his followers.

Some material relating to the unconscious psyche and Jung's personal "confrontations with the unconscious" will undoubtedly seem strange to the uninitiated. This is only natural, because the psychic force called the unconscious, with its power to fascinate and compel, is a strange and, at times, seemingly mystical force. Appreciating the power of this psychic force is necessary so when you witness the power of an archetypal image or motif in advertising, you'll understand whence comes this power.

The chapter subsequently discusses why people need mythologies and the continuing need for mythologies in a modern, scientific world. The chapter concludes by exploring the role of advertising in creating and perpetuating mythologies.

• • •
What Is Mythology?

Most people associate the term *myth* with something that never occurred (something that is made up). Take, for example, the book entitled *JFK: The Man and the Myth*, by Victor Lasky. As the title suggests, the book tries to separate the facts—what is known to be true about John F. Kennedy—from hearsay, made up stories, or myths.

The other most common association with myths or mythology is some recollection of Classic Greek or Roman mythology. Remember how Perseus foiled Medusa by using his shield as a mirror? Myths are wonderfully appealing stories for young and old alike.

In Western European cultures, the term *mythology* has become synonymous with Greek and Roman mythologies. This is hardly surprising, because they are generally the only mythologies to which Americans are exposed—a function of our Eurocentrism. There are in fact many mythologies—Asian, African, Norse, and Arabian, among others. But in all fairness, our fascination with Greek and Roman mythologies is not simply a function of our Eurocentrism; it is also a function of their excellence—the fact that Greek and Roman mythologies are outstanding examples of rich, fertile mythologies that yield many insights into the nature of the human soul or psyche.

• •

"There are in fact many mythologies—Asian, African, Norse, and Arabian, among others. . . .our fascination with Greek and Roman mythologies is not simply a function of our Eurocentrism; it is also a function of their excellence."

• •

Writing on the mythology of the ancient Greeks, Edith Hamilton talks about the "the Greek miracle" (Hamilton, 1969, p. 14):

... in the earliest Greek poets a new point of view dawned, never dreamed of in the world before them, but never to leave the world after them. With the coming forward of Greece, mankind became the center of the universe, the most important thing in it. This was a revolution in thought. Human beings had counted for little heretofore. In Greece man first realized what mankind was. (Hamilton, 1969, p. 16).

It is also important to understand that a definition of mythology in its broadest sense is not limited to what we formally identify as mythology; it encompasses anything that in some sense mythologizes or "dresses up reality." Moby Dick is a mythology. So is the Budweiser commercial you watched during last night's game.

Everything as Myth

Roland Barthes, a French literary critic, postulated that myth is a "form of speech," "a semiological system," and "a mode of signification" (Barthes, 1957) Barthes' book, *Mythologies,* was inspired by ". . . a feeling of impatience at the sight of the 'naturalness' with which newspapers, art, and common sense, constantly dress up a reality which, even though it is the one we live in, is undoubtedly determined by history" (Barthes, 1957, p. 11).

Barthes came to believe that everything is, in effect, a mythology (Barthes, 1957, p. 109). His book, written over a period of 10 years, is a collection of essays on some of the myths he encountered in everyday French life. Barthes' essays cover a broad and varied range of topics, from steak and wine to wrestling matches and striptease acts. For example, writing on the mythology of wrestling, Barthes says "The virtue of all-in wrestling is that it is the spectacle of excess." Continuing, Barthes says that winning and losing, or the question of whether it is staged or real, is of less importance to the public than their enjoyment of "the great spectacle of Suffering, Defeat and Justice" (Barthes, 1957 p. 19).

Barthes' notion that everything is a mythology is in synch with the postmodern sensibility, which, in the wake of Immanuel Kant, believes that there is no objective reality—all is perception. Kant believed that the mind does not passively absorb knowledge but rather actively interprets it. Thus, all knowledge is ultimately interpretive.

On the other hand, the mythologies that seem to be most meaningful are those that do more than simply alter or dress up reality. Mythologies help us to feel spiritually centered, shape our lives, and nourish our soul. Mythologization that goes beyond dressing up reality, that gives us a view of the soul, is the genre of the artist—and sometimes the adperson.

In a recent essay, "The Mystique of the Nonrational," James Heisig discusses the meaning of the word "mythologizing." Heisig explains that mythologizing can be summed up to include" . . . all forms of symbolic narrative fictions that show universal, collective, and recurrent patterns of psychic response to the experiences of life . . . any human representation seen from the viewpoint of soul" (Heisig, 1989, p.194).

This definition of mythologizing seems to be particularly well suited to advertising. Advertising is a storied form of communiation, a narrative fiction that, in addition to communicating information about the product, tries to reflect the values, lifestyles, and sensibilities of the target consumer and/or culture. As such, advertising often deals with issues of soul.

Mythologist and scholar Joseph Campbell says that myths function on different levels:

"Mystical Function"	". . . realizing what a wonder the universe is, and what a wonder you are, and experiencing awe before this mystery."
"Cosmological Function"	"helping us to understand the universe and our place in it."
"Sociological Function"	"supporting and validating a certain social order."
"Pedagogical"	". . . how to live a human lifetime under any circumstances" (Campbell, 1988, p. 31).

Modern Human Beings and the Mythological Experience

Formal mythologies like those of the Ancient Greeks and Romans are essentially a storied form of *explanation*—a way of explaining the universe and our place in it through the heroic stories of the divinities. Mythology played an important role in prescientific cultures like those of the ancient Greeks and Romans. However, science has essentially replaced mythology in contemporary societies, and it has become increasingly difficult for modern people to comprehend the significance and importance of mythology. We have lost conscious touch with the mythological experience and our mythological roots.

The Hungarian scholar, C. Kerenyi, says that science, with its interpretations and explanations, has blocked modern humans' sense of spirituality:

> We have lost our immediate feeling for the great realities of the spirit—and to this world all true mythology belongs—lost it precisely because of our all-too-willing, helpful, and efficient science. It explained our drink in the cup to us so well that we knew all about it beforehand, far better than the good old drinkers; we even have to ask ourselves: Is an immediate experience and enjoyment of mythology still in any sense possible? (Kerenyi, 1949, p. 1).

Carl Jung explains why the mythological approach is, in some ways, superior to the scientific:

What we are to our inward vision, and what man appears to be *subspecie aeternitatis*, can only be espressed by way of myth. Myth is more individual and expresses life more precisely than does science. Science works with concepts of averages which are far too general to do justice to the subjective variety of an individual life (Jung, 1989, p. 3).

Today's world has been demythologized and disenchanted by science and technology. We are no longer open to the magical song of the universe. We no longer feel connected to nature, to the mountains, streams, and trees. The forest is no longer an enchanted place where we might encounter nymphs and fairies. Joseph Campbell in his wonderful book, *The Power of Myth*, published a copy of a letter from a Native American tribal chief, Seattle, to the president of the United States, that illustrates the chasm between mythopoeic and modern man. The letter was written in 1852 in response to an inquiry from the U.S. government about buying tribal lands. Chief Seattle begins the letter by saying that he can't understand how the land can be bought or sold. The concept of land ownership is clearly incomprehensible to him because, as a mythopoeic man, he perceives the land, sky, and all of nature, as sacred and alive: he perceives himself and his people as connected to it.

Every part of this earth is sacred to my people. Every shining pine needle, every sandy shore, every mist in the dark woods, every meadow, every humming insect. All are holy in the memory and experience of my people.

We know the sap which courses through the trees as we know the blood that courses through our veins. We are part of the earth and it is part of us. The perfumed flowers are our sisters. The bear, the deer, the great eagle, these are our brothers. The rocky crests, the juices in the meadow, the body heat of the pony, and man, all belong to the same family.

The shining water that moves in the streams and rivers is not just water, but the blood of our ancestors. If we sell you our land, you must remember that it is sacred. Each ghostly reflection in the clear waters of the lakes tells of events and memories in the life of my people. The water's murmur is the voice of my father's father (Campbell, 1988, p.34).

In contrast to Chief Seattle's paleolithic sensibility and mythopoeic experience of the world, modern people view themselves as separate from the land and the animals, and believe that the land and animals were placed here to be exploited. Ann Baring and Jules Cashford, in *The Myth of the*

Goddess, trace this "modern sensibility" back to the Judeo-Christian mythology, which views human beings as dominant over the animals: "Be fruitful and multiply, and replenish the earth, and subdue it: and have dominion over the fish of the sea, and over the fowl of the air, and over every living thing that moveth upon the earth" (Genesis I: 28) (Baring and Cashford, 1991, p. 426).

The mythopoeic human experiences the world instinctively and intuitively—in the depths of the soul. In this sense, the mythopoeic imagination is also the realm of the artist, who also experiences the world mythopoeically, then tries to communicate that soul experience in art.

In his introductory comments to *Moby Dick,* Harold Beaver describes Ishmael's mind as "instinctively prescientific, prerationalistic, preanalytic—moving in closed and circular modes to reel in the universe" (Melville, 1986, p. 27). Beaver explains how Melville uses different devices to capture and convey Ishmael's mythopoeic experience of life:

> Melville, the myth-maker, needs only the age-old devices of symmetry, symbolic inversions and permutations, contrasts, antitheses, dissociations and binomial groupings to order, interpret and transmit his experience of life. His whale is explicitly "mystical marked"; for at its core, as in the earliest ritual myths, blazes the sun, a flash of gold, Promethean fire (Melville, 1986, pp. 27-28).

And later, Beaver suggests that the mythopoeic imagination may in fact be the theme of *Moby Dick*: "His very theme is the mythopoeic imagination . . . Mythopoeia, in fact, far from contriving a mask, or prophylactic screen, is shown by Melville (as later by Jung) to disclose the deepest layers of psychological awareness" (Melville, 1986, p. 28).

• •

" the ancient Greek myths are not simply entertaining little stories; they represent archetypal patterns of human experience."

• •

The Source of the Mythological Experience

The deepest layers of psychological awareness alluded to by Beaver are contained in the unconscious psyche—the source of our dreams and our mythologies. Campbell says that mythology is literally the stuff that dreams are made of: "Myths and dreams come from the same place . . . myths are the world's dreams . . . the song of the universe" (Campbell, 1988, p. 32). Carl Jung says that myths are psychic projections: "Myths are first and foremost psychic phenomena that reveal the nature of the soul. . . ." (Jung, 1968, p. 6).

In other words, the ancient Greek myths are not simply entertaining little stories; they represent *archetypal patterns of human experience* that have existed since the remotest times and across all cultures. Their seeming simplicity belies their profundity. In their mythologies and pantheon of Gods, the Greeks projected their own dreams and fears—and in so doing, gave us a glimpse of the human soul.

Mythology provides a window into the unconscious psyche—the nonrational, intuitive aspect of the human psyche. Mythology grants us a glimpse of the human soul, our instinctual nature that lays hidden beneath the veneer of civilization. Being in touch with our unconscious psyche helps us to feel grounded and human, and it is a rich, vital source of creative energy and insights. Campbell says that "inspiration comes from the unconscious . . . " He describes the creative process as an opening up: " . . . anyone writing a creative work knows that you open, you yield yourself, and the book talks to you and builds itself" (Campbell, 1988, p.58). Indeed, many authors and copy writers have experienced this "opening up process." At some point in the creative process it is as if someone else or some unseen force is writing. The piece seems to take on a life of its own, and it takes you to places that you could never have imagined beforehand.

Johann Jakob Bachofen, a Swiss social philosopher, describes myth as

> . . . the exegesis of the symbol. It unfolds in a series of outwardly connected actions what the symbol embodies in a unity. It resembles a discursive philosophical treatise insofar as it splits the idea into a number of connected images and then leaves it to the reader to draw the ultimate inference (Bachofen, 1992, p. 48).

M. Esther Harding, a psychoanalyst and disciple of Carl Jung, points to myths and folktales as a way into the unconscious and an alternative to the intellectual approach—a source of enlightenment: "When intellectual acumen fails us in this way, we have to turn to unconscious products for enlightenment and see whether a study of symbols and instinctive ways of acting may not throw some light on the obscurity" (Harding, 1971, p. 19).

• • •
The Unconscious Psyche: A Mythological Realm

Clearly, then, to understand and appreciate the power of myth, advertisers must have some understanding of the powerful, unseen, psychic force called the *unconscious*. The human psyche has both a conscious component and an unconscious component. The conscious component is the normal everyday consciousness, the ego, or "I" that functions in the world. The unconscious psyche and the "nonordinary" states of consciousness can be experienced in dreams, mystical states, or through the use of drugs. It was Sigmund Freud who discovered the unconscious component of the human psyche. The importance of Freud's discovery of the unconscious is often compared to Copernicus' finding that the earth is not the center of the universe and Darwin's finding that Homo sapiens evolved from nature along with all the other animals. All three discoveries were met with tremendous resistance when they were first revealed, and with good reason—they have had a humbling effect on humankind. They revealed that humans are not the center of the universe, not separate from the other animals, and not even completely in control of their behavior.

Today these discoveries are widely accepted. However, some people who say they understand and accept Freud's idea of the unconscious do not fully grasp its significance—that human behavior is influenced and controlled from behind the scenes by an unseen psychic force: the unconscious. To understand the significance of an unconscious psychic force, not intellectually but viscerally, in one's gut, is unsettling.

● ●
"The collective unconscious does not develop
individually, but is inherited. "
● ●

Freud's discovery of the unconscious was further developed by Carl Jung, who spent his life trying to understand the unconscious. In his work with psychiatric patients, Jung was struck by the fact that similar, often archaic imagery was expressed by many of his patients. Drawing from his observations, Jung developed the idea of the "collective unconscious"; that the unconscious contains archetypal (universal) images that can be traced back to the origin of the human species and that are the same in all people. To Jung, the archetypal images contained in the unconscious are essentially hard-wired into the human species, inherited, and function somewhat like instincts to influence and control our behavior. The archetypal image is the cornerstone of Jung's work and the key to our understanding the link between mythology and the human psyche.

Archetypes

The concept of archetypes can be traced back to the ancient Greeks, to the dialogues of Plato and his Doctrine of Forms. The Greeks perceived the world in terms of universal forms—essences or archetypes—that underlay the world of day-to-day reality, and gave their "Kosmos" order and meaning. The Greeks perceived not only the immediate reality of a thing, a specific sword, but also the idea of "swordness," the universal form or archetype that defines all swords.

Moreover, the Greeks believed that these transcendent ideals or archetypes had an independent existence and that through the human intellect, humans could perceive these archetypes and in that way attain true knowledge. In other words, the Greeks believed that the essence of "swordness," the idea of an archetypal sword, exists within the universe—independent of human consciousness.

Archetypes were explored further by Carl Jung. Jung's concept of archetypes is similar to that of the early Greeks, with one important difference. Jung maintained that the archetypal forms or images existed not out there in the cosmos, but inside the human psyche, in humans' collective unconscious. Jung describes the collective unconscious:

> ... there exists a second psychic system of a collective, universal, and impersonal nature which is identical in all individuals. This collective unconscious does not develop individually but is inherited. It consists of pre-existent forms, the archetypes, which can only become conscious secondarily and which give definite form to cerain psychic contents (Jung, 1968, p. 43).

Jung's archetypes exist within the unconscious; they cannot be seen directly. The archetypes of Jung's collective unconscious function somewhat like an instinct to drive and shape our behaviors. What we can see are expressions of the archetype in the form of archetypal images and symbols. In other words, any archetype may manifest itself in an infinite number of ways. For example, the basic Warrior archetype that represents the instinct for war and aggression can be revealed by many expressions (Roman soldier, knight, U.S. Marine, and so on).

● ●

"... transcendent ideals or archetypes had an independent existence and that through the human intellect, humans could perceive these archetypes and in that way attain true knowledge."

● ●

Jung's idea of archetypal images is related to Freud's discovery of "archaic remnants" in the dreams of his patients. (Freud was fishing while standing on whale—he completely missed the significance of their archaic remnants.) Jung described the archaic remnants found in dreams as "mental forms whose presence cannot be explained by anything in the individual's

●●

Figure 2.1

Warrior Archetype

life and that seem to be aboriginal, innate, and inherited shapes of the human mind" (Jung, 1964, p. 67).

Archetypal imagery goes to the heart of mythology. Humanity's universal drama is captured and played out in a series of archetypal images and mythical moments. Erich Neumann, a disciple of Jung, says that, in the course of life, everyone must pass through "the same archetypal stages which determine the evolution of consciousness in the life of humanity" (Neumann, 1970, p. xvi).

In his classic work *The Great Mother,* Neumann explains the significance of the archetypal image in the life of early humans:

Early man perceives the world mythologically . . . by forming archetypal images that he projects on it. The child, for example, experiences
in his mother the archetype of the Great Mother, that is, the reality of
an all-powerful numinous woman on whom he is dependent in all
things, and not the objective reality of his personal mother, this
particular historical woman which his mother becomes for him later
when his ego and consciousness are more developed" (Neumann,
1973, p. 15).

In other words, an infant nursing at its mother's breast does not yet know
its personal mother. What the infant experiences is "motherness"—the Great
Mother archetype, a big, warm, nurturing Great Mother—the eternal nurturer
and provider. The archetypal image of a mother nursing her child is a
universally recognizable image found throughout human history and across
all cultures. It is a visual representation of the maternal instinct. Each
archetype has its own symbol group or symbol canon that is also created and
directed by the unconscious. The powerful appeal of an archetypal image
like the mother-child image is that humans respond to it not only on a
conscious level but also on a deeper, instinctive, and unconscious level.

In a similar vein, Jung makes a distinction between the personal,
idiosyncratic dream and the archetypal dream, which is a universal dream,
the kind that is projected into mythological stories. The archetypal dream
contains archetypal images or deals with universal (mythic) events or
situations. Joseph Campbell uses the example of someone dreaming about
contemplating marriage or worrying about passing an exam:

"Will I pass the exam?" or "Should I marry this girl?"—that is
purely personal. But on another level, the problem of passing an
exam is not simply a personal problem. Everyone has to pass a
threshold of some kind. That is an archetypal thing. So there is a
basic mythological theme there even though it is a personal dream
(Campbell, 1988, p. 40).

Both Freud and Jung believed that there was a connection between the
mythologies and folklore of prescientific cultures and neurosis. But Jung
conceived the idea that the archetypal images were the common link
between the two—the idea that the individual archetypal images that
emanate from the unconscious component of the human psyche and appear
in our dreams are "inherited" and are the same images that inspired the
mythologies and folklore of prescientific cultures: "The same archetypal
images that appear in my dreams spring from the same human capacity that
gave rise to ancient mythologies among our remote ancestors" (Downing,
1991, p. xiii).

Confrontations with the Unconscious

Intrigued by his findings, Jung decided that the only way to understand the collective unconscious was to experience it for himself. Jung's entire life was a courageous experiment—an attempt to understand the unconscious by looking deeply into the abyss.

However, Jung understood at the outset the danger of direct "confrontations with the unconscious." The archetypal images of the unconscious are "the same images which fatally confuse the mental patient." The images often appear in dreams or as visions or apparitions. The danger is that the visions can be fascinating and compelling to the point that one can get caught up in them and lose one's hold on reality:

> Although everything is experienced in image form, i.e., symbolically, it is by no means a question of fictitious dangers but of very real risks upon which the fate of a whole life may depend. The chief danger is that of succumbing to the fascinating influence of the archetypes. . . . If there is already a predisposition to psychosis, it may even happen that the archetypal figures, which are endowed with a natural numinosity, will escape from conscious control altogether and become completely independent, thus producing the phenomenon of possession (Jung, 1968, p. 39).

In his biography *Memoires, Dreams, Reflections,* which was recorded and edited by Aniela Jaffe when Jung was 81 years old, Jung describes his struggle to maintain his hold on reality during his confrontations with the unconscious:

> It is of course ironical that I, a psychiatrist, should at almost every step of my experiment have run into the same psychic material which is the stuff of psychosis and is found in the insane. This is the fund of the unconscious images which fatally confuse the mental patient. But it is also the matrix of a mythopoeic imagination which has vanished from our rational age.
>
> The unconscious contents could have driven me out of my wits. But my family, and the knowledge: I have a medical diploma from a Swiss University, I must help my patients, I have a wife and five children, I live at 228 Seestrasse in Kusnacht—these were actualities which made demands upon me and proved to me again and again that I really existed . . . (Jung, 1989, pp. 188-89).

Direct confrontations with the archetypal images in the unconscious can also be very frightening. We have all experienced the frightening power of archetypal images in dreams—nightmares. Dream imagery comes right out of the unconscious. One can also encounter the archetypal imagery of the unconscious in visions or apparitions, which occur while the person is awake. Visions were a fairly common occurence among mythopoeic humans. For Eskimos and Native Americans of the plains, visionary experiences were an accepted and important part of their cultures. Native Americans called them "big dreams."

Within the unconscious there is a whole other world, of which most people have little or no awareness. Jung describes how he entered the world of the unconscious psyche, an unimaginably fascinating netherworld, a transpersonal, mythological realm that reaches back in space and time, the *tao* (the beyond that is within), a realm inhabited by daemons, ghosts, and all sorts of fantastic archetypal entities and imagery. In his memoires, Jung recalls the propitious moment when he decided to enter the shadow world of the unconscious psyche:

> It was during Advent of the year 1913—December 12th, to be exact—that I resolved upon the decisive step. I was sitting at my desk once more, thinking over my fears. Then I let myself drop. Suddenly it was as though the ground literally gave way beneath my feet, and I plunged down into dark depths. . .   After a while my eyes grew accustomed to the gloom, which was rather like a deep twilight. Before me was the entrance to a dark cave, in which stood a dwarf with a leathery skin, as if he were mummified. I squeezed past him through the narrow . . . (Jung, 1989, p. 179).

There are also many examples of visionary experiences in the early history of European cultures. In his autobiography, Benevenuto Cellini, the sixteenth-century Italian artist, recounts how he decided to enlist the aid of a necromancer to help him win the love of his latest paramour. (In Cellini's times, most folks believed in demons and spirits.) Cellini describes how right before his eyes, the necromancer conjures up hundreds of demons ". . . the most dangerous denizens of hell" (Cellini, 1927 p. 118). Saint Paul's vision, which is described in the Bible, is one of the more famous examples of a visionary experience.

However, in our modern, scientific world, the visionary experience is generally looked on with skepticism or ridicule. Most modern people do not believe in visions or apparitions, and they have little or no understanding of the unconscious psyche. But sometimes during a period of severe emotional stress or a spiritual crisis, their unconscious psyche may erupt into their consciousness in the form of an intense dream, vision, apparition, or nonordinary state of consciousness. For the nonbeliever, a first-time, direct confrontation with the unconscious psyche usually comes as a tremendous shock. People like to believe that they live in the here and now, and that they are in control. Discovering that there is a powerful aspect of the human psyche that is uncontrollable can be frightening and is often accompanied by a sense of panic; the person may feel that he or she is becoming insane.

An inability to tell dreams from reality is fairly common in children. Up to the age of eleven years, the thinking of children is characterized by strong eidetic imagery. *Eidetic images* are hallucinatory images that are so vivid that they may compete with reality (Haber and Haber, 1964). The evidence would suggest that during early development, children experience the world in much the same way as the prescientific, mythopoeic man.

In *The Mythic Imagination,* psychoanalyst Stephen Larsen describes the "mythic imagination" of the child. He recounts a story from cartoonist Gary Larson's ("The Far Side") personal remembrances of a childhood experience that captures ". . . the ultimate torture of the childhood mythic imagination: His older brother would lock him in the basement and, as little Gary stood pleading at the door above that well of darkness, intone, "They're coming, Gary, *they're coming. . ."* The cruelly clever lad knew he needn't even specify what "they" were; his younger brother's mind would do the rest" (Larsen, p. xxi).

● ●
"We like to believe that we live in the here and now,
and that we are in control"
● ●

Jung continued to experience visions throughout his life and indeed his writings are full of these " confrontations with the unconscious" and how they helped him to understand the unconscious. In *Alchemical Studies,* Jung explores the work of the alchemist Paracelsus in order to better understand his own explorations. Jung found that alchemists like Paracelsus inevitably confronted the unconscious psyche in their quest to find the "prima materia."

> I do not know how many or how few people today can imagine what
> "coming to terms with the unconscious'" means. I fear they are only
> too few. . . . It is on the one hand an endeavour to understand the
> archetypal world of the psyche, on the other hand a struggle against
> the sanity-threatening danger of fascination by the measureless heights
> and depths and paradoxes of psychic truth . . . Here the human mind
> is confronted with its origins, the archetype; the finite consciousness
> with its archaic foundations; the mortal ego with the immortal self. . . .
> Here we must feel our way with Paracelsus into a question that was
> never openly asked before in our culture and was never clearly put,

partly from sheer unconsciousness, partly from holy dread" (Jung, 1983, pp. 170-71).

Jung believed that most Europeans lacked the "stomach" for direct confrontations with the unconscious. A wonderful scene at the opening of Goethe's *Faust* seems to confirm Jung's suspicions. Faust is in his study despairing because all of his scientific knowledge has not brought him any closer to understanding the secrets of the universe. He has "turned to magic lore" in order ". . . that I may perceive whatever holds the world together in its inmost folds, see all its seeds, its working power..." (Goethe, 1952, p. 11).

Faust longs to get in touch with the spirit world, which he believes will provide the ultimate knowledge he seeks. But when his incantations actually do bring forth a vision of the "Earth Spirit," Faust is terrifed, and the spirit begins to needle Faust for his lack of courage:

Where art thou, Faust, whose voice rang out to me,
Who toward me pressed with all thy energy?
Is it thou who, by my breath surrounded,
In all the deeps of being art confounded?
A frightened, fleeing, writhing worm? (von Goethe, 1952, p. 14)

There are some apparent similarities between the experiences people report in their encounters with the unconscious psyche and experiences reported by people who use hallucinogenic drugs such as LSD. Indeed, this idea is supported by the work of Stanislav Grof, a psychoanalytic psychiatrist who used LSD as well as a number of powerful nondrug techniques to activate the unconscious psyches of his patients. (Grof also developed a technique called "holotropic breathing" that he says is as effective in activating the unconscious as LSD.) Grof's findings, based on thousands of therapeutic sessions, seem to confirm Jung's idea of archetypes and the existence of archaic archetypal imagery within the unconscious. During LSD sessions with patients, Grof found that "individuals unsophisticated in anthropology and mythology experience—without any programming—images, episodes, and even entire thematic sequences that bear a striking similarity to the descriptions of the posthumous journey of the soul and the death-rebirth mysteries of various cultures" (Grof, 1977, p. 175).

Although Grof's work seemed to have enormous therapeutic value for many of his patients, unsupervised confrontations with the mythological realm of the unconscious psyche, with or without LSD, can be frightening. Again, for the uninitiated, discovering that there is a whole other world inside of us that is full of archetypal figures and entities that are uncontrollable comes as a tremendous shock. Anyone who has had a direct confrontation with the unconscious psyche, in the form of a vision/apparition, will immediately understand the basis for this fear. The image appears frighteningly real (in the room with the person) and it is *not* under one's control. Jung often described the spirit-like archetypal images encountered in visions and dreams as "numen" or "numinous," that is, they are autonomous and appear to be charged or alive:

> . . . a numen to which neither human expectations nor the machina-
> tions of the will have given life. It lives of itself, and a shudder runs
> through the man who thought that "spirit" was merely what he
> believes, what he makes himself, what is said in books, or what people
> talk about. But when it happens spontaneously it is a spookish thing,
> and the primitive fear seizes the naive mind (Jung, 1968, p. 17).

In "The Mystique of the Nonrational," Jungian analyst James Heisig describes what its like to enter the world of the unconscious:

> It is an experience of an unknown and uncontrollable, yet awesome
> and enchanting, takeover of the everyday self by a force so sheerly
> other that we speak of it only by denying it our words. Jung, as is well
> known, welcomed Otto's descriptions [*mysterium tremendum et
> fascinans*] as pointing to the very events that had most impressed him
> about the psyche, and frequently spoke himself of the "numinosum,"
> not only in association with extraordinary religious and mystical
> experiences but also in referring to the commonplace experiences of
> dreams and fantasies and the allurement of symbols" (Heisig, 1989, p.
> 187).

Confrontations with the unconscious psyche often have a mystical quality about them. Six weeks after his father's death, Jung's father came to him in a dream. Jung described the experience as "so real that it forced me to think about life after death" (Jung, 1989, p. 97).

The person having an encounter with the unconscious cannot be sure whether the image is real or imagined. It is very unsettling. Those people who experienced this are forced to conclude that either there really are spirits, ghosts, and "things that go bump in the night," or have to recognize that there really is a part of the psyche that is autonomous and full of spirits, chimaera, ancient daemons, and so on, which can erupt into our consciousness. And with this comes the frightening realization that the line between sanity and madness is thin indeed, as Jung summarizes: "In the realm of consciousness we are our own masters; we seem to be the 'factors' themselves. But if we step through the door of the shadow we discover with terror that we are the objects of unseen factors. To know this is decidedly unpleasant, for nothing is more disillusioning than the discovery of our own inadequacy" (Jung, 1968, p. 23).

The Unconscious Psyche as a Creative Force

The previous discussion tried to convey a sense of the power as well as the danger and terror associated with direct confrontations with the unconscious, but the unconscious is also "where our treasures lie." It is the creative life force humans all share, the godhead, the creative wellspring of the human imagination. Joseph Campbell describes both the terror and the fascination of the mythological realm called the unconscious:

> The unconscious sends all sorts of vapors, odd beings, terrors, and deluding images up into the mind—whether in dream, broad daylight, or insanity; for the human kingdom beneath the floor of the comparatively neat little dwelling we call our consciousness goes down into unsuspected Aladdin caves. There are not only jewels but also dangerous jinn abide. . . . They are fiendishly fascinating too, for they carry the keys that open the whole realm of the desired and feared adventure of the discovery of the self. . . . That is, the lure, the promise and terror, of these disturbing night visitants form the mythological realm that we carry within" (Campbell, 1968, p. 8).

The artist (like the shaman) must learn how to draw from the well of the unconscious and to channel his or her mythopoeic imagination into his art: "The poet needs to synthesise the powerful images and tropes coming from the unconscious and place them in a meaningful context" (Sellery, 1989, p. 101).

The artist must ultimately turn inward—look into his or her own soul for inspiration. The Japanese believe that people can look into their souls by gazing into a mirror. They believe that in the mirror, individuals see their own eyes as the "door" of their soul.

In mythology this looking inward is often depicted as looking into a pool of water. The water represents the unconscious. By looking deeply into the water (the unconscious), one confronts one's own soul. *Moby Dick* has been described as "an epic quest of inner consciousness" (Melville, 1986, p. 26).

> Take almost any path you please, and ten to one it carries you down in a dale, and leaves you there by a pool in the stream. There is magic in it (Melville, 1986, p. 94).

In his commentary on Moby Dick, Harold Beaver explains that understanding the magic and fascination of water is the key to understanding the symbolic significance of Moby Dick. Like Narcissus, what we seek is ". . . the image of the ungraspable phantom of life" (Melville, 1986, p. 701).

And finally, Beaver sums up the book's epic theme:

> The quest for Moby Dick, then, is to be read as a pastoral turned daemonic, an extension of the Narcissus myth in which the whole ocean becomes the mirror image of man. In its pastoral opening the valley of the Saco lies "thus tranced"—a pine-tree shaking sighs like leaves upon some shepherd's head: in its sea, the picture yet again lies

"tranced." Amid nightmares, day-dreams, enchantments, the book moves from trance to trance. In the end is the beginning (Melville, 1986, p. 701).

Many great examples of creative works seem to emerge straight from the unconscious. Mozart claimed that his symphonies appeared to him already completed in his mind. Jazz musicians often report that musical riffs seem to come to them from nowhere. Other artists have reported that their creations were a divine gift from God. For example, Giacomo Puccini claimed that *Madame Butterfly* was given to him by God.

But one of my favorite examples of a work that seems to have sprung right out of the mythological realm of the unconscious is "Der Erlkönig" ("The Erlking"), a German folksong created by Franz Schubert in 1815 when he was only 18 years old. Schubert put Goethe's verses to music. The verses are based on the legend of the King of Elves, which says that anyone who is touched by the elf must die. Living in the twentieth century, it is easy to lose sight of the fact that as early as 200 years ago, it was widely believed among common folk that the forests were inhabited by elves and fairies. And Grof reports that during states of nonordinary consciousness, which he induces with his holotropic breathing technique, people often report encounters with elves, fairies, trolls, mermaids:

> ... in many cases, where people had no previous knowledge of certain mythological figures, they were not only able to experience them accurately and with great detail but were able to draw pictures with details that perfectly matched ancient descriptions of those figures (Grof, 1992, p. 161).

● ●
" Many great examples of creative works seem to
emerge straight from the unconscious."
● ●

Jungian analyst Stephen Larsen talks about spontaneous mythmaking experiences (what Freud referred to as "primary process" events), which "can occur when the intentional mind is 'taking time off ': a night dream, a daydream, or a hypnagogic fragment, such as a vividly perceived (eidetic) image at the threshold of sleep" (Larsen, 1990, p. 22).

Mary Shelley's *Frankenstein* is a terrific example of a creative work that seemed to spring directly from the creator's unconscious mind. While staying at a villa in Geneva, the Shelleys and some of their literary friends were amusing themselves by making up ghost stories. For several days Mary had been trying unsuccessfully to come up with a ghost story that would outdo the others. Finally, one night when she went to sleep,

. . . when I placed my head on my pillow I did not sleep, nor could I be said to think. My imagination, unbidden, possessed and guided me, gifting the successive images that arose in my mind with a vividness far beyond the usual bounds of reverie. I saw—with shut eyes, but acute mental vision—I saw the pale student of unhallowed arts kneeling beside the thing he had put together. I saw the hideous phantasm of a man stretched...he opens his eyes; behold the horrid thing stands at his bedside. ....I opened mine in terror. The idea so possessed my mind that a thrill of fear ran through me . . . (Shelley, 1991, p.xxv).

Poet Samuel Taylor Coleridge often used opium to stimulate and activate his unconscious psyche, which he referred to as "the primary imagination" and which he believed was the source of inspiration and creativity. Coleridge recounts how "Kubla Khan," one of his best-known poems, appeared to him fully formed in a vision while awaking from one of his opium episodes. Coleridge explained that as he hurried to copy it down, he was interrupted by a persistent caller from the neighboring, now infamous, town of Porlock, and some of the poem was lost (Holmes, 1990, p. 165).

In his commentary on *Kubla Khan*, Richard Holmes describes Coleridge's poem:

Kubla Khan is a pagan celebration of creative force in the universe, which the poet shares in the moment—perhaps irrevocable—of trance-like inspiration. In the sudden release of unconscious images, which Coleridge credited to his opium "reverie," the poet becomes both the controlling magus of this power, and also perhaps its sacrificial victim (Holmes, 1990, p. 166).

Camille Paglia describes what is perhaps Coleridge's most famous work, "The Rime of the Ancient Mariner" as a "mystery poem" in which " . . .the daemonic expresses itself nakedly." Paglia compares Coleridge with Edgar Allan Poe and asserts: "Coleridge and Poe are seized by visions that transcend language, that belong to the dream experience beyond language" (Paglia, 1990, p. 322).

Coleridge's "Ancient Mariner" is a sea journey into the shadowy underworld of the unconscious—a confrontation with an evil-avenging spirit in a watery realm full of hallucinations and "a thousand slimy things" (Holmes, 1990, p. 140).

The Mythological Experience is Ultimately a Spiritual Experience

C. Kerenyi, classical scholar and contemporary of Jung, connects the spiritual experience of the unconscious back to the mythological experience.

Kerenyi states that the mythological experience is ultimately a spiritual experience, something we experience in the inner depth of our soul, an encounter with the "divine":

> [T]o encounter the divine in absolute immediacy. . . . [as the mytho-logical vision or experience becomes more archetypal] we move out of the sphere of mythology and into the sphere of mysticism (Jung and Kerenyi, 1949, pp. 22-23).

In one of his more famous mystical experiences, Jung recounts how the "ghosts" of his unconscious began "haunting" him to write a work that he later title *Septem Sermones*.

Jung says that Freud, too, was afraid that the unconscious could open the door to mysticism and the occult. Freud intimated to Jung that he felt it was necessary to make a "dogma" of his sexual theory, "an unshakable bulwark" against the "black tide of occultism" (Jung, 1989, p. 150).

In their encounters with the unconscious, artists often delve into mysticism. William Butler Yeats is perhaps one of the better-known artists whose creative work has been strongly influenced by mysticism and the occult. Yeats' poetry was often inspired by his mythopoeic visions, and he was fascinated by magic and the occult. Yeats often attended seances, and in 1925 he revealed the source of his creative genius: ". . . an unknown writer who communicated with him through his wife's automatic writing or words spoken while she was asleep or in a trance" (Peterson, 1982, p. 197).

• • •
Why Do People Need Mythologies?

This chapter delves deeply into the unconscious psyche because it is ultimately both the source and the repository for the mythological experi-ence. The power of mythology, and the symbols that drive it (archetypal images), comes from the unconscious psyche—our primeval, instinctual soul. The universal images and patterns of human behavior that we see projected in mythology emanate from the unconscious psyche, and they represent humanity's soul-felt experience of the world. The power of myth and symbols lies in its ability to break through our intellectual armor, to touch our soul.

Mythologies can work on different levels. At the simplest level, my-thologies can simply be viewed as enduring stories that entertain and amuse. On a higher level, some mythologies represent universal images and themes that are found across cultures. Mythologies often deal with perennial, existential questions: Who am I? Why am I here? What is important? Mythology helps people in their struggle to understand the universe and their place in it. Humans take comfort and guidance in the mythological stories   depicting others who have struggled before them. Mythology ultimately helps people to understand who they are. A sense of identity has become increasingly important in a modern world where it is easy to lose one's way. People need to feel rooted and spiritually centered.

In his book *Cry for Myth,* psychologist Rollo May uses a wonderful quote from Arthur Miller's *Death of a Salesman* to capture and convey the modern human struggle for identity. The quote is taken from Willy Loman's funeral, where his neighbor Charlie is admonishing Willy Loman's son for being angry because he feels that his father has betrayed him: "Nobody dast blame this man. . . . Willy was a salesman—a man way out there in the blue, riding on a smile and a shoeshine" (May, 1991 p. 43).

In a consumptive society driven to continually increase growth and profits, we are all struggling to maintain our identity. We are *all* salespeople "riding on a smile and a shoeshine" (I trust the irony of an adperson telling you this has not been lost).

One could argue that in contemporary Western cultures driven by materialism and consumerism, the spiritual benefits provided by mythologies have become more important than ever. Mythologies not only help to provide humans with a sense of identity, they also help people understand what is important and how people should conduct their lives. By presenting archetypal or universal patterns of human behavior, mythologies offer a blueprint for life.

Life is a heroic journey. Humans begin life as water creatures. They struggle to be born. They struggle to find their own path through life and then they die. They could use some help.

On yet another level, mythologies work to provide the ethos or guiding set of beliefs that define human culture. This definition helps people to understand what is important, what we as a culture value. Without a mythology we have no ethos, no values or beliefs to guide us. Unfortunately, today people live in an increasingly demythologized, disenchanted world. Rollo May attributes the increase in violence in American society, and Americans' obsession to make money, to their "mythlessness" (May, 1991, pp. 122-24).

• • •

Who Is Responsible for the "Care and Feeding" of Myths?

In pretechnological cultures, mythmaking is the purview of the shaman or medicine man. (By the way, in pretechnological cultures, the shaman or medicine man is held in very high esteem.) Campbell defines the shaman as "a person, male or female, who in his late childhood/early youth has an overwhelming psychological experience that turns him totally inward. It's kind of a schizophrenic crack-up. The whole unconsciousness opens up, and the Shaman falls into it—they are particularly gifted people whose ears are open to the song of the universe" (Campbell, 1988, p. 85).

The role of shamans is "making both visible and public the systems of symbolic fantasy that are present in the psyche of every adult member of their society" (Campbell, 1949, p. 101). In the contemporary world of mass communications, this is the role of the artist: "The function of the artist is the mythologization of the environment and the world" (Campbell, 1988, p. 85). Hollywood is in the business of mythmaking, and so is Madison Avenue.

With the introduction and proliferation of electronic media, advertising has become a dominant art form and a powerful force in American culture and our lives. Television is the magic mirror that both creates and reflects our dreams and fantasies. Because it is so intrusive, pervasive, and of-the-moment, advertising plays an important role in mythmaking. In contemporary, technological cultures, the advertising person has replaced the shaman. The advertising whiz has become the new mythmaker (albeit unwittingly), weaving commercial magic in the blue glow of electronic space and in the consumer's psyche.

●●●●●●●●●●●●●●●●●●●●●●●●●●●●●●●●●●

> " With the introduction and proliferation of electronic media, advertising has become a dominant art form and a powerful force in American culture and our lives."

●●●●●●●●●●●●●●●●●●●●●●●●●●●●●●●●●●

It is understandable that some people may be appalled by the idea that America as a culture must turn to Hollywood—and worse yet, Madison Avenue, for our mythologies. But consumerism, with all its warts and wen, is the cornerstone of American culture. Like it or not, consumerism permeates every aspect of society and Americans' lives. Even our politics are driven by presidential promises of increased growth and profits. It is therefore only fitting that advertising should come to play a role in creating and reinforcing the mythologies that shape our lives. The Greeks had their pantheon of gods; Americans have brands.

● ● ●
Advertising as a Form of Mythmaking

In some sense, virtually all advertising is a form of mythologizing. Each advertisement or commercial represents an individual mythology, which also contributes to the overall brand mythology. As Chapter 1 stressed, a brand is a perceptual entity that exists in psychological space—in the consumer's mind. Advertising can be used to fill this perceptual brand space, to create mytho-symbolic worlds into which humans project dreams, fears, and fantasies. In creating these mytho-symbolic worlds, the art director and copy writer must look to the unconscious psyche, to their intuitive feelings and instincts for inspiration. The people who create advertising must literally get out of their heads, their day-to-day consciousness, in order to tap into their unconscious psyche, the mythological realm, the magical place of childhood, the place of dreams. This is the creative matrix, the secret hidden pool that lies deeply buried in the inner labyrinth of the human mind. It is the seminal font, the source of human creativity. Like art, poetry, and music, great advertising springs from the unconscious psyche. The brand mythology stems from the brand's unique perceptual inventory of images, feelings, and associations—what the brand stands for in the consumer's mind. As with any mythology, advertising mythologies can work on different levels. Most brand mythologies function on a basic level to engage, entertain, and amuse the consumer by "dressing up reality" and/or communicating product attributes and/or benefits. Many brand mythologies also function on a sociological level to reflect and reinforce our cultural values. Sometimes, brand mythologies even work on a spiritual or cosmological level to nourish the soul.

McDonald's as a Microcosm of America

Advertising's role in creating and maintaining the myths and mythical worlds that reflect peoples' dreams and fantasies as well as our cultural sensibilities and ethos is most evident when one looks at the advertising for megabrands like McDonald's and Coca Cola. Megabrand advertising doesn't just sell product, it creates an emotional bond between the brand and the consumer. Advertising creates this bond by mythologizing the product; by humanizing it; and by giving the product a distinct identity, personality, and sensibility. Advertising mythologizes brands by wrapping them in consumers' dreams and fantasies.

Through advertising, McDonald's has created the perception that it is much more than a fast food restaurant. McDonald's advertising has created a mythical world, a wondrous, magical place where everyone is welcome, safe, happy, loved, kind, caring, sharing, and forever young or young-at-heart. McDonald's has wrapped itself in America's mythology. McDonald's is a microcosm of everything America was supposed to be.

At the same time, McDonald's has created and reinforced the perception that it is an important part of American lives and culture. When advertisers ask consumers about McDonald's advertising, they say that a lot of the McDonald's commericals leave them with "a warm, fuzzy feeling... they are very appealing and heartwarming." I remember interviewing one woman who, when asked to describe McDonald's advertising, said, "McDonald's advertising makes me feel as if I died and went to heaven."

Coca Cola as a Cultural Catalyst

Coca Cola advertising is another great example of advertising that satisfies the human need for myths. In 30 seconds, the original "I'd like to teach the world to sing" campaign captured not only the ethos, but the spirit of a generation. Again, the mythical world created by this advertising is a wonderfully appealing world where people put aside their differences and come together. In this mythical world, Coke is the catalyst that brings people together. Having a Coke becomes a shared cultural experience, which has the power to bring people together regardless of racial, cultural, or generational differences.

● ●

> " Megabrand advertising doesn't just sell product, it creates an emotional bond between the brand and the consumer."

● ●

Advertising That's Good for the Soul

The myths and the mythical worlds created by advertising not only reflect and sustain American's cultural sensibilities, they can also work on a deeper level to nourish the soul.

Advertising often uses a mythological motif that works on several levels. The recent New York Telephone "we're all connected" campaign is a wonderful example of advertising using a mythical motif that works on different levels. At the prima facie level, "we're all connected" refers to the fact that people are all connected by telephone wires, presumably New York Telephone's.

On another level, "we're all connected" communicates the idea that people are *emotionally* connected to family and friends—through New York Telephone.

On yet another level, the "we're all connected" campaign can also be interpreted to mean that all humankind, indeed all life, is connected. The notion of oneness and the idea that people are all part of the same life force is a powerful, pervasive mythological motif that runs through many cultures.

Thus, at the heart of New York Telephone's advertising is a mythological motif, a golden nugget, that not only works to help New York Telephone sell its service but also to build an emotional bond with consumers by leaving them with a good feeling about the company.

Part II

• • • • • • • • •

Mythologies

The objective of Part II is to explore the mythologies that have shaped American culture (cultural mythologies) and Americans' lives, and at the same time to see how they are reflected in the mythologies created around advertising brands (brand mythologies).

Chapters 3, 4, and 5 comprise Part II. Chapters 3 and 4 explore the dominant western cultural mythologies, which, until recently, have been very different for men and women. People live in a world of opposites, male and female, Yin and Yang. A sense of maleness and female-ness permeates human culture and sensibilities. There-fore, in Chapters 3 and 4, the prevailing cultural mytholo-gies are split into female and male, respectively. Chapters 3 (Female Mythologies) and 4 (Male Mythologies) at-tempt to explore the most dominant and pervasive cul-tural mythologies from the perspective of gender.

There is another reason for separating cultural mytholo-gies into female and male. Advertisers are frequently called on to create advertising that is gender specific (appeals specifically to women or men). In a world where the roles and images of the sexes are in a state of flux, an understanding of masculinity and femininity transcending fashion and trends—an understanding of the male and female soul—can obviously be very helpful. Granted, the issues surrounding gender identity are controversial and politically charged. However, gender identity is an important aspect of advertising, and it is often critical to building brands.

Chapter 3 introduces an investigative technique (analogic) that is used to further the understanding of female and male mythologies. The analogic investigative technique, a technique favored by Carl Jung, is used because the traditional scientific approach does not work when we are dealing with issues of soul (mythologies spring from the unconscious psyche or soul). The analogic approach seeks to further people's understanding of the issue at hand through mythological amplification, by drawing from ancient mythologies, psychoanalysis, and other mythopoeic (soul-felt) sources.

Although there are many different mythologies— African, Celtic, Chinese, and Arabian are notable examples—the myths used herein to provide mythological amplification are drawn predominantly from ancient Greek mythology. There are two reasons for this decision: An exploration of world mythologies is not feasible in the space of this book; and, more to the point, Greek mythology (and Roman mythology, which essentially mirrors the Greek) is the one that has most greatly impacted western culture. Many of our cultural mythologies and sensibilities are rooted in Greek mythology. However, Chapters 3 and 4 will also draw from some of the numerous different cultural mythologies to help readers appreciate the richness of other cultural mythologies and the universality of such themes.

Chapters 3 and 4 explore the archetypal (universal) images traditionally associated with male and female mythologies. These two chapters clarify that at the core of most mythologies there is an archetypal image or theme, a universal image or pattern of thinking that comes out of the unconscious psyche. The archetypal images encountered in ancient mythologies and fairy tales still exist in the human psyche. These chapters explain how archetypes have shaped the American culture and consumers' lives. They illustrate the powerful, instinctual appeal of archetypes. At the same time they also point up the danger of archetypes being used as one-dimensional stereotypes that prevent men and women from becoming fully realized human beings. Chapters 3 and 4 ultimately try to reconcile the powerful, instinctual pull of these archetypes with the diverse societal and lifestyle changes made possible by technology.

And finally, Chapters 3 and 4 set the stage for Chapter 5, which explores some of the more familiar brand mythologies created mostly through advertising. Brand mythologies often mirror cultural mythologies. Advertisers try to appeal to consumers by reflecting their values, lifestyles, and sensibilities. The same archetypal images that shaped Americans' cultural mythologies are encountered in the various brand mythologies. For example, the image of the Warrior, an ancient archetypal image across many cultures and one at the core of most male mythologies, is the same archetypal image on which many brand mythologies depend. The Marlboro Man and the Bud Man are both manifestations of the male Warrior archetype.

An understanding of the gender-related archetypes and how brand mythologies exploit these instinctive reactions sets the stage for constructing new brand mythologies and strengthening existing ones—the subject of Part III.

Chapter 3
• • • • • • • • • • •

Female Mythologies

One of the first things advertisers must do is identify and define their target consumer. Advertisers need to know who will be the recipient of their advertising message. Who an ad will "speak to" has an important bearing on the advertising message (what advertisers wish to communicate) and their choice of media (how they will get their message to the consumer). Because gender identity generally plays a critical role in shaping a person's overall identity, it is an important consideration in developing advertising mythologies.

• • •
Gender Identity

Gender identity refers to those aspects of an individual's identity or self-concept that are tied to gender. The psychodevelopment of each individual proceeds from an undefined, unconscious being to a being with a conscious sense of self (ego). The developing person and emerging ego consciousness strive to develop a sense of self or identity that helps him or her to understand who they are, their place in society. Gender identity (a sense of maleness/femaleness) is an important aspect of a person's overall identity.

Gender identity is also an important issue in creating advertising. Are the target consumers male? Female? Both male and female? Depending on the product, most brand mythologies can be categorized as male, female, or not gender specific.

Many advertising brands create mythologies that serve to reflect and reinforce the consumer's identity. The hope is that the consumer will identify with the *user imagery* (the type of person portrayed as using the product) created by the advertising: "The person using that product is a lot like me (or the person I would like to be), so maybe I should be using that product." In some highly emblematic categories like beer, the consumer wears the brand like a badge— "I'm a Bud man." Advertisers' ability to create advertising that serves as an identity holder presupposes that they understand the consumer's identity needs—that they understand what would be an appropriate, appealing identity for this particular consumer. This in turn presupposes that advertisers understand the gender identity (maleness and femaleness) that generally dominates the consumer's sense of self.

Because of the women's movement, gender identity issues have become a hot topic and a political minefield. It has become politically incorrect to say anything that sounds like it is not a whole-hearted endorsement of the women's movement (especially if the comment is made by a man). The controversy and tension surrounding gender identity and the battle of the sexes have made it difficult for advertisers to create *gender-specific advertising,* advertising that is geared to appeal uniquely to men or to women. For example, an advertiser with a woman's product who is trying to create advertising that will appeal to women has to ask, "What kind of woman do I want to portray in my advertising?" If an advertiser's female user imagery and female mythology is out of synch with the values, sensibilities, and lifestyles of the intended target women, the product most likely will be rejected.

At the same time, advertisers can employ gender-specific advertising to reinforce the consumer's sense of masculinity or femininity, which can be a powerful inducement to use a brand. For many brands, gender identity is an important aspect of the brand identity and overall brand mythology. Budweiser has created a powerful brand mythology based not only on its quality heritage but also on its ability to provide male beer drinkers with a sense of masculine identity. Oil of Olay has also created a powerful brand mythology by providing women with a sense of feminine identity. One of the biggest challenges faced by both these brands is the tricky business of managing male/female identities in a world where ideas about gender identity have become politically charged and are rapidly changing.

In order to create gender-specific advertising in today's world, advertisers have to maintain a constant awareness of how male and female values and lifestyles are changing. At the same time, they need to have a deep understanding of the male/female soul or psyche, an understanding that transcends cultural trends and fashions. All the people involved in creating ads need to understand what is important to males and females—their similarities and differences, their mythologies, and how their mythologies have come to shape their perceptions and their lives. This chapter begins that exploration of female archetypes.

• • •
An Analogic Approach

Chapters 3 and 4, and the remainder of this book, use an *analogic* approach. This is something we all do instinctively and intuitively. For example: in describing how awful last night's party was, someone might say, "It was like a funeral," or, "It was a party from hell." Analogies provide comforting means of expressing new ideas by linking them with familiar ones. Bachofen, Campbell, Jung, and many of Jung's followers used essentially this same technique of amplifying by analogy, but they drew their analogies specifically from classical mythology and other mythopoeic sources.

Early mythological investigators like Bachofen and Jung were highly creative, seminal thinkers who used an investigative technique that enabled them to illuminate by analogy, through a process of mythological amplification. Jung drew his analogies from classic mythologies, alchemy, and other ancient writings because he felt they came out of the mythopoeic experience, which is grounded in the unconscious psyche (art, music, and literature are other sources that draw from the unconscious psyche). Jung sought to further the understanding of a subject by surrounding it with analogous imagery and symbolism, which he often left open to interpretation so the reader could benefit from experiencing first-hand the full power of the imagery and symbolism. This kind of investigative technique is especially helpful in dealing with issues and questions that do not lend themselves to traditional scientific inquiry—questions of soul.

Jung drew heavily from mythology and other mythopoeic sources that might reveal humankind's soulfelt experience of the world and self because he believed it paralleled the way the unconscious psyche works. The unconscious psyche does not work in a linear, logical fashion, like the conscious psyche. The unconscious psyche does not achieve understanding through the use of logic and reason, but rather by looking at the canon of symbolism and imagery that is appropriate to the inquiry.

The analogic approach is somewhat like going on a psychic archaeological dig, wherein the explorers sort through various primeval, archaic, and mythopoeic material in the hopes of deepening their understanding of an issue or question. The analogical approach represents a different path to knowledge than the scientific approach; it represents a different way of knowing:

> There are two roads to knowledge—the longer, slower, more
> arduous road of rational combination and the shorter path of the

imagination, traversed with the force and swiftness of electricity. Aroused by direct contact with the ancient remains, the imagination [Phantasie] grasps the truth at one stroke, without intermediary links. The knowledge acquired in this second way is infinitely more living and colorful than the products of the understanding [Verstand] (Bachofen, 1992, p. xxvii).

The analogical approach is a prescientific, intuitive approach that examines symbolic material from mythology and various other mythopoeic sources (folklore, art, literature, and psychoanalysis) to provide a mythological perspective. People must be careful not to bring a scientific mindset to their interpretation of mythologies. Joseph Campbell refers to Bachofen, who says "Mythologies arise from and are governed by the same psychological laws that control our own profoundest sentiments, the surest way to interpret them is not through intellectual ratiocination but the exercise of our psychologically cognate imagination" (Bachofen, 1992, p. xxvii).

Keep in mind that the analogic approach, which seeks to amplify by analogy, requires an examination of many different symbols. Any one symbol, taken alone, may be insufficient and misleading. Here readers must examine the "canon of symbolism," what Neumann calls "the coherent symbol group" surrounding our subject:

The way of the unconscious is different. Symbols gather round the thing to be explained, understood, interpreted. . . . Each symbol lays bare another essential side of the object to be grasped, points to another facet of meaning. Only the canon of these symbols congregating about the center in question, the coherent symbol group, can lead to an understanding of what the symbols point to and of what they are trying to express (Neumann, 1970, p. 7).

The symbolic material found in mythology and other mythopoeic sources often brings insights and a depth of understanding that would be impossible using traditional research techniques. According to Jung, all symbolic material emanates from the deeper layers of the collective unconscious that speak to us in archetypal images. They are not the product of our consciousness, that aspect of the psyche that is logical and ordered. Rather, the symbols of myth are a product of human intuitive, soulfelt, unconscious psyche. Bachofen points up the unique power of the symbol:

• •

" The way of the unconscious is different. Symbols gather round the thing to be explained, understood, interpreted . . ."

• •

The symbol awakens intimations; speech can only explain. The symbol plucks all the strings of the human spirit at once; speech is compelled to take up a single thought at a time. The symbol strikes its roots in the most secret depths of the soul; language skims the surface of understanding like a soft breeze. The symbol aims inward; language outward (Bachofen, 1992, p. 50).

And Neumann says the symbol is "an analogy, more an equivalence than an equation, and therein lies its wealth of meanings, but also its elusiveness. Only the symbol group, compact of partly contradictory analogies, can make something unknown and beyond the grasp of consciousness, more intelligible and more capable of becoming conscious" (Neumann, 1970).

• • •

Aspects of Femininity

At the heart of most mythologies is a symbol, an archetypal image that essentially drives the mythology, which, in turn, shapes people's lives. The unconscious psyche speaks through symbolic, archetypal images and patterns of human thought that are the basis of mythology. Jung believed that the unconscious psyche contains archetypes that exist in both sexes and that represent aspects of both masculinity and femininity. For example, men and women both have an instinct for aggression, a warring instinct that is represented by the Warrior archetype. And men and women both have a nurturing instinct, the maternal instinct that is represented by the Great Mother archetype. However, in western cultures certain archetypes are associated with and have come to dominate people's perceptions of what is male and female.

How Cultural Myths Shape Lives

We live in a world of opposites where gender identity permeates every aspect of human life. Gender identity is an important aspect of both cultural and advertising mythologies. For example, men and women who are in their forties or older grew up with John Wayne and Donna Reed myths, respectively. The John Wayne myth is based on the Warrior archetype, whose virtues are courageousness, independence, and strength. In the John Wayne myth, men are like the characters John Wayne played in his movies: strong, silent types who hang tough and don't cry or show their feelings. In the Donna Reed myth, women are supposed to be selfless nurturers who live for their children and husbands. The Donna Reed myth is based on the Great Mother archetype, whose virtues are nurturance, protectiveness, and love.

Myths shape people's lives even when no one is conscious of their influence. In his autobiographical book, *Goodbye Darkness*, author/biographer William Manchester states that a lot of the young men who joined the

Marines and fought in World War II said they could trace their decision to join the Marines (a risky decision during wartime) back to a war movie: "He had joined the Marines on impulse after seeing John Payne, Randolph Scott, and Maureen O'Hara in *To the Shores of Tripoli,* a gung-ho movie that conned a lot of guys into boot camp" (Manchester, 1980, p. 199).

The archetypes that are so often the basis for cultural myths also play an important role in Madison Avenue's mythmaking. Advertising that creates brand mythologies around appealing mythical characters or appealing user imagery often uses (albeit unwittingly) archetypal images. For example, many advertisements traditionally directed to female homemakers are based on the Great Mother archetype, an image that represents "motherness," the maternal instinct in all of us. The powerful appeal of an archetypal image is that people respond to it not only on a conscious level but also on a deeper, instinctive, emotional level. The human response to archetypes is almost always emotional.

• • •

"Feminine" Archetypes

Building on the work of Jung and Neumann, Jungian analyst Gareth Hill developed a useful schema that can help readers grasp the different aspects of the masculine and feminine. Hill distinguishes two aspects of both the masculine and the feminine: "The static masculine and the dynamic masculine;" and "the static feminine and the dynamic feminine" (Hill, 1992, p. 4).

The Static Feminine: "The Great Mother"

In his classic work, *The Great Mother,* Erich Neumann describes the static feminine aspect (Neumann uses the term *elementary character*) of the female image as "containing" (Neumann, 1991, p. 65). According to Neumann, the central feminine symbol is the vessel. "The basic symbolic equation: Woman = body = vessel corresponds to what is perhaps mankind's—man's as well as woman's—most elemental experience of the feminine" (Neumann, 1991, p. 39). And Hill says, "The static aspect of the feminine principle takes its elemental image from the containing uterus—moist, dark, surrounding, holding fast to what is gestating within it" (Hill, 1992, p. 4).

The static aspect of the feminine is expressed in the archetypal image of the Great Mother. The Great Mother is a universal image of woman as the eternal womb and nurturer. It is an image of woman that has existed since the remotest times, across all cultures. In one of his innumerable insights, Bachofen points to the universal, sacrosanct love between a mother and her child as the one "bright spot" amid the squalor and brutality of early humans:

"At the lowest, darkest stages of human existence the love between the mother and her offspring is the bright spot in life" (Bachofen, 1992, p. 79). Bachofen posits the "primacy of mother love" as compared to paternal love, which was a later development requiring a higher moral order (Bachofen, 1992, p. 79).

Early males were no doubt impressed with the specialness of the love between a mother and her child. This is why, according to Bachofen, despite his greater physical strength, early man both feared and worshiped woman. Virtually all of the pre-Hellenic cultures worshipped goddesses and were matriarchal, with most of the wealth and power being handed down from mother to daughter:

> The elevation of woman over man arouses our amazement most especially by its contradiction to the relation of physical strength. The law of nature confers the scepter of power on the stronger. If it is torn away from him by feebler hands, other aspects of human nature must have been at work, deeper powers must have made their influence felt (Bachofen, 1992, p. 85).

The Great Mother archetype that represents the static feminine has both positive and negative elements. At the positive pole, the archetype represents the primordial womb of life, the giver of life, nourishment, warmth, and protection. According to Jung, the archetype ". . . refers to a place of origin, to nature. . . . It also means the unconscious, our natural and instinctive life, the physiological realm, the body in which we dwell or are contained; for the 'mother' is also the matrix, the hollow form, the vessel that carries and nourishes, and it thus stands psychologically for the foundations of consciousness" (Jung, 1985, p. 158).

Like all archetypes, the Great Mother has its own symbol canon: "Anything deep—abyss, valley, ground, also the sea and the bottom of the sea, fountains, lakes, and pools, the earth, the underworld, the cave, the house, and the city—all are parts of this archetype. Anything big and embracing that contains, surrounds, enwraps, shelters, preserves, and nourishes anything small belongs to the primordial matriarchal realm" (Jung, 1985, p. 158). There is a fairly obvious connection between the Great Mother and the earth. Most pretechnological cultures worshipped earth goddesses in some form or other. The earth is perceived as a Great Mother who, through her bounty, nourishes and sustains all of earth's creatures. (Figure 3.1) In Greek mythology, the goddess Gaia was the earth itself (her husband was Uranus—the sky). Gaia's counterpart in Roman mythology was Tellumo. The Iroquois Indian worshiped an earth goddess named Eithinoha, which means "our mother." And the Algonquin Indian name for earth is *nokomis*, which means "grandmother." The Chinese goddess Hou T'u represents the spirit of the earth, as does the Aztec goddess Coatlicue.

The Great Mother also represents fecundity, symbolized by the pig. Pigs

Figure 3.1

Earth Goddess

Credit: Special Collections, Augustus C. Long Health Sciences Library, Columbia University

have lots of piglets; note too that the Greek and Latin word for pig is *cunt* (Hall, 1980, p. 81). In pre-Hellenic matriarchal societies, the sexuality of the goddess was sacred, believed to lead to human, animal, and agricultural fertility. In her book, *In the Wake of the Goddesses,* Tikva Frymer-Kensky says ancient hymns to goddesses often used graphic language to celebrate the sexuality of the goddess. This was ". . . not an indication of sexual prurience or pornographic interest. On the contrary, these hymns are a celebration of Inanna as vulva, of the goddess as 'cosmic cunt'" (Frymer-Kensky, 1992, p. 57).

Generally, the males in primitive (pretechnological) cultures stand in awe of woman's body and her sexuality. Early males must have been shocked and bewildered by the fact that a woman's body bleeds in periodic cycles that somehow are mysteriously tied to the moon's cycles. And even more bewildering, females' behavior seemed to be tied to and influenced by these mysterious cycles. The same woman who rejected his sexual advances a few days ago might suddenly and inexplicably seek his sexual favors. Consequently, early males believed women were possessed by an "evil spirit." Esther Harding, a disciple of Jung, describes the power of women's evil spirit to "bewitch" men:

> The female "animal," far from rejecting the advances of the male at the season of heat, desires and seeks his company. No taboo restrains her in the exercise of her charms. All the males of the species from far and wide are attracted to her and are unable to attend to any other interest so long as she is in that condition. Whoever has kept a female dog will know how powerful is the "evil spirit" with which she is possessed. The males who seek her out forego sleep and food and neglect their "duties" in their own homes. They are indeed bewitched (Harding, 1990, p. 60).

Most women experience a "season of heat," or estrus (a Greek word that means "frenzied") either a few days before or a few days after ovulation. It is a uniquely feminine experience, an aspect of femininity that ties woman to all that is wild and untamed in nature. In modern society, it has become an aspect of femininity no longer acknowledged or revered, only vulgarized and trivialized. It is an aspect of femininity that has been used against women, to put them down as proof of their irrationality and their inability to control their behavior. Or worse, thousands of women have been put to death because they were believed to be witches—women with insatiable lust. In *The Malleus Maleficarum,* an encyclopedia of witch beliefs written in 1486, the Dominican priest concluded: "All witchcraft comes from carnal lust, which in women is insatiable" (Kors and Peters, 1976, p. 127).

Males have both worshiped and feared the seductive power of woman's sexuality, her procreative fecundity, and her mysterious ties to nature. That this sexuality operates both on a cosmic level—humankind emerging from the primeval womb of mother nature—and also on a more personal level—the individual emerging from the womb of his personal, biological mother—must have come as a shock. The tender, caring "mother" who bore them also has a cold, unfeeling, dark side.

The male fears that ultimately, woman answers only to Mother Nature, who calls to her through her loins. The male, any male, is merely her instrument, her plaything. She seduces him, uses him, amuses herself with him, and then (like the spider) she devours him to nourish her body, which, energized by the male's sperm, is already preparing itself for a new brood. (There is actually a species of spiders in which, after mating with the female, the male offers himself up as her food.)

The early, matriarchal goddess cultures were replaced by male Warrior cultures in which males dominated. Just as the male Warrior was expected to protect and defend the village, each male was expected to protect and defend his family, with his own life, if necessary. In taking on these responsibilities, the male naturally assumed the role of head of his family and demanded that his wife and children obey him and be accountable to him. But the male's need to control and possess is threatened and undermined by a female sexuality that is driven by the unseen, unfeeling, instinctive force of nature. On the one hand the male is afraid of succumbing to the seductive power of the female's sexuality and, in so doing, losing control as he becomes nature's instrument. On the other hand, the male is also afraid that he will not be able to control the female's sexuality; he fears that she may seek out other males.

The male perceives a female in heat as dangerous because it makes her unpredictable and uncontrollable (the "unpredictable, irrational nature of woman" can ultimately be traced to the fact that her sexuality is tied to nature, to her estrus cycle). The male fears that a "female in heat," driven by her need to satisfy her sexual lust, will betray him, will make him a cuckold by mating with any available male. She may become pregnant by another man and deceive him into believing that the child is his own. Males really have no way of knowing for sure if their children are really their own.

The male perceives a woman in heat as treacherous. She may betray his trust by sleeping with his enemy. History and mythology are full of stories about women who betray men by sleeping with other men.

Males may have intuitively looked to omnipotent, juridical "sky gods" that replaced the early goddesses, because males needed a force that could help them control and rule over the power of nature—and women as "nature's whores." The perception of women as untrustworthy and treacherous is deeply rooted in the patriarchal, Judeo-Christian mythologies. This is clear in the story of Adam and Eve, in which Eve is seduced by the serpent. In Christianity, the serpent symbolizes the anti-Christ, the devil. However, the serpent is an ancient, prebiblical symbol found in many cultures, including the early Sumerian and Babylonian cultures, where it generally represents the Great Mother. Thus, symbolically, the serpent's seduction of Eve can be interpreted as Eve being taken over by natural feminine instincts, giving into her female sexuality. Because female sexuality is tied to nature, the male's sky god is intended to rule over nature and female sexuality. Eve's sin is that she obeyed nature's call; she gave in to her sexual feelings. In doing this, she defied Yahweh and seduced man.

Males have tried to control women's sexuality through male-generated laws, various religious and social institutions, and whatever means males considered necessary. Edward Rice quotes Captain Richard Burton's description of how Somali, Abyssinian, and various other peoples tried to preserve the chastity of their women:

> They sew up the lips of the girl's private parts either with a leather lace, or, more often, with one of horse-hair. A female slave, whom the Arabs call *Kadimah* and the Somalis, *Midgan*, cuts the girl's clitoris and nymphae with a large knife; when the excision has been made she takes a needle and sews up the lips with a continuous series of large stitches. A small passage for passing water is left with the lower part, . . . if a man wishes to fornicate with the girl, and she is shameless enough to permit it, he unpicks the stitches; a husband, on the other hand, will take great pains to increase and amplify his physical strength by a meat diet, and at night when he goes to bed with his newly wed bride will strain to break through the blockage with his sword of love . . . (Rice, 1991, pp. 304-5).

It is easy to see why women may have tried to downplay certain aspects of femininity and female sexuality. But for some women, it may be time to once again acknowledge and celebrate this uniquely feminine experience—to throw back their heads and howl at the moon. This is the message in Clarissa Pinkola Estes' book, *Women Who Run with Wolves,* which emphasizes the importance of women getting in touch with the wild, sensory aspects of their nature: "A woman's heat is not a state of sexual arousal but a state of intense sensory awareness that includes, but is not limited to, her sexuality" (Estes, 1992, p. 334).

The Great Mother is the protectress and nourisher of all life, including man. She reigns over the animal kingdom. The Greek goddess Artemis (Diana to the Romans) represents this aspect of the Great Mother archetype. Artemis is the "Lady of the Wild Things, Huntsman-in-chief to the Gods . . . the protectress of dewy youth" (Hamilton, 1969, p. 31). She is usually depicted with a bow and arrow and surrounded by wild animals.

The Great Mother also rules over all vegetative growth, a world of continual transformation—a swampy, primordial world with endless cycles of birth and decay. This representation appeared in the image of Demeter, goddess of the harvest, and in the ancient festivals worshiping the goddess Cybele, where male priests castrated themselves before her to emulate the castration of her son Attis and to symbolize the cutting of trees and corn. The image of the Earth Mother Goddess ultimately symbolizes the power of mother nature, the unifying life force that humans all share.

There are many examples of manifestations of the Great Mother archetype from many different cultures and periods. Some of the more well-known examples are these goddesses:

- Venus of Willendorf (Paleolithic)
- Gaia (one of the most ancient Greek deities)
- Hestia (Greek)
- Isis (Egyptian)
- Ixquic (Mayan)

Hestia is a particularly appropriate goddess for female homemakers. Hestia represents the home's spiritual center, the goddess of the home and hearth. Hestia is associated with warmth, family, and security. And the image of the Egyptian Great Mother, Isis, holding and suckling her divine son Horus, an image that prefigures the Madonna and child revered by Christianity, epitomizes the sacrosanct bond between mother and child.

Mothers and Daughters

Luke uses the ancient Greek myth of Demeter and Kore to provide a mythological perspective and amplification of the archetypal mother-daughter relationship and transformation from maiden to mother. Psychoanalysts explain that the mother-daughter relationship is very different than the mother-son relationship. Because the son is male, he learns at an early age that he cannot be like mother. In order to achieve his own sense of masculine identity, he must separate himself from his mother. The daughter, on the other hand, continues to identify with her mother. She sees in her mother a reflection of herself, and the mother sees her daughter as an extension of herself. In order to achieve her own identity, the daughter must separate herself from her mother. She must become the mother. "On an archetypal level the son carries for the mother the image of her inner quest, but the daughter is the extension of her self. . . ." (Luke, 1991, p. 80).

Initially, the Kore (the primordial maiden), represented by Persephone, lives in the protective shadow of her mother. Persephone is picking flowers and playing with her friends. She is not yet conscious of her destiny, her transformation from daughter to mother. Intoxicated by the scent of the flowers, she strays from her friends and is seized and raped by Hades, the lord of the underworld. Her intoxication symbolizes an awakening of her consciousness. To make the transformation from maiden to mother, she must break away from the protective circle of her mother; she must put her childhood behind her and become a mother herself. Luke says:

> The moment of breakthrough for a woman is always symbolically a rape—a necessity—something that takes hold with overmastering power and brooks no resistance. The lord of the underworld is he who arises, bursts forth from the unconscious with all the tremendous power of instinct. He comes with his "immortal horses" and sweeps the maiden (anima in a man) from the surface life of her childish paradise into the depths, into the kingdom of the dead—for a woman's total giving of her heart, of herself, in her experience of her instincts is a kind of death (Luke, 1991, p. 82).

Thus, the young maiden must be transformed from her passive, protected state ". . . into the vital passivity of opening herself up to receive the seed, transition point being marked actually or symbolically by the violent breaking of her virginity" (Luke, 1991, p. 81). The male's phallic sword is nature's instrument in cutting the mother-daughter tie, transforming the maiden into the mother. Maidenhood must be forcibly ended, symbolized by the male's penis penetrating the hymen.

The Terrible Mother

The static aspect of the feminine archetype represented by the Great Mother also has a negative aspect: "the Great Container, tends to hold fast to everything that springs from it and surround it like an eternal substance. Everything born of it belongs to it and remains subject to it; and even if the individual becomes independent, the Archetypal Feminine relativizes his independence into a nonessential variant of her own perpetual being" (Neumann, 1991, p. 25). The terrible Earth Mother archetype has its origins in nature's endless cycles of renewal and decay. The same earth that, like a Great Mother, nourishes us and gives us life also brings death and dismemberment. Birth and life are inextricably tied to death and decay:

> Castration, death, and dismemberment on this level are all equivalent. They are all correlated with the decay of vegetation, with harvesting, and the felling of trees. Castration and tree felling, closely associated in myth, are symbolically identical (Neumann, 1970, p 58).

What makes the Terrible Mother aspect of the Great Mother archetype so sinister is that she can be appealing and seductive. Like the spider (one of her symbols), she lures the unsuspecting into her deadly trap: ". . . She is also the goddess who drives mad and fascinates, the seducer and bringer of delight, the sovereign enchantress. The fascination of sex and the drunken orgy culminating in unconsciousness and death are inextricably combined in her" (Neumann, 1970, p. 60).

In the fertility cults of ancient Moon goddesses, the priests attending the goddesses were often eunuchs. The male denied his masculinity by castrating himself in front of the Great Mother. Sometimes the male priest's castration was symbolic, as in cutting his hair or shaving his head. But in some cases it was an actual castration. During the three-day festival worshiping the Moon goddess, Cybele, young males castrated themselves in an orgiastic ritual. The ritual castration was done to celebrate Cybele's grief for her son Attis (he too was a moon God, shown wearing the crescent moon), who castrated himself before the Great Mother.

Harding describes how, in the worship of Cybele, young men ritually castrated themselves in imitation of her son:

> . . . Singing and wailing intermingled and the emotional abandon
> rode to orgiastic heights. Then in a religious frenzy young men
> began to wound themselves with knives; some even performed the
> final sacrifice, castrating themselves before the image of the goddess
> and throwing the bloody parts upon her statue. Others ran bleeding
> through the streets and flung the severed organs into some house
> that they passed. This household was then obliged to supply the
> young man, now become a eunuch priest, with women's clothes.
> These emasculated priests were called "Galloi." After their castra-
> tion they wore long hair and dressed in female clothing (Harding,
> 1990, p. 142).

By wearing women's clothing (a practice still seen in the garments worn by Catholic priests) the eunuch priest denies his masculinity and gives himself over completely to the Great Mother—he becomes her maricon.

A powerful representation of the negative aspect of the feminine archetype is revealed in the Indian culture's goddess, Kali. In Greek and Roman mythology, the negative aspect of the Great Mother is often represented by winged gorgons that devour monsters with snakes for hair, beards, and outthrust tongues (Neumann, 1991, p. 169). All hero myths symbolically represent the human struggle to become free from the ensnaring clutches of the Terrible Mother. For example, Perseus must slay Medusa (the terrible devouring mother) before he can win the hand of Andromeda. Perseus is a typical Hero myth that represents humans' heroic ascent from the unconscious.

For obvious reasons, Madison Avenue has generally chosen to focus on the positive, Great Mother aspect of the overall feminine archetype. Betty Crocker, the corporate symbol for General Mills, is a good example of a recognizable brand character who is based on the positive aspects of the

Great Mother archetype (Betty Crocker will be examined in much greater detail in Chapter 5).

The "Dynamic" Feminine: "Virgin/Maiden"

The other feminine archetype that dominates Western culture and is often used in advertising mythologies is the virgin or maiden. This archetype represents the other side of the overall Great Mother archetype. (See Figure 3.2.) In *The Heroine's Journey,* Maureen Murdoch quotes a woman who sums up her feelings about the feminine images that dominated her childhood: "The images of the feminine that were presented to us in my childhood were either of the sex object Marilyn Monroe or of the great selfless provider. Either way you ended up as the big tit" (Murdoch, 1990, p. 23).

The notion of woman as an alluring, enchanting, seductive creature is, like the nurturing mother archetype, a primordial, archetypal image of woman. Examples of the maiden archetype can be found in literature's muses, fairies, and young virgins; they are enchanting, feminine creatures who inspire men to greatness. The Blessed Virgin is perhaps the most well-known example of the Maiden/Virgin archetype, sans sexuality.

Beauty has always been an important aspect of femininity. A woman's beauty is tied to a woman's overall sense of self-worth and is also a source of power over men. Young girls realize early on that they have a powerful effect on men. However, in the 1960s, the women's movement attacked existing concepts on feminine beauty and sexuality. Feminists reacted in part to the "dumb blonde, Barbie doll look" that had become a cultural stereotype, and they attacked the idea of feminine beauty as "passive." The women's movement tried to bring about a general denial of feminine beauty and sexuality as an aspect of femininity—an aspect that women seemed to enjoy and that afforded them enormous power over men.

The pendulum has swung again in the 1990s. In *Sex, Art, and American Culture,* Camille Paglia says that women can be strong and assertive but also "very sexy." Paglia points to Donna Mills, who played the character Abby Ewing on the nighttime soap "Knots Landing," as a "contemporary woman . . . this total businesswoman is shrewd, mentally alert, and keen, and then also very sexy..." (Paglia, 1992, p. 286). Paglia says she sees a going back toward acceptance of feminine beauty.

My recent research among teenage girls seems to confirm Paglia's point of view: Today's young women are, indeed, very concerned with feminine beauty. In a national study of American teenagers (boys and girls 12 to 17 years old), a series of two-hour focus groups were conducted across America, and it included extensive discussions with teenagers as well as with "teen experts"—people who have a lot of experience and expertise in dealing with teenagers (school counselors, teachers, psychologists, clergy, and so on).

Teenage girls were asked: "What do teen boys and girls obsess about, that is, spend most of their time, energy, and money on" Teen girls readily admitted that girls are obsessed with how they look and spend most of their time shopping and doing things that will enhance their appearance. This was in contrast to what the girls believe teenage boys are preoccupied with: their cars and sports.

Paglia takes the feminists to task for "reducing" the image of a woman's beauty and the power of her sexuality to "passivity":

> I just think it's so sad if we're at that point where you have 10,000 ships destroyed for the beauty of a woman, when you have old men on the gates of Troy in Homer looking at her and, like, they haven't felt any sexual desire in years, in decades, and they look at her and they say, "Look at that beautiful woman. It was worth it." If that's what we're reduced to, taking one of the greatest, most dominant images of mythology of the power of a woman's sexuality and reducing this to "passivity," what a sad and totalitarian life we're living now, with no literature and no art and nothing but these sermonizing lessons that we must learn! (Paglia, 1992, p. 289).

Negative Aspects of the Dynamic Feminine
Maiden Archetype: The Virgin or Harlot

Like all archetypes, the maiden archetype has both negative and positive aspects. The polar opposite of the Virgin/Maiden archetype is the harlot or whore. Again, whenever we confront an archetype, its shadow emerges. In the patriarchal Judeo-Christian mythologies, the unmarried woman is perceived as a threat. More specifically, her undomesticated sexuality threatens the established order of the patriarchal family structure.

In her fascinating book on the Virgin Mary, *Alone of All Her Sex,* Marina Warner explains that in Christianity the unmarried women is portrayed either as a virgin (Virgin Mary) or a penitent whore (Mary Magdalene). To Warner, these two biblical images "[typify] Christian society's attitudes to women and to sex. Both female figures are perceived in sexual terms: Mary as a virgin and Mary Magdalene as a whore—until her repentance. The Magdalene, like Eve, was brought into existence by the powerful undertow of misogyny in Christianity, which associates women with the dangers and degradation of the flesh . . ." (Warner, 1983, p. 225).

In classical mythology, the negative expression of the dynamic feminine maiden takes the form of nixies (mythical, feminine water creatures), sirens, and wood nymphs who seduce young men and suck the life out of them. The Lorelei (from Germanic mythology), enchanting feminine creatures who inhabit the Rhine River and who lure sailors and their ships onto the rocks, are example of the negative aspect of the Virgin/Harlot archetype.

Figure 3.2

Archetypical Female Images

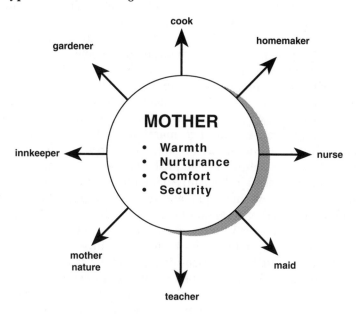

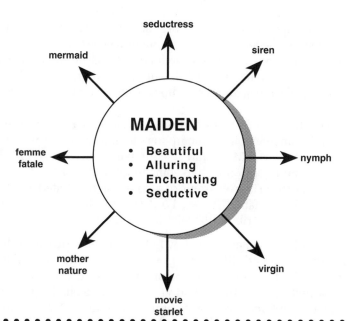

The mermaid is another mythological figure (Figure 3.3) that represents the negative aspect of the feminine—an extension of the Terrible Mother, the witch who devours her children. The fishlike nature of the mermaid symbolizes the inhuman, instinctual, unfeeling aspect of the feminine. The fish, the leviathan (Moby Dick), represents the instinctive force of nature. In ancient Egypt the word for *abomination* was symbolized by the fish (Neumann, 1970, p. 71). And in Jewish legend the deep waters of the ocean are "the territorial waters of the Terrible Mother . . . the child-eating Lilith, the adversary of man, who refuses to submit to Adam, and withdraws to a place called the 'gorge of the sea'" (Neumann, 1970, p. 71).

According to some ancient scriptures, Lilith, not Eve, was actually the first woman. This character is no longer mentioned in the Old Testament, but in the Zohar, thirteenth-century writings about the Torah, we find that Lilith was Adam's first wife. Lilith was vanquished because she defied Jehovah, and because she refused to lie beneath Adam during sexual intercourse; she believed that she was Adam's equal and refused to submit to his wishes. Lilith is often depicted as a demon or a witch. There is a version of the archetypal Lilith character in the ancient Sumerian culture as well: the unmarried, undomesticated goddess Inanna who loved making war and love. Inanna enjoyed using and discarding men in the same way that some men enjoy using and discarding women. Inanna is often described as the goddess who behaved more like a man than a woman. During her festivals, cross-dressing was the order of the day. A more contemporary version of the archetypal, man-eating Lilith appeared in the television show "Cheers"— Frazier's wife, who, appropriately, is named Lilith.

The contemporary equivalent of mermaids, nymphs, and other free-willed females is the femme fatale, a women whose beauty and mysterious feminine charm have a hypnotic, seductive effect on men—usually with disastrous results. In the Judeo-Christian history of the world, Eve was the first femme fatale and seductress, who caused the couple's expulsion from Paradise.

Mata Hari, the exotic dancer who became a German secret agent during World War I, is an infamous, contemporary femme fatale. Known as "the spy with the velvet eyes," Mata Hari's seductive beauty proved fatal for the British officers unlucky enough to come under her spell.

Marlene Dietrich is an example of a femme fatale created on celluloid— a Hollywood femme fatale. A *New York Times* article that appeared at the time of her death described "the Dietrich image":

> The Dietrich image personified by Lola-Lola, the seductive cabaret singer in top hat and silk stockings whom she portrayed in *The Blue Angel,* was that of a liberated woman of the world who chose her men, earned her own living, and viewed sex as a challenge. Audiences were captivated by this creature out of no one's experience but out of everyone's imagination (New York Times, 1992, p. A1).

Figure 3.3

Temptress Archetype: Mermaid

On some level, the femme fatale represents the male's fear of being sucked back into the primordial ooze, of being devoured by the licentious, unfeeling, procreative power of the Great Mother. The femme fatale is ". . . not a fiction but an extrapolation of biologic realities in women that remain constant" (Paglia, 1990, p. 14). Paglia points to the toothed vagina myth *(vagina dentata)* of the North American Indians, which she describes as "a gruesomely direct transcription of female power and male fear. Metaphorically, every vagina has secret teeth, for the male exits as less than when he entered. . . . In sex, the male is consumed and released again by the toothed power that bore him, the female dragon of nature" (Paglia, 1990, pp. 14-15).

Sexuality Versus Sexism: A Fine Line

The women's movement has done a good job of making sexism one of the big bugaboos of our times. No one wants to be accused of being a sexist. At the same time, America is a culture preoccupied with sex. We are a sexy culture. Sexy is good. The old axiom in advertising, "Sex sells," is no less true today. Most of us have no objection to advertising that is *sexy* so long as it is not *sexist*—it does not demean or dehumanize women (or men). Of course, the problem is that sexuality is subjective and interpretive. Advertising that one consumer perceives as sexy may strike another as sexist. Moreover, our perceptions of what is sexy or sexist continue to change. Advertising that was considered sexy in the past may now be considered sexist.

● ●

" Advertising that one consumer perceives as sexy may strike another as sexist."

● ●

There is nothing inherently wrong with advertising that uses sexuality (female or male) to sell products. Humans live in a free society, and everyone enjoys looking at a sexy man or woman. Creating advertising that is sexy and appealing, as opposed to sexist and offensive, is ultimately a judgment call. If an advertiser has any doubts about whether the advertising is offensive, the company can, and should, conduct consumer research that will reveal whether the advertising is indeed offensive. For example, in 1955, *Life Magazine* refused to run the famous "Does she . . . or doesn't she?" ad created by Shirley Polykoff at Foote, Cone, and Belding. The magazine people were afraid the ad might be too risqué or might offend some women. Polykoff persuaded the people at *Life* to conduct a poll among its female employees to see whether in fact women found the ad offensive. They didn't, and the Clairol campaign ran for 15 years.

In any case, the consumer always has the final say. If enough consumers feel an advertisement is offensive, they can make this known to the advertiser. Most advertisers are sensitive to negative press, and they will pull an ad rather than run the risk of offending consumers or creating bad publicity. In today's media-intensive world, a world where there are no secrets, American businesses have, in effect, a built-in system of checks and balances that serves to mediate any differences of opinion between advertiser and consumer.

• • •
The Archetypal Journey

Life is a sacred journey. As we travel its roads, all of us, consciously or unconsciously, live through a series of archetypes and archetypal experiences that define and shape our lives. We all start out by living the Child archetype that represents innocence. We then progress to the Orphan and through various other archetypes. In *The Hero Within,* Carol S. Pearson describes some of the main archetypes:

> Each of the archetypes carries with it a world view, and with that different life goals and theories about what gives life meaning. Orphans seek safety and fear exploitation and abandonment. Martyrs want to be good, and see the world as a conflict between good (care and responsibility) and bad (selfishness and exploitation). Wanderers want independence and fear conformity. Warriors strive to be strong, to have an impact upon the world, and to avoid ineffectiveness and passivity. Magicians aim to be true to their inner wisdom and to be in balance with the energies of the universe. Conversely, they try to avoid the inauthentic and the superficial (Pearson, 1989, p. 5).

However, Pearson believes that the pattern of archetypes that we embrace and that helps shape our lives has generally been different for men and women. In western cultures, warrior virtues are associated with masculinity and, therefore, men are pushed into the Warrior archetype at a very early age. Little boys are encouraged to be strong and independent: "Be strong, don't cry, hang tough." Males learn early on to suppress their nurturing, feeling side because it is perceived as unmanly. Women, on the other hand, are pushed into the martyr, caretaking role. Little girls are encouraged to be polite, sensitive, kind, and caring. The caretaker role continues into marriage, where women embrace the Mother archetype, which again requires caretaking and nurturing. Until recently, women have generally shunned the Warrior archetype in the same way that men have shunned archetypes that would allow them to express their caring, nurturing side. Cultural stereotypes can limit women and men to one-dimensional lives preventing them from becoming fully functional, fully realized human beings. One of the really important achievements of the women's movement is that it has encouraged women to break away from the traditional "feminine archetypes" to experience life as warriors and wanderers. At the same time, seeing women in nontraditional roles has worked to encourage males acknowledge their own nurturing, feeling side and to embrace caretaker archetypes that traditionally have been associated only with women.

History provides some great examples of Warrior-Hero women: Joan of Arc, the symbol of French nationalism, was the farm girl who answered to the call to lead the fight against England and was burned at the stake; Catherine the Great ruled an empire when she was only 13 years old; Boudicca, a legendary warrior heroine, symbolizes the British spirit. During the first century, Boudicca led the Icini tribe against the Romans, choosing to die like a warrior rather than surrender.

However, most young women growing up in contemporary, western cultures have very few Warrior-Hero role models, whereas, male role models have been based almost exclusively on the Warrior-Hero archetype. Unfortunately, most Americans have been led to believe that the archetypal Warrior-Hero, the Lone Ranger, Superman-type superhero, whose values are independence, strength, and courage, is inherently better than other archetypal role models that emphasize values like nurturing, compassion, and creativity. This is simply not true everywhere. For example, the Lone Ranger myth and the Warrior-Cowboy mentality it represents are not prized in Japan, a culture that prizes harmony and a strong sense of community over the aggressive, "rugged individualism" represented by the Cowboy-Hero archetype.

There are two ways to approach the role model issue: Advertisers can try to create more Warrior-Hero role models for women (which is what society is doing now), or Americans can change their cultural values to de-emphasize the importance of aggression and competitiveness, to create a society that places equal value on compassion, kindness, and caring—the female archetypal values. Too much emphasis on androcentric, Warrior-Hero values has already left humanity a world full of aggression and hostility. Pearson says that people are suffering from an absence of the Caregiving archetype:

> In earlier periods of patriarchal history, men's emphasis on Warrioring was balanced by women's caregiving roles. In part, the contemporary women's movement was motivated because women were assigned most of the caretaking, nurturing functions for the society, but that work was not, and is not now, respected or rewarded. As many women have stopped nurturing and caring for others full-time—seeking roles that would give greater rewards— men have not moved in to fill the void. So we have a crisis. Who will care for the children? Who will maintain our homes? Who will care for the elderly? Who will create community and help people know they matter? (Pearson, 1991, p. 275).

The perennially provocative Dr. Spock shocked parents (again) when he suggested that Little League be abolished, that there is too much emphasis in this country on aggression and competitiveness. Dr. Spock proffered that kids should also be encouraged to spend at least as much time learning to be compassionate and caring by, for example, doing volunteer work in hospitals and nursing homes.

Amazonism

Amazonism is an extreme expression of the female Warrior. The Amazonian sensibility sees patriarchy and men as inherently oppressive. In ancient mythology, the female warrior was often represented by the Amazon woman. The word *amazon* means "without breast": Legend has it that the Amazon women removed one of their breasts so they could draw their archery bows better. Amazon legends are pre-Homeric, and it remains unclear whether they actually existed or were mythical figures. In some sense it really doesn't matter; the fact that Amazon women exist in the human unconscious psyche is significant.

One of the more enduring Amazonian myths concerns the women of Lemnos. The women of Lemnos offended Aphrodite, who in revenge cursed them with an awful body odor. Their husbands couldn't stand their smell and took up with the women from Thrace. This, in turn, enraged the women of Lemnos, who killed their husbands and fathers, except that Hypsipyle hid and protected her father from harm. Hypsipyle was also the Queen of Lemnos. When Jason and the Argonauts later landed on Lemnos, Hypsipyle slept with Jason and bore him two sons. Bachofen explains the symbolic significance of the myth of the women of Lemnos:

> Aphrodite was hostile to the women of Lemnos because they had neglected her cult. The meaning is evident. The women of Lemnos found greater pleasure in the warlike life of the Amazon than in the fulfillment of their feminine calling. The law of Aphrodite, according to which marriage and childbearing are women's highest duty, was not fulfilled. Warlike valor was set above motherhood. . . . Warlike valor destroys all woman's charms (Bachofen, 1992, p. 174).

Bachofen maintains that "Amazonism is a universal phenomenon. It is not based on the special physical or historical circumstances of any particular people, but on conditions that are characteristic of all human existence" (Bachofen, 1992, p. 105). Amazonism is invariably precipitated by "a previous degradation of woman" (Bachofen, 1992, p. 104). In other words, Bachofen believes that instances of Amazonism can be found in any culture in which women have been subjected to degradation and abuse.

Elements of Amazonism have emerged in U.S. culture. For example, the film *Thelma and Louise,* in which two women embark on a wild adventure, exhibits an undercurrent of Amazonism. The main character in the film *Basic Instinct* comes right out of the Amazonian archetype: a bisexual, unfeeling, man-murdering woman who brings herself to orgasm while killing her male lovers with a phallic ice pick as she is straddling them during intercourse.

• • •
The Changing Role of Women

The role of women in American society is changing. Women are pursuing permanent careers outside the home and entering jobs and professions that were once open only to men. Women are struggling to overcome and eliminate the inequities inherent in a patriarchal society built on traditional male values. They have begun flexing their muscles—literally and figuratively, and they have begun to seize control of their lives and their bodies. In order to achieve a psychic wholeness, women must embrace and develop the masculine aspect of their psyche, what Jung called the *animus*. Indeed, as women mature and grow older there is generally a masculinization process that takes place both physically and psychologically. For example, after menopause, it is not unusual for women to develop facial hair. On a more psychological level, many women who have lived their younger years as traditional homemakers may come to embrace their masculine side *(logos)* in their later years. They may become more world-involved or they may discover and develop latent talents, start businesses, and so on.

Embracing the Feminine and the Masculine

Men, too, go through a feminization process, a decrease in male hormones and muscle mass. On a more psychological level, as men grow older they begin to get in touch with their feelings and their intuitive side. However, women have generally done a much better job of embracing their masculine side (animus) than men have done in embracing their feminine side, their *anima*. Women are more secure in their femaleness and womanhood than men are in their masculinity and manhood. Moreover, by developing her masculine side (animus) the female becomes more world-involved and empowered.

The male, on the other hand, feels threatened by the idea of embracing his feminine side (anima) because he fears he will lose his hard-won sense of masculinity. Chapter 4 discusses the male's life-long struggle to establish his masculinity and achieve a level of manhood. Moreover, in the American culture, masculinity and male (Warrior) values are generally valued more

Figure 3.4

Rosy The Riveter, We Can Do It

Courtesy of the National Archives

highly than feminine values like compassion and nurturance. Thus, unlike the female who becomes empowered by embracing her masculine side, the male who embraces his feminine side feels he is relinquishing some of his worldly power; he has a lot to lose. Of course, by embracing his feminine side, the male ultimately gains: His creative powers increase and he becomes a whole person. But most males don't see it this way, and they are therefore threatened by the idea of embracing their feminine side.

On the other hand, the danger for women is that the empowerment that comes with the development of their masculine side can be intoxicating. Women can sometimes become too enthusiastic in embracing their masculine side, to the detriment of their feminine side. Psychoanalyst Emma Jung, (Carl Jung's daughter) contrasts the woman who has successfully integrated her masculine side (animus) with her feminine nature, with a woman who has failed to integrate her masculine principle (animus) with her feminine nature:

> . . . there are also women in whom this aspect of masculinity is already harmoniously coordinated with the feminine principle and lending it effective aid. These are the active, energetic, brave, and forceful women. But also there are those in whom the integration has failed, in whom masculine behavior has overrun and suppressed the feminine principle. These are the overenergetic, ruthless, brutal men-women, the Xantippes who are not only active but aggressive (Jung, 1957, p. 4).

Indeed, as they entered the 1990s, women increasingly began to reject the Superwoman myth and began to experience a sense of ennui. Psychoanalyst Maureen Murdoch says she has encountered a lot of dissatisfaction among 30- to 50-year-old career women: "These women have embraced the stereotypical male heroic journey and have attained academic, artistic, or financial success; yet for many the question remains, 'what is all this for?'" (Murdoch, 1990, p.1). Murdoch reports that women have been so busy competing as men in a man's world that they have lost touch with their own femininity: "The sense of loss these women express is a yearning for the feminine, a longing for a sense of 'home' within their own bodies and community" (Murdoch, 1990, p. 73). Female psychoanalysts like Murdoch warn that unless women once again embrace their femininity, they will never feel whole.

Women in Search of a New Mythology

Prompted by the women's movement, women have rejected the old definitions of femininity, but they have failed to devise a viable new definition of femininity and a new female mythology. Nowhere is this more evident than among today's young women. One of the most interesting findings in the national teen study cited earlier is that teenage girls have no idea what it means to be feminine. They associate femininity with "old-fashioned ideas" about girls being "passive," "modest," and "waiting at home for some boy to call them." Without a new feminine mythology to replace the old one, teen girls have no guidelines about what is appropriate behavior for a young woman.

The study asked the teen experts: "If one could become a 16-year-old once again, what would be different or changed in the world of today's teens?" Their response was essentially the same in every part of the country: "Teen girls are much more sexually aggressive now." Teachers and counselors reported numerous complaints from parents that the teen girls badger their sons or leave lewd messages on the answering machine. Some reports cited single-parent mothers who double-date with their daughters and have both their boyfriends sleep over. Other teen experts who work in the social services note the increasing numbers of 13- and 14-year-old girls who contract syphilis and gonorrhea or become pregnant because "there is just no selectiveness in whom they date."

Many of the teachers who have been teaching teenagers for more than 10 years said they were shocked by the profanity and even more shocked by the increase of violence among teen girls. Without a feminine mythology, many teen girls believe they should behave just like boys do. This idea is being reinforced in the media, where women are increasingly being portrayed as violent. To counter the idea that women are "passive," television shows and films portray women as violent—punching, kicking, shooting, and killing just like men.

Not to be outdone by their girlfriends, teen boys feel they have to be even more macho and violent in order to differentiate themselves from the girls. Thus, the softening, tempering effects of being around women are being negated. Americans are becoming a Warrior culture in the extreme, a culture that only respects power and violence.

If there are important differences between males and females that go beyond anatomical differences, people need to understand them. Certainly people should not, in the name of equality, disregard important male-female differences that might mislead our young people and create havoc in their lives.

Promiscuity in women threatens to bring about a degeneration of our social structure, a return to *haeterism,* a term coined by Bachofen to refer to the premarital, sexual promiscuity that existed in the earliest prematriarchal, communal cultures (Bachofen, 1992, p. xviii). A woman's uterus is a "temenos," a sacred place, an inner sanctum where human life is created. Paglia sums it up, "a girl is a sealed vessel that must be broken into by force. the prototype of all sacred spaces. . . the Holy of Holies" (Paglia, 1990, p. 23). Paglia speculates whether there is a good reason for the double standard regarding male and female sexuality:

It is in nature's best interests to goad dominant males into indis-
criminate spreading of their seed. But nature also profits from
female purity. . . Women hold themselves in reserve because the
female body is a reservoir, a virgin patch of still, pooled water
where the fetus comes to term. Male chase and female flight are not
just a social game. The double standard may be one of nature's
organic laws (Paglia, 1990, p. 27).

M. Ester Harding says women must not lose touch with their uniquely
feminine life experience. For example, she says that among women today,
the prevailing attitude toward menstruation is that it is a nuisance, "the
curse" (Harding, 1990, p. 73), a handicap that may prevent them from
competing effectively with men. This is in direct contrast to women in so-
called primitive, pretechnological cultures who withdraw from the daily
routine of life and go into isolation during menstruation. Women need a
sense of feminine space away from men, a chance to get in touch with "the
dark powers of her own feminine instinct" (Harding, 1990, p. 73).

Teen girls desperately need a new feminine mythology to replace the old
one; without a mythology they not only see themselves as equal to boys, but
also see themselves as being the same as boys. This point was driven home
in one group session in which teen girls complained that, "It ain't fair that
girls have to suffer with periods and cramps" whereas the boys do not. This
same resentment, this "ain't fair" attitude, also fuels some of the angry
feminist rhetoric.

Women are beginning to realize that they must get back in touch with
their own unique, feminine powers. Now this book is *not* suggesting that
women give up their struggle for equal rights or go back to nature, to the dark
ages of the Earth Mother. Technology has, to some extent, freed women (and
men) from the tyranny of human instincts. Women must continue to move
forward and assume greater power and responsibility in shaping the world.
Emma Jung says this is not simply an ". . . idiotic aping of man, or a
competitive drive betokening megalomania" (Jung, 1957, p. 5). Continuing,
Jung says that the world has changed and women have no choice but to
change.

● ●

" Women are beginning to realize that they must
get back in touch with their own unique, feminine
powers."

● ●

Connie Zweig's essay, "The Conscious Feminine: Birth of a New
Archetype," identified a newly emerging feminine archetype ("the conscious feminine") that celebrates the uniquely feminine powers of women.

Zweig says that women must get back in touch with their own unique, feminine powers: "The world has never known the . . . archetype of conscious mature woman" (Zweig, 1991, p. 191). Zweig quotes Jungian analyst Marion Woodman, who says we need to bring feminine values into the world "because the power that drives the patriarchy, the power that is raping the earth, the power drive behind addictions has to be transformed. There has to be a counterbalance to all that frenzy, annihilation, ambition, competition, and materialism" (Zweig, 1991, p. 191).

Women (and men) are in a tough spot. They're damned if they do and damned if they don't. Women have to embrace their masculine side to become a whole person, but if they do too good a job of it, they may lose touch with their femininity. On the other hand, in order to achieve wholeness, men have to do a better job of embracing their feminine side, but they are afraid of losing their hard-won sense of masculinity and manhood. Somehow humans need to strike a balance between their masculine and feminine sides while maintaining a separate sense of masculine and feminine space, a sense of what is uniquely masculine and feminine. It won't be easy.

And there is no shortage of naysayers, such as Allan Bloom who, in *The Closing of the American Mind,* expressed the thesis that the great social experiment is doomed to fail:

> The souls of men—their ambitious, warlike, protective, possessive character—must be dismantled in order to liberate women from their domination. . . . With machismo discredited, the positive task is to make men caring, sensitive, even nurturing, to fit the restructured family. Thus once again men must be re-educated according to an abstract project. They must accept the "feminine elements" in their nature. A host of Dustin Hoffman and Meryl Streep types invade the schools, popular psychology, TV, and the movies, making the project respectable. Men tend to undergo this re-education somewhat sullenly but studiously, in order to avoid the opprobrium of the sexist label and to keep the peace with their wives and girlfriends. And it is indeed possible to soften men. But to make them "care" is another thing, and the project must inevitably fail (Bloom, 1987, p. 129).

• • •
The Newly Emerging Female Mythologies

Despite the naysayers and cautionary notes about women maintaining a sense of femininity and feminine space, these are exciting, heady times for women. Women are moving into uncharted territory, literally redefining the image of women and their place in society. One thing is certain: the old feminine mythologies are too limiting. Women are searching for new ones that reflect the changing needs and roles of contemporary society.

Perhaps the key to understanding the newly emerging female mythologies lies in greater diversity and pluralism, in breaking away from the traditional roles and images of women—those that limited them to supportive, caretaker roles in society. To be sure, the new female mythologies will undoubtedly retain the traditional archetypal images of women as mothers and maidens, but they will expand beyond these as well to include feminine imagery based on archetypes like the warrior, wanderer, and magician. This opens up exciting new possibilities, both in terms of the way women are perceived as well as their roles in society.

The emerging female mythologies will create a new ethos or set of guiding beliefs, which in turn will give women greater freedom and diversity in the conduct of their lives. For example, the dual role of women as both powerful leaders and loving mothers has already gained widespread acceptance in American culture. We may also see more women who, like Murphy Brown, eschew the traditional ideas of marriage and family and opt to have a child through artificial insemination. Women have taken the lead, and what we are witnessing is nothing short of a social revolution—one that will touch all our lives.

The new female mythologies will allow for diverse, pluralistic lifestyles and sensibilities that may be radically different than anything people have seen before. This will, in turn, force men to change their mythologies, to move beyond the Warrior archetype, to embrace alternate archetypes that allow them to acknowledge the kinder, nurturing, more creative aspects of their psyches. Some men have already indeed assumed greater roles at home, taking care of children, and so on.

The new diversity and greater acceptance of different values, cultures, and lifestyles pioneered by the women's movement will undoubtedly also include a greater acceptance of lesbians and gays. And, as Part III shows, advertisers have a responsibility to be sensitive to these social changes and to reflect them in their brand mythologies.

Chapter 4
• • • • • • • • • •

Male Mythologies

In contrast to the fairly extensive, well-developed literature on various aspects of femininity, feminine archetypes, the Great Mother, and so on, there is a relative paucity of material about masculinity and male archetypes. One might expect that in a patriarchal culture it would be the reverse, but that is not the case. For example, Jung and Neumann covered the Great Mother and Maiden archetypes in detail, but their information regarding masculine archetypes was scattered and less well-developed. However, the material in this chapter is structured so that, where possible, it parallels the material on female mythologies.

• • •
The Dawn of Consciousness

To early humans the world must have been a scary place. Neumann artfully describes the helplessness and vulnerability of man's emerging ego-consciousness and the terrors he faced, both from the world without and the world within:

> The ego-consciousness . . . feels itself a tiny, defenseless speck, enveloped and helplessly dependent, a little island floating on the vast expanse of the primal ocean. At this stage, consciousness has not yet wrested any firm foothold from the flood of unconscious being. . . .
>
> Exposed to the dark forces of the world and the unconscious, early man's life feeling is necessarily one of constant endangerment. Life in the psychic cosmos of the primitive is a life full of danger and

uncertainty; and the daemonism of the external world, with its sickness and death, famines and floods, droughts and earthquakes, is heightened beyond measure when contaminated with what we call the inner world. The terrors of a world ruled by the irrationality of chance and mitigated by no knowledge of the laws of causality, are made even more sinister by the spirits of the dead, demons and gods, witches and magicians (Neumann, 1970, p. 40).

Once they became conscious of their own mortality, early humans must have been awed by the God-like power of nature with its endless cycles of growth and decay. And males were no doubt equally awed and impressed by the fact that females, with their body's cycles and power to create life in their bodies, were mysteriously connected to nature. Early males did not realize that pregnancy came as a result of sexual intercourse. They believed that it was the work of God or some mysterious power—the same power that was responsible for the fecundity of the earth. Thus, early males believed that women were somehow strangely allied with nature—a force they both feared and revered. Women must have seemed strange to men, and vice versa. One African creation myth says man and woman were created separately, and when they saw each other, they laughed.

Static Masculine: "The Great Father"

Like femininity, masculinity has both "static" (elementary) and "dynamic" (transformative) aspects, and each aspect has both a positive and negative side. The static masculine character is represented by "logos" (order and reason), by the Great Father and Senex archetypes. *Senex* is Latin for "old man" and represents "all that is old, ordered, and established" (Hillman, 1990, p. 19). The positive traits of the Great Father archetype center around organizing, establishing rules, laws, and a sense of hierarchical order. Manifestations of the Great Father archetype occur in social systems as well as, on a more personal level, in the patriarchal family structure. The Great Father provides and protects. He is also caring and loving. Other manifestations of the Great Father are the king, and teacher/mentor.

Fatherhood and patriarchal consciousness represent the development of a higher consciousness and moral order. According to Bachofen, human culture has gone through three different phases:

1.   The *tellurian phase,* which represents motherhood without marriage—a time of sexual promiscuity during which males mated with any available females.

2.   The *lunar* or *matriarchal phase,* which represents "conjugal

motherhood and authentic birth," that is, a time when bloodlines were carried through the mother's lineage, from mother to daughter.

3. The *solar* or *patriarchal phase* (the current situation), represented by "conjugal father rights," or the bloodlines being carried through the father's lineage, from father to son (Bachofen, 1992, p. 178).

The lunar phase, when goddess worship flourished, also brought with it agriculture and communities, and matriarchies evolved not only because man stood in awe of woman, but also because women needed to free themselves from the constant sexual demands of males, which in a nonconjugal, communal society with lots of unattached males roaming around, must have been intense.

Patriarchal consciousness represents humankind's spiritual side, the ascension from matriarchal consciousness, which represents humankind's corporal side and is rooted in the endless cycles of nature:

. . . the triumph of paternity brings with it the liberation of the spirit from the manifestations of nature, a sublimation of human existence over the laws of material life. . . (Bachofen, 1992, pp. 109-10).

The ancient Greek gods Cronus and Zeus are two of the earliest and most enduring examples of the Great Father archetype, the image of a Universal Father, an all-powerful male God who is a just defender of the weak and helpless. Greek mythology reveals the struggles of humankind to free itself from the primordial stew, and at the same time displays the growing emergence of a patriarchal sensibility.

The Greeks believed that in the beginning there was only formless confusion, chaos, and darkness. Chaos gave birth (inexplicably) to Night and Erebus, "the unfathomable depth where death dwells" (Hamilton, 1969, p. 63). Miraculously, out of this dark nothingness came Love:

Black Winged Night
Into the bosom of Erebus dark and deep
Laid a wind born egg, and as the seasons rolled
Forth sprang Love, the longed for, shining, with
Wings of gold (Aristophanes)

Love created Light and Day. The earth was created, and its first inhabitants were Gaia (Mother Earth) and Ouranos (Father Heaven). (Similar creation myths are found in other cultural mythologies.) They gave birth to three multiheaded monsters, three other monsters who each had one oversized eye (Cyclops), and the more beneficent Titans. Father Heaven hated the monsters even though they were his sons (just picture ol' Cronus taking one look at the monsters and saying "these can't be *my* kids!"), so he locked them away in a secret place, but he allowed his other sons, the Cyclops and Titans, to roam free.

Mother Earth was upset that her monster sons were locked away, and she cried for help. Cronus, the Titan Son of Father Heaven, was the only one who was bold enough to defy his Father. He ambushed his father and killed him by cutting off his genitals and flinging them into the sea. Cronus with his sister Queen Rhea became the new rulers of Heaven and Earth. But Cronus heard that one of his own children was destined to dethrone him. He tried to prevent this by devouring his children as they were born. However, when his sixth child was born, his wife tricked him, giving him a stone wrapped in swaddling clothes that he swallowed thinking it was his child.

Rhea's sixth son was Zeus, who grew up and with his awesome lightning bolt became the supreme ruler, the God of Gods. In Zeus emerges the male patriarchal sensibility based on the exclusionary idea of one supreme, male God.

The notion of an omnipotent, male sky god like Zeus with his lightning bolt, and the patriarchal, Judeo-Christian God who has come to dominate western culture and sensibilities, is prefigured in the ancient Babylonian God Marduk, who wielded a lightning bolt and emerged as the first male Warrior-Hero God.

Like the Great Mother archetype and Earth Goddesses, the Great Father archetype and the Sky Gods are found in most cultural mythologies. For example, plains Indians like the Sioux worshiped The Great Spirit or "Father of the Sky." In Chinese mythology, Lao-Tien-Yeh is "Father Heaven," who made human beings by molding them out of clay (much like the Judeo-Christian Sky God). Thor, the Norse God of Thunder, eldest son of Odin, with his magical hammer Mjollnir (it always came back to his hand after he threw it), is remarkably similar to Zeus. Also, like Ouranos from Greek mythology, sky gods representing the Great Father archetype are often paired with earth goddesses representing the Great Mother archetype. For example, in Polynesian mythology, the sky god Rangi is paired with the earth goddess Papa.

• • •
Modern Fatherhood

The concept of "fatherhood" changed and evolved over time. Early notions of fatherhood were generally patriarchal and modeled after the Judeo-Christian religions. The father was the head of his family and household in much the same way the God ruled over the church and His peoples. However, during the 1800s a more modern version of fatherhood emerged. E. Anthony Rotundo, in "American Fatherhood," outlines two major periods of American fatherhood: patriarchal fatherhood (1620 to 1800) and modern fatherhood (1800 to the present). Today, a third style of fatherhood—androgynous fatherhood—seems to be evolving (Rotundo, 1985, pp. 7-25).

According to Rotundo, androgynous fatherhood represents a new form of fatherhood in which there has been a blurring and overlapping of traditional father/mother roles, where the father and mother work and both share equally in the day-to-day caring of children and home. Thus, the concept of fatherhood has evolved from a patriarchal style, in which fathers had absolute power and authority, to a more modern style, in which power and authority are shared equally by fathers and mothers. At the same time, there has also been a parallel trend toward greater emotional involvement and participation in child rearing by fathers. Unlike the patriarchal father who took responsibility for his children's moral values but who was generally distant, detached, and a strict disciplinarian, the modern father's relationship is closer and more involved. The concept of fatherhood has been shaped—and continues to be shaped—by the prevailing social, economic, and political forces of the culture. For example, the patriarchal style of fatherhood is clearly rooted in this country's agrarian past, when American families worked and lived together on the farms. The patriarchal father's power grew out of his control of the family property. Dad owned the farm, and if you didn't live by his rules, you were cut off (Rotundo, 1985, pp. 7-25).

Galvanizing Impact of the Industrial Revolution

Father's absolute power and authority was undermined by the Industrial Revolution. Urbanized, mechanized cultures needed a work force to tend its growing industrial machine. Increasing numbers of Americans left the farm to work in factories and offices, and the so-called traditional breadwinner and homemaker roles grew out of industrial America's need for a stable workforce. Having mom home to take care of the children while dad worked in factories and offices was an arrangement that suited the needs of growing industrial economies.

World War II: Women Go to Work

Father's power and authority was further undermined by World War II, which forced women into the workplace, and the women's movement, which raised women's consciousness and challenged them to redefine and reshape their role in society. Consequently, men were forced to reexamine their own roles. The "traditional breadwinner-homemaker roles" gave way to shared responsibilities both inside and outside the home. Fathers have been forced to share in the responsibilities of running households and raising families. Thus, the distinction between fathers' and mothers' roles is less clear.

In fact, the only aspect of patriarchal fatherhood that still exists is the fact that children carry their fathers' surname, and as evidenced by all the hyphenated surnames, even that has come under attack. America is a patriarchal culture in name only. In day-to-day practice, most marriages function more like a matriarchy than a patriarchy. Although today's male shares in the household responsibilities and the raising of the children, the woman still has the upper hand when it comes to raising children and "feathering the nest." The primacy of mother's rights is still recognized by the U.S. legal system, which, in divorce cases, generally awards the children, the home, and a sizable share of the man's wealth to the mother. Additionally, because of the naturally strong bond between a woman and her mother, most married men live matrilocally—they wind up spending more time with their wife's family than their own.

•••••••••••••••••••••••••••••••
" New appeal is to advertise with
positive male energy . . . "
•••••••••••••••••••••••••••••••

On the other hand, the male's involvement with his children seems to be greater than ever before. This is not to deny the fact that there are still lots of "deadbeat dads," but today's fathers are more involved with their children and are not ashamed to admit it. It's ironic that the megaforces that imposed a definition of fatherhood—one that distanced fathers from their children—have come full circle and brought them back together. It has now become socially acceptable for men to be emotionally involved with their children and to participate in all aspects of child rearing. Men are discovering that being involved parents is hard work, but, at the same time, they are also discovering the special joys and love that the involvement brings. And, in the process, maybe men are also learning something about themselves, that humans are all complex creatures with many needs, including the need to be nurturing, loving, and caring. Men should not submit to an imposed definition of fatherhood that deprives them of an important part of their humanity.

• • •
Father Figures in the Media

It is surprising, given the fact that America is supposed to be a patriarchal culture, that there are relatively few examples of father figures in advertising or in the media at large. There were a few television series like "My Three Sons" and "The Rifleman" that were based on the Great Father archetype and that explored the father-son relationship. One of the more memorable, archetypal father figures was the character played by Robert Young in "Father Knows Best." Father was portrayed as a wise and loving dad on whom everyone could depend for love and guidance. Robert Young brought essentially this same character to another hit television series, wherein he played Dr. Welby, a paternal, caring doctor. This in turn ultimately led to Robert Young being chosen as a spokesman for Sanka Coffee. Madison Avenue used Robert Young, the archetypal fatherly doctor, to advise consumers about the dangers of too much caffeine.

A more recent example of an appealing father figure in advertising with lots of positive male energy is Bill Cosby. Cosby serves double duty because he is black, and young black males desperately need positive male role models. Cosby has a natural appeal among kids and he has consequently been the spokesman for quite a few products designed to appeal to children (Jell-O Pudding Pops, and so on).

Where's Dad?

The absence of father figures in television advertising might be partly explained by the fact that most early television commercials were directed at the female homemaker. Advertisers simply didn't need to present a father figure in their advertising. But, on another level, this may also be a reflection of a deeper, cultural reality: Dad wasn't around. Dad had become an absentee father who spent most of his time toiling away in corporate America's factories and offices. Now mom has joined dad, and she too has become an absentee parent.

Robert Bly, a contemporary poet who has captured attention for his advocacy of the "men's movement," argues that American's do not have a true patriarchy, but rather ". . . a system of industrial domination which is not patriarchal and honor is given neither to the male nor to the female" (Bly, 1992, p. 6). Men have been duped by the industrial/ military complex, and now their sisters are "free" to join them.

In *Iron John,* Bly says one of the things he has heard repeatedly from men in his seminars is, "There is not enough father." There is not enough "positive male energy," what the Greeks called "Zeus energy" (Bly, 1990, p. 22).

● ●

"What do you do all day at work, Dad? "

● ●

Most of this absence has been blamed on the Industrial Revolution, which physically removed fathers from their families. Most children do not see their fathers during the day, and they do not see what their father does.

Whose children have not asked, "What do you do all day at work, Dad?" And when Dad finally does come home, it's not much better:

> The successful father brings home a manic mood, the unsuccessful father, depression. What does the son receive? A bad disposition, springing from powerlessness and despair mingled with long-standing shame and the numbness peculiar to those who hate their jobs. Fathers in earlier times could often break through their own defective dispositions by teaching rope making, fishing, post-hole digging, grain cutting, drumming, harness making, animal care, even singing and storytelling (Bly, 1990, p. 5).

Fathers and Sons

Bly maintains that not only is father physically absent, there is also a *spiritual* absence of father in this culture. According to Hillman, the result is a society with too many ungrounded young males or *Puer aeternus* (eternal youths). The Puer archetype (eternal youth) is the polar opposite of the Senex archetype (old man) (Hillman, 1990, p. 173). Again, all archetypes are bipolar or bivalent. When an archetype is constellated, we immediately become aware of its "shadow"—its bipolar/bivalent opposite lurking in the wings. The Puer is a man who behaves like a butterfly, flitting from one thing to another. He fears responsibility and hard work, anything that might bring him down. Psychoanalyst Dan Kiley refers to the Puer aeternus complex as "the Peter Pan Syndrome" (Kiley, 1983, p. 26).

In her classic work, *Puer Aeternus,* Marie Louise von Franz describes the puer aeternus as a man who "... remains too long in adolescent psychology; that is, all those characteristics that are normal in a youth of 17 or 18 are continued into later life, coupled in most cases with too great a dependence on the mother" (von Franz, 1981, p. 1). Von Franz states that the two most typical disturbances associated with this complex are "homosexuality and Don Juanism" (von Franz, 1981, p. 1), which makes for a lot of unhappy females.

The father is responsible for the son's initiation into manhood and the world of men. At some point—usually around the time of adolescence— young males are generally taken away from the protective circle of the mother and initiated into the male world. Many of the initiation rituals include a physical transformation such as circumcision, which signifies the young man's rebirth, his crossing over into the man's world. Eventually, most cultures initiate young men into warriorhood, either by proving their courage in battle or in confronting a dangerous predatory animal. Thus, males not only have to prove their manhood before the Great Mother but also have to prove their manhood before other males.

The initiation into the male world may take many forms. The father takes the boy under his wing and becomes both his mentor and role model. Shoulder to shoulder, father teaches son about making arrows, auto repair, or the fine points of fishing. The father represents logos (order and reason) and patriarchal consciousness. The boy must make the transition from matriarchal consciousness to patriarchal consciousness—a recapitulation of humanity's evolution from matriarchal consciousness to patriarchal consciousness.

How It Used to Be

Sherwood Anderson wrote an essay in 1939 describing his own "silent but stormy" initiation into the male world. The essay does such a wonderful job of capturing the poignant, unspoken bond between the father and son, and the saturnic sadness of the father, it is reprinted here for the readers' enjoyment.

The Night I Became the Son of My Father

There came a certain night. Mother was away from home when Father came in and he was alone. He'd been off for two or three weeks.

He came silently into the house. It was raining outside. It may be there was church that night and Mother had gone there. I had a book before me and was sitting alone in the house, reading by the kitchen table.

Father had been walking in the rain and was very wet. He sat and looked at me. I was startled, for on that night there was on his face the saddest look I have ever seen on a human face. For a long time he sat looking at me, not saying a word.

He was sad and looking at him made me sad. He sat for a time, saying nothing, his clothes dripping. He must have been walking for a long time in the rain. He got up out of his chair.

"You come on, you come with me," he said. I was filled with wonder but, although he had suddenly become like a stranger to me, I wasn't afraid. We went down a long street and out of the town.

Finally we came to a pond. We stood at the edge. We had come in silence. It was still raining hard and there were flashes of lightning followed by thunder. My father spoke, and in the darkness and rain his voice sounded strange. It was the only time after we had left the house that he did speak to me.

"Take off your clothes," he said. Still filled with wonder, I began to undress. There was a flash of lightning. I saw that he was already naked.

And so naked we went into the pond. He did not speak or explain. Taking my hand, he led me down to the pond's edge and pulled me in. It may be that I was too frightened, too full of a feeling of strangeness to speak. Before that night my father had never seemed to pay attention to me.

And what was he up to now? I kept asking myself. It was as though the man, my father I had not wanted as father, had got suddenly some kind of power over me.

I was afraid and then right away, I wasn't afraid. It was a large pond and I didn't swim very well but he had put my hand on his shoulder. Still he did not speak but struck out at once onto the darkness.

He was a man with very big shoulder muscles and was a powerful swimmer. In the darkness I could feel the movement of his muscles. The rain poured down on us. The wind blew. There were flashes of lightning followed by the peals of thunder.

And so we swam, I will never know for how long. It seemed hours to me. There was rain on our faces. Sometimes my father turned and swam on his back; and when he did, he took my hand in his large powerful one and moved it over so that it rested always on his shoulder. I could look into his face. There would be a flash of lightning, and I could see his face clearly.

It was as it was when he had come earlier into the kitchen where I sat reading the book. It was a face filled with sadness. In me there was a feeling I had never known before that night. It was a feeling of closeness. It was something strange. It was as though I had been jerked suddenly out of myself, out of a world of a school boy, out of a place where I had been judging my father.

He had become blood of my blood. He the stronger swimmer and I the boy clinging to him in the darkness. We went back along the road to the town and our house.

It had become a strange house to me. There was the little porch at the front where on so many nights my father had sat with the men. There was the tree by the spring and the shed at the back. There was a lamp in the kitchen and when we came in, the water dripping from us, there was my mother. She smiled at us. I remember that she called us "boys." What have you boys been up to?" she asked, but my father did not answer. As he had begun the evening's experience with me in silence, so he ended it. He turned and looked at me, and then he went, I thought, with a new and strange dignity out of the room.

He went upstairs to his room to get out of his wet clothes, and I climbed the stairs to my own room. I undressed in the darkness and got into bed. I was still in the grip of the feelings of strangeness that had taken possession of me in the darkness of the pond. I couldn't sleep and did not want to sleep. For the first time I had come to know that I was the son of my father and that I would be a story-teller like himself. There in the darkness of my bed in the room I knew that I would never again be wanting of another father (Anderson, 1992, p. 79).

Reprinted with permission of Harold Uber Associates, Inc. Copyright © 1942, 1969, by Eleanor Anderson.

Unfortunately, males live in a world where it is increasingly difficult to connect with their fathers, both physically and spiritually—a world where a sense of masculine or feminine identity is being supplanted by a unisex sensibility, by androgynous rock stars and muscular female body builders. Traditional male and female roles have been blurred. People's sense of what is uniquely masculine or feminine, our sense of masculine and feminine space, has been diminished. Even the locker room, the jock's inner sanctum, has been invaded by female reporters. Males (and females) are desperately trying to maintain a sense of masculine identity. It is not surprising that more men are sporting beards and facial hair (as evidenced by the increasing number of male models, actors, and regular guys with beards and shadow stubble). Facial hair is one of the few exclusively male things left.

Earlier in this century, there was lots of male space. (There was also lots of female space.) There were pool halls and local "shot and a beer" joints, which were only inhabited by men. Men shot pool, drank beer, cussed, smoked, and spat into brass spittoons. There used to be male barbershops with red-and-white-striped barber poles where men congregated for a shave and a chance to shoot the breeze with other men.

The Disappearance of Male Rites and Rituals

Many male rites and rituals have disappeared. With the exception of the Jewish Bar Mitzvah, our culture does not have any rituals that officially recognize a boy's passage into manhood. Military service used to function as a male rite of passage, but this stopped with the elimination of the draft. In fact there are few male rites and rituals remaining in our culture. On the negative side, the need for male rites and rituals has, among inner-city males, found expression in gang cultures where gang initiations (usually violent) have replaced traditional rites and rituals.

And yet, because manhood is not a given (it must be achieved), there is a need for male rites and rituals that recognize and affirm the young male's passage into manhood. The process of becoming a man is difficult, with lots of pitfalls that can derail the process. Parents intuitively understand this; that's why they are reluctant to let Johnny play with dolls. The American culture can accept the idea of having a daughter who is a "tomboy" ("she's got a lot of spunk"), but not the idea of having a son who is a "sissy." Almost from day one, there is enormous pressure on boys to not do anything that might be considered even remotely effeminate. In our society, gay men are looked upon with much more scorn and derisiveness than are lesbians.

The male learns early on not to show pain, not to cry, and not to show his feelings, because these actions will be taken as a sign of weakness by other boys, and they will make his life miserable. And it never ends. President Bush's "handlers" told him to stop flitting his hands when he spoke because it looked effeminate. The U.S. culture demands a male to be strong and masculine. And women are often the worst offenders. They are turned off by men who seem weak and turned on by strong, slightly dangerous males. These are the same women who keep wondering why men can't be more sensitive and more in touch with their feelings.

Achieving manhood seems to have become more elusive than ever. Younger men need to be initiated into the world of men, and according to Bly (and the prevailing psychoanalytic view), this initiation must be done by a male—the father or a father figure. ". . . only men can initiate men, as only women can initiate women . . . When women, even women with the best intentions, bring up a boy alone, he may in some way have no male face, or he may have no face at all" (Bly, 1992, pp. 16-17). A mythological representation of this fatherless figure occurs in *The Odyssey*. Odysseus's son Telemachus, who has grown up without his father, doesn't know how to deal with the male intruders who are badgering his mother.

And in a PBS television show ("Frontline: In Search of Our Fathers," which aired on November 24, 1992), a 30-year-old documentary maker, Marco Williams, examined the impact of the fact that about half of America's black families do not have fathers in the home. Williams himself grew up in a household of women—four generations of women who raised children without a father in the home. In a society where the number of single women raising children has increased dramatically, one can only wonder what the consequences may be.

Of course, girls also undergo initiation ceremonies: They are initiated into "the cave of womanhood." But Joseph Campbell states:

> It's harder for the boy than for the girl, because life overtakes the
> girl. She becomes a woman whether she intends it or not, but the
> little boy has to intend to be a man. At the first menstruation, the
> girl is a woman. The next thing she knows, she's pregnant, she's a

mother. The boy first has to disengage himself from his mother, get his energy into himself, and start forth. That's what the myth of "Young man go find your father" is all about (Campbell, 1988, p. 138).

• • •
The Father Quest

The father quest is a mythic, universal theme. "Telemachus was told by Athena, 'Go find your father.' That father quest is a major hero adventure for young people. That is the adventure of finding what your career is, what your nature is, what your source is" (Campbell, 1988, p. 129). Campbell says, "The finding of the father has to do with finding your own character and destiny. There's a notion that the character is inherited from the father, and the body and very often the mind from the mother. But it's your character that is the mystery, and your character is your destiny. So it is the discovery of your destiny that is symbolized by the father quest" (Campbell, 1988, p. 166).

In Greek mythology, the story of Phaethon, as told by the Latin poet Ovid, provides another wonderful mythological amplification of the father quest. Phaethon grows up in a single-parent household, without a father. His mother is a mortal (Clymene), but his father (whom he has never seen), is the Sun God Apollo. Phaethon's mother tells her son to go seek out his father and tell Apollo that Phaethon is his son. Phaethon goes in search of his father and finds that his father is indeed the God who carries the sun in his chariot across the sky every day. The father acknowledges Phaethon as his son and then promises to grant him anything he wishes. The young boy is excited by his father's fiery chariot, so he asks to ride across the sky in his father's fiery chariot. Apollo tells Phaethon that he is not ready to ride the chariot. But the boy insists, and a promise is a promise. Dad finally caves in and, against his better judgment, lets Phaethon drive his chariot. The boy is indeed not ready and he crashes to his fiery death.

The Phaethon myth not only captures the father quest, it also points up the dangers surrounding the rite of passage into the world of adulthood, symbolically represented by the boy wanting to drive his father's chariot. In modern cultures this is symbolized by getting the keys to the family car. The myth teaches that the boy or girl must be ready to take on the responsibility of adulthood; otherwise, driving a powerful vehicle may have disastrous consequences.

In order to establish his own identity, the boy must break away from his mother and find his father, and thereby his own identity and masculine center. But finding his father is only the beginning. In order to establish his own identity, the boy must eventually *challenge* his father. In his essay,

"Sons and Fathers: Or Why Son Is a Verb," T. Mark Ledbetter describes three stages the son must pass through in his relationship with his father:

- Stage 1: "Fathers can do no wrong in the eyes of their sons, at least for a while. In turn, the young adolescent is content, encouraged, and safe" (Ledbetter, 1991, p. 70). At this stage, the father often refers to the son as his "buddy" or "best friend."

- Stage 2: The son grows out of adolescence. There is a complete reversal in the son's attitude. He now feels "The father can do no right." And he rejects all the traditional values that he previously shared with his father (Ledbetter, 1991, p. 70). The father feels rejected; the son feels betrayed. "The son has to reject the father in order to become his own person. Sons decide, soon after their adolescent years, that they cannot become their fathers; furthermore, sons decide that they do not *want* to become their fathers" (Ledbetter, 1991, pp. 71-72).

- Stage 3: "The sons return to fathers when they see their own reflections in their fathers' faces. Perhaps failure unites the two. The father fails to make life easy for the son. The son fails to achieve the seemingly fantastic life promised by his father. Therein lies the connection. While both men may never be fathers, both men are sons" (Ledbetter, 1991, p. 74).

In *The Odyssey,* after being away for 20 years, Odysseus returns to find his own father. When he finds his father, tending grapevines in his vineyard, he's a grief-stricken old man wearing patched clothes. Odysseus is moved to tears.

A scene in the original *Godfather* film is reminiscent of this archetypal scene. Don Corleone, now old, grieves in his garden with his son Michael over the death of his son Sonny.

Father's Daughters

Daughters who model their careers after their fathers' seem to have increased as a result of the women's movement. Some younger women have rejected their mothers because they represent the "passive, limiting lifestyles" of an earlier feminine sensibility. Such young women find they can relate better to their world-involved fathers.

Maureen Murdoch quotes Lynda Schmidt ("How the Father's Daughter Found Her Mother"), who describes the father's daughter as:

. . . the daughter with a powerful, positive relationship with her father, probably to the exclusion of her mother. Such a young woman will orient herself around men as she grows up, and will have a somewhat deprecatory attitude toward women. Father's daughters organize their lives around the masculine principle, either remaining connected to an outer man or being driven from within by a masculine mode . . . (Murdoch, 1990, pp. 29-30).

To be sure, a strong father-daughter relationship is desirable and healthy. Fathers often play an important role in their daughters' initiation into the world. Fathers often function as an ally and a mentor in what is still primarily a male world built around male values. The danger with father's daughters is that in rejecting their mothers, they also reject and lose touch with their own feminine center. Moreover, they often have difficulty finding a man that can fill their father's shoes.

Daddy's Little Girl

The image of Daddy's little girl is one of a sweet little girl devoted to her father and vice versa. The father instinctively wants to cherish and protect the sweetness and wonderfulness of his little girl. It is an endearing image; however, it also has a dark, dysfunctional side. There is an underlying implicit contract between the father and daughter that says, in effect: "Daddy will give his daughter everything in his power to give, and, in exchange, she will never reject or challenge his authority. In other words, she may grow old, but she may not grow up" (Carter, 1992, p. 121).

The Terrible Father

The Terrible Father, symbolized in classical mythology by Cronus-Saturn, is the devouring father, the male who tries to prevent his offspring from growing, from finding their own path and becoming their own people. The devouring aspect of the father archetype is also manifested in the rigidity of the existing patriarchal order, its rules and laws that confine and restrain the developing ego. Every new generation must confront its parents.

In Greek mythology, the castration of Ouranos by his son Cronus-Saturn symbolizes the new generation challenging the established order of the old. Castration is an inevitability that must be faced by each succeeding new generation. Right after he castrated his father, Cronus began devouring his *own* children because he feared that one of them would replace him. "Father and son see in each other what is in store for them—unavoidable old age and decadence for the youth, confiscation and discredit for the old" (Vitale, 1990, p. 51).

....ᴠ Masculine: The Warrior-Hero

The transformative/dynamic aspect of masculinity is represented by the Warrior-Hero archetype, whose positive traits include independence, courage, and strength. (See Figure 4.1) The Good Warrior is the selfless defender of truth and justice, he who is willing to die for what he believes in and/or in the service of those who cannot defend themselves. The spiritual side of the Good Warrior finds expression in the scientist, the philosopher—truthseekers who search for knowledge, who try to penetrate the secrets of the universe for the benefit of all humans.

The "dynamic" or "transformative" aspect of masculinity is the polar opposite of the static aspect of femininity. In contrast to the "static" or elementary feminine character, which Neumann described as "containing," the dynamic masculine character is projecting and "penetrating." The male's projecting/penetrating character emanates from his penis, which projects outward and is used to penetrate the female. The "dynamic" or transformative aspect of masculinity is aggressive, hard-driving, and goal-oriented.

Within the overall constellation of archetypes, the Warrior-Hero archetype emerges as the most pervasive and enduring universal male image. (Zeus was a warrior figure as well as a father figure.) See Figure 4.2. From mythical heroes like Marduk, Achilles, and Hercules to modern warriors like John Wayne, Rambo, and General Norman Schwartzkopf, the male Warrior-Hero, with its emphasis on independence, strength, and courage, has dominated the psyches and sensibilities of western cultures. On the positive side, the Warrior-Hero is the protector, a selfless defender of all that is good. The Warrior-Hero has the courage to fight the good fight, to fight for what he believes, to confront "the dragon" and lay down his life if necessary. He stands ready to defend his family and his country. On the negative side, the Warrior archetype is manifested in unprovoked hostility, violence, killing, rape, and war.

Fundamental Male Role

Stripped of all intellectual and sociological pretense, the fundamental role of the male is to impregnate the female, and the fundamental role of the female is to get pregnant. Nature conspires to drive us to fulfill these biological roles to ensure species survival.

The female is more complete and self-contained than the male. She awaits only the male spark to ignite the powers of her procreative furnace. She holds the power of life within her womb. The male's phallus is his source of power, the power to penetrate and impregnate the female.

Figure 4.1

Archetypal Masculine Images

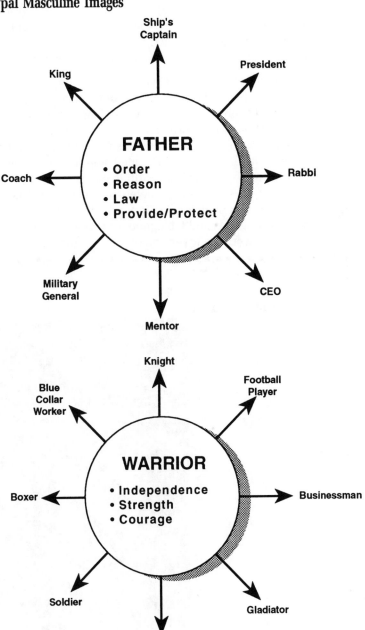

In her wonderfully illuminating, provocative book, *Sexual Personae,* Camille Paglia argues that the male's projective character stems not only from his anatomy, but also from his need to separate himself from the "Dionysian Great Mother," who threatens at every turn to engulf him and suck him back into the primordial womb from which he sprang. Paglia further asserts that the spectacular achievements of Western civilization were "invented" by males as "a defense against female nature:"

> Woman was an idol of belly-magic. Woman seemed to swell and give birth by her own law. From the beginning of time, woman has seemed an uncanny being. Man honored but feared her. She was the black maw that had spat him forth and would devour him anew. Men, bonding together, invented culture as a defense against female nature. Sky-cult was the most sophisticated step in this process, for its switch of the creative locus from earth to sky is a shift from belly-magic to head-magic. And from this defensive head-magic has come the spectacular glory of male civilization, which has lifted woman with it. The very language and logic modern women use to assail patriarchal culture were the invention of men (Paglia, 1990, p. 9).

Figure 4.2

Perseus Holding Head of Medusa

Credit: Alinari Art Resource, New York

Closer to home, the male's projective character is also driven by his more immediate need of having to separate himself from his personal mother. Beginning with Freud, psychoanalysts have pointed out that the psychodevelopment of males is different than that of females. The masculine identity depends on the male separating himself from his female mother, whereas the developing female identifies with her mother. Carol Gilligan states that because of these critical developmental differences, "relationships and particularly issues of dependency are experienced differently by women and men." Gilligan explains that:

Since masculinity is defined through separation while femininity is defined through attachment, male gender is threatened by intimacy while female gender is threatened by separation. Thus, males tend to have difficulty with relationships, while females tend to have problems with individuation (Gilligan, 1982, p. 8).

Gilligan cites the "web" as a model for the way females interact. Females interact by attracting and networking. Male interactions tend to be "hierarchical" (Gilligan, 1982, p. 62). Males compete for dominance, one-upmanship.

Femaleness, like the night, is primary and self-evident. In the beginning there was only the primordial darkness of the unformed universe, which each person re-experiences on a more personal level in the primordial darkness of mother's womb. In contrast to femaleness, maleness, like the light of day that emerges from darkness (daylight and sun symbolize patriarchal consciousness), is secondary: The male is born of female, and his manhood is not self-evident; it must be proven.

Menstruation and pregnancy are visible manifestations of womanhood and the life-creating power of woman, and they occur naturally. Becoming a woman seems to be the most natural thing in the world, at least to a man. To be sure, a woman must use her charms and wiles to attract a male so she may fulfill her biological destiny. But in contrast to the essence of femaleness—which, like the egg, is self-contained, dark, silent, brooding, waiting to be energized by the male sperm—maleness requires action. Maleness is goal-oriented. Maleness means getting the job done, for which nature gave the male a "special tool." Maleness means passing muster, "getting it up." If the male doesn't get an erection and successfully impregnate the female, the species will die out. Every male must prove his manhood before the Great Mother.

The male's role in procreation is obviously necessary, but it is only a momentary, supporting role. It's really the female's show. Moreover, as Bachofen points out, the connection between the mother and child is obvious, something that can be verified by the senses. Anyone can actually see the child emerging from the mother. The connection between the father and child cannot be verified by the senses. The father-child connection seems more tenuous; it must be "mediated by the child's mother" and always retains "a certain fictive character" (Bachofen, 1992, p. 109).

The female takes center stage, and the male is left standing around with his hands in his pockets trying to figure out what to do with himself. Men began to hook up with other men to form groups (male bonding), partly to escape the all-consuming power of women and partly to define their own sense of masculine space, to figure out what men are supposed to do. With the women often indisposed because of pregnancy and child care, hunting and the establishment of tribal rituals and laws fell to the men. Men developed a separate male society based on hunting and warfare. Turning Freud's idea of penis envy on its head, psychoanalyst Karen Horney talks about "womb envy," which may also be behind man's drive to create.

Male bashing and technology bashing are currently popular as well as politically correct. Males and technology have been blamed for "raping the earth," and there is clearly justification for the allegation. In their heroic, headlong efforts to transcend nature, males created a science and technology that has been insensitive to the needs of the planet. People are just beginning to understand the importance of using science and technology intelligently, in harmony with the environment. On the other hand, technology has lifted humankind from the unfeeling horrors of Mother Nature. Nobody would wish to go back to a world without science and technology. Technology has given people more control over their lives and a quality of life undreamed of in ancient times.

Our technological world, with all its wonders and horrors, was fashioned mostly by men. Skeptics of the women's movement raise the question why women's contribution to the world has been so small. The most obvious explanation is that women have been busy having children and raising them. One could also justifiably argue that both nature and men have exploited women by using their bodies and maternal instincts to keep the species going and to satisfy the patriarchy, without giving women an opportunity to explore and develop other aspects of their lives.

On the other hand, women also may have been too smug and self-satisfied in their procreative powers. Neumann says that woman:

> . . . lives her femininity outwardly . . . she loves, becomes pregnant, bears, nourishes, cherishes. . . . This tendency may explain the smallness of her spiritual achievements as compared to men, her lack of creative productivity. It seems to a woman (rightly or wrongly?) that to be the source of life in pregnancy and birth is creative enough (Neumann, 1990, p. 227).

Historically, women seem to have regarded men's struggles with an air of condescension. They looked on in amusement while men struggled to create a world based on science and technology ("they're like little boys playing"). Women watched with a mixture of horror and excitement as men killed each other in battle. Anything men did paled by comparison to woman's ability to create life in their bodies. Then one day the women looked around and said: "Hey, the boys have created a pretty nice world . . . and they look like they're having much more fun . . . we don't want to be tied to this childbirth thing anymore." Indeed, science and technology have created a world in which it's now possible for women to achieve fulfillment outside of childbirth.

The Emergence of Male Warrior Cultures

Male Warrior cultures undoubtedly evolved from the early male hunting groups. Some of the earliest evidence (30,000 BC) of hunting rituals and societies has been found in the drawings in the caves at Lascaux, France. The early male hunting groups seem to have coexisted with goddess worship and the goddess mythologies it spawned. Early male hunting mythologies were still part of the goddess mythology, and indeed hunting and killing were done in the service of the goddess. In their book, *The Myth of the Goddess.* Anne Baring and Jules Cashford describe how the generally peaceful reign of the early goddesses was interrupted around 4500 BC when nomadic, warring Aryan (Indo-European) and Semitic (Hebrew) tribes invaded and destroyed much of their civilization: "These people, who led a nomadic life, worshiped sky gods who wielded the thunderbolt and the axe, and rode the horse, which they domesticated as early as 5000 BC, enabling them to cover vast distances at a previously unimaginable speed. Suddenly, the battle-axe and the dagger appear in the Old European sites" (Baring and Cashford, 1991, p. 79).

Beginning in the Bronze Age (3500-1250 BC) and gaining momentum in the Iron Age (beginning around 1250 BC), we see the emergence and growing dominance of patriarchal warrior cultures and the diminishing power and status of goddesses and women. Baring and Cashford describe how the patriarchal, Semitic tribes regarded women:

> . . . the Semitic tribes regarded women as possessions of men.
> Fathers and husbands claimed the power of life and death over
> daughters and wives. Sons inherited from their fathers, whereas
> daughters inherited nothing, and could be sold into slavery by their
> fathers and brothers. The birth of a son was hailed as a blessing,
> while a daughter could be exposed to die (Baring and Cashford,
> 1991, p. 159).

Baring and Cashford maintain that the devaluation of women can also be seen in Judeo-Christian creation myths. There are several different versions of Genesis. "In one version, man and woman are created together that suggests that Elohim is imagined as both male and female" (Baring and Cashford, 1991, p. 423). However, in the version of Genesis that has become the standard for the Judeo-Christian mythology, woman (Eve) appears "as an afterthought" (Baring and Cashford, 1991, p. 425). In this version of Genesis, God creates Adam in his own image and breathes the soul of life into him. Then He makes the animals. And then He thinks that it might be a good idea for Adam to have a "helpmate," and he fashions Eve from one of Adam's ribs. In creating woman from man, a total reversal and usurping of the procreative powers of the goddess occurs.

The shift from the lunar, cyclical mythologies of the goddesses to solar, Warrior, male god mythologies brings with it a shift from a focus on the goddess to a focus on the son of the goddess—male Warrior gods. All Warrior-Hero myths are solar myths in that, like the sun, the Warrior-Hero must defeat the powers of darkness.

The Sumerian Epic of Gilgamesh—the earliest recorded hero myth, found written on tablets in the ruins of the Assyrian king Assurbanipal's library—tells the story of the "Enuma Elish," the ancient Babylonian god Marduk, and herein we see the overthrow of the goddess mythology and the emergence of a patriarchal creation myth:

> The mythological roots of all three patriarchal religions descend from the "Enuma Elish." . . . The violent image of conquest in the "Enuma Elish" sets the paradigm of the Iron Age as one of conflict between the older mythology of the mother goddess and the new myths of the Aryan and Semitic father gods. . . Marduk was the first god to vanquish the mother goddess and take her place as creator of life (Baring and Cashford, 1991, p. 275).

The seed of male-dominant Warrior cultures was sewn in the male's aggressive, warring, territorial instinct. All that was needed were the right conditions for the seed to sprout and take hold. When agriculture and cities began to replace nomadic hunting and gathering, the potential for conflict over territories and stored foods intensified. And the discovery of metals for weapon making and the domesticated horse (and horse-drawn chariot) greatly amplified the male warrior's war-making capabilities and made cataclysmic warfare a reality. Cities became vulnerable to armed invaders who could swiftly swoop down and plunder the city, kill its men, and rape and enslave its women. There was an enormous need for the "strong arm of the warrior" to protect the cities. In war and their increasing power to take human life, men had finally found something that could match the procreative power of women. Drop for drop, the life-sapping blood that flowed from his eviscerated enemies could more than match the fecund, menstrual blood of woman. There could be no turning back. The death-dealing power of the armed, male Warrior on horseback became the most awesome power on earth, a power that rivaled and overshadowed the life-giving power of the goddess.

• • •

The Irrepressible Goddess

The Judeo-Christian mythology, which is based on the idea of a single, omnipotent male god and a distinctly patriarchal sensibility, essentially eliminated the idea of goddess worship and relegated women to second-class status. However, the need for a goddess is not easily repressed. The need for an archetypal feminine spirit/life force seems to be deeply rooted in the human psyche, and it has continued to manifest itself. In *Alone of All Her Sex,* Marina Warner explains how the need for a female deity in an otherwise all-male Christian religion manifested itself in the form of a growing cult worship around the figure of the Virgin Mary. In some sense, the Virgin Mary served the same function as the early pagan goddesses. Indeed, there are many similarities linking the early goddesses and the Virgin Mary. For example, one interpretation of the etymology of her name, *Maria,* suggests that it can be traced back to the sea, the primordial origin of all goddesses. The Virgin Mary was called *Stella Maris* or Star of the Sea. She was revered by fishermen and other seafaring peoples. And some of the older paintings and statues of the Virgin Mary feature symbolism such as the crescent moon and stars circling her head, which is reminiscent of the images of the early pagan goddesses like Inanna-Ishtar. Even the Eastern Star, which guided the wise men in the birth of Christ, had an earlier association with the pagan goddesses. The eastern star was often shown above the head of seated Sumerian goddesses.

Warner traces the growing importance of the Virgin Mary among Christians; at the same time, Warner explains how the Catholic Church, which seemed to intuitively understand the people's need to have a feminine presence in the Catholic religion, gradually increased the stature and power of the Virgin Mary until, in 1950, Pope Pius XII issued the Catholic dogma of the Assumption, that the body and soul of the Virgin Mary was taken up to heaven.

• • •

Amplification of the Warrior-Hero Archetype: Odysseus

Greek mythology has had an enormous influence on western cultures. The western patriarchal sensibility can be traced back to Hellenic Greece, specifically to Homer's *Odyssey*. What makes it all the more remarkable is the fact that the *Odyssey* is one of the first examples of a true literary work, one of the first sagas. It is a story that has left a lasting imprint on western civilization. The *Odyssey* is an adventure story, a Warrior-Hero myth. On one level it is a story about a man who leaves his wife and newborn son to go off and fight a war. On another level, the *Odyssey*, like all myths, is also a journey of self-discovery.

●●●●●●●●●●●●●●●●●●●●●●●●●●●●●●●●

" On another level, *The Odyssey*, like all myths, is also a journey of self-discovery."

●●●●●●●●●●●●●●●●●●●●●●●●●●●●●●●

The image of the Warrior is archetypal and exists across time and cultures. The earliest recorded Warrior epic is "The Epic of Gilgamesh," a story about a Sumerian warrior/king written 4,000 years ago (an epic is generally a blend of history, myth, and legend). In fact, many historians believe the Epic of Gilgamesh was the prototype for the Greek warrior-hero myths (Odysseus, Hercules, Achilles, and so on). And epics like the Epic of Gilgamesh and the Odyssey are found in other cultures as well. For example, the African culture, provides an epic story about a Warrior-hero named Maghan Sundiata ("Sundiata: An Epic of Old Mali"). Like the Greek epics, the story of Sundiata was handed down by storytellers (griots). And, like the Greek warrior-hero epics, the epic story of Sundiata is full of heroic adventures and battles (often against supernatural beings).

There is an interesting example of a Warrior epic from the Irish culture. In Irish mythology, "The Voyage of Bran," a story about an Irish warrior-prince, is remarkably similar to The *Odyssey*. Bran has an incredible series of adventures while sailing home to Ireland—a voyage that takes more than 100 years.

In *The Odyssey,* a mythical Greek king named Odysseus lives on the mythical Greek Isle of Ithaca. Odysseus is called to leave his home and family to fight in the Trojan War, which lasts 10 years. On his way home from the war he has a series of incredible adventures with gods, monsters, sirens, and so on, which keep him detained another 10 years. While he is away, his faithful wife Penelope is badgered and harassed by would-be suitors. The uninvited guests hang around Odysseus' house drinking his wine, killing and eating his livestock, and hoping to marry his unwilling wife. His son, now a young man, wants to help his mother and protect his inheritance, but he doesn't know how to deal with the intruders. The son goes in search of his father (the father quest).

When Odysseus finally makes his way back to Ithaca, he comes in disguise to surprise his antagonists and also to see whether his wife and servants have been faithful. His wife has indeed been incredibly faithful (20 years!), but some of his servants have betrayed him. The only one who recognizes him is his dog who comes to greet him and then dies of old age.

The dog has evidently been hanging on all these years, waiting for his master to return. Odysseus is reunited with his son, who then tells his father about the unwanted intruders. Odysseus tells his son that with his help he will take vengeance on them. The son protests that there are too many of them, and some of them are pretty tough characters. His father tells him to take heart. With his loyal son by his side, Odysseus courageously confronts the intruders. He draws his long bow and mercilessly deals death to the 40 some odd malingerers. He also kills the unfaithful servants, including the women servants who consorted with the malingerers, and anyone else who had in any way been unfaithful to him.

The Odyssey is a Warrior myth. And like all hero myths, it is ultimately a paradigm for the process of self-discovery. Joseph Campbell states:

> The standard path of the mythological adventure of the heroes is a magnification of the formula represented in the rites of passage: separation—initiation—return: . . . . A hero ventures forth from the world of common day into a region of supernatural wonder: fabulous forces are there encountered and a decisive victory is won: The hero comes back from this mysterious adventure with the power to bestow boons on his fellow man (Campbell, 1968, p. 30).

On another level, The Odyssey is the ultimate patriarchal fantasy/mythology. It has everything a guy could want:

- To be a strong, brave warrior who is victorious in battle.

- To be respected, admired, and feared by other men.

- To have a beautiful, faithful wife who will wait forever for your return.

- To have a loyal son who will stand by your side and carry on your great name.

- To own a big house and property.

- To even own a loyal dog who waits 20 years for his master's return.

The story of Odysseus is the blueprint for western patriarchal culture and sensibility. Until the recent advent of the women's movement, our cultural mythology seemed to have come right out of the Odyssey.

This is just beginning to be an emergence of feminine sensibility. When Vice President Dan Quayle attacked Murphy Brown for undermining family values, what he really meant was patriarchal family values and, in that, he was essentially correct. In her decision to have a baby out of wedlock, without a participating father, and to raise it as a single parent, Murphy

Brown's values and lifestyle represent a radical departure from the traditional patriarchal family structure. The media harangued Vice President Quayle for attacking a "fictitious character in a fictional television series," but in fact television shows like Murphy Brown are a form of mythologizing that tries to reflect our cultural sensibilities and values. Regardless of the vice president's views or his philosophy, television shows like "Murphy Brown" *are significant* in that if we see a value shift in television shows, it is likely that it is a reflection of a value shift that is occurring within U.S. culture.

The incidence of women choosing to have and raise babies without fathers has increased significantly and will probably continue to increase. Even lesbian women can now have babies through artificial insemination; there are even "donor catalogs" describing the backgrounds and attributes of various anonymous male donors. New technologies have given women enormous flexibility in choosing the kind of lifestyle they want, and even to create an entirely different society. For example, it is possible to create a matriarchal society without males (except for a few that would be kept around to produce sperm).

Why Has the Image of the Male Warrior Come to Dominate the American Culture and Sensibilities?

The Warrior archetype is so pervasive and enduring that it raises the question: Why has this image come to dominate U.S. culture and our sensibilities?

It is difficult, standing at the end of the twentieth century, to appreciate the truly awesome power of the pretechnological Warrior and his impact on the human psyche. Our image of this figure has been neutered and dwarfed by technology. The power of a strong arm wielding a sword has been eclipsed by machines. The modern Warrior is essentially a technician, a machine operator.

This holds true for female Warriors as well. One of the issues currently facing the military is whether women should be given active combat duty. One could argue that technology has now made it possible for women to have an equal role in warfare. Except in hand-to-hand combat, where men usually have a size and physical strength advantage, there is no reason why females in the armed forces shouldn't serve in combat. Women can shoot a gun, operate a fighter plane, or drive a tank as well as men can.

On the other hand, women who participate in combat go against their most basic instinct, which is to create life. Women who engage in combat must put aside naturally strong, life-giving, life-affirming instincts and become destroyers of human life. These women become the Terrible Mother who devours her sons and daughters. And because women create human life in their bodies, women may have to pay a greater price in terms of the psychic conflict and inner strife that comes with killing other human beings.

At any rate, the pretechnological Warrior lived in a world dominated by and dependent on people power. In this world people traveled on foot or horse and lit their homes with candles to hold back the terror of the night. Imagine living in a pretechnological world and confronting an Arnold Schwartzenegger wielding a sword.

One of the few places where Americans can still encounter the pure warrior is in the movies. There's a wonderful moment in the film *Dances with Wolves* when a U.S. Cavalry soldier (Kevin Costner) first encounters an Indian brave in full war paint and feathers, charging on a horse while waving a tomahawk and screaming. Costner stands gaping, transfixed by an image that is at once beautiful and terrifying.

It is hard to imagine the fierceness and fury of the pretechnological warrior who had to dismember and disembowel his enemy in hand-to-hand combat, with his sword, tomahawk, or spear, while looking the person in the eye. After a battle, warriors would be so full of rage and battle frenzy that they had to be isolated from the rest of the village. In *The Code of the Warrior,* Rick Fields cites a passage from the old Irish Epic, *The Tain,* where the warrior Chu Chulainn had to be submerged into a series of vats of cold water in order to dissipate his "martial heat" after a battle (Fields, 1991, p. 64).

Achilles, the mythical Greek warrior, a Warrior's warrior, was also consumed with battle frenzy when he found out that his friend Patroclus was killed by Hector. Warriors usually respect their fallen enemy, but Achilles, in his battle rage, dragged Hector's body around the city in defiance of the Gods, for which he was eventually sent to Hades (killed).

Achilles was a fierce warrior who was almost invulnerable in battle. His mother was a goddess who dipped him in the river Styx (the river in Hades) when he was an infant to make him invulnerable in battle. The place where she held him by his ankle was the one spot where he was vulnerable, and where the cowardly Paris, waiting in ambush, shot him with an arrow, "a cowardly weapon" (in the warrior world of hand-to-hand combat, the bow was considered the most cowardly weapon).

● ●

" The power of a strong arm wielding a sword has been eclipsed by machines."

● ●

Fields makes reference to the "beserkirs," warriors who covered themselves with a bearskin or wolfskin in order to take on the identity and fierceness of that particular animal: ". . . Like the shamans, they danced themselves into identity with bear and wolf, shambling, loping, wrapping themselves in fur, wearing masks, wrapping themselves in pelts, howling, grunting, growling" (Fields, 1991, p. 63). Thus transformed, the beserkirs were often put at the front of the battle lines where, snarling and gnashing their teeth, they would unleash their fury against the enemy. If they managed to survive the battle, it was often difficult to bring them back to their normal state, and sometimes they had to be killed.

"Hoka Hey"

The pure Warrior is someone who is ready to die for what he believes. Native American Chief Crazy Horse used to rally his braves with the battle cry "Hoka Hey," which means "It's a great day to die." The Warrior is not only willing but happy to die. To die bravely in battle is the Warrior's highest honor. The Warrior has crossed the line, undergone a spiritual transformation through a confrontation with his own death:

> For most people death is the great terror, the great enemy, the invincible enemy. But for the truly heroic warrior, death—his own death—is also the worthiest opponent. The noble warrior fights other men and takes their lives with his own hand, but the noblest of the noble warriors, the best—the "aristoi"—demonstrate bravery in the unequal contest with their own death, and this, finally, is what allows him to hold his head above all others (Fields, 1991, p. 73).

In embracing his own death, the Warrior becomes numb to his own feelings and the life-giving, life-affirming, feminine side of his soul. He must remain emotionless, with no commitments, no attachments. He is, in effect, already dead, given over to another world. His life is committed to "slaying some dragon," to a cause, for which he is willing to die. In the Japanese culture, the Samurai warrior lived according to the Bushido, a warrior ethos that not only glories in death but often requires the Warrior to kill himself. If a Samurai believes he has been dishonored, he can recover his honor by committing Hara Kiri (belly cutting), a ritualized form of suicide in which he disembowels himself with his sword. Although this is very painful, he must not cry out in pain. He must literally spill his guts without crying out. To ensure that he will not cry out and dishonor himself, the Samurai usually has a "second," a friend standing by with a Katana (a large "killing sword") ready to cut off the Samurai's head if he looks like he is about to cry out.

Women find the Warrior dangerously exciting, but no woman can reach him, for he is already wedded to death. In *The Demon Lover,* Robin Morgan points to the terrorist (who is almost always male) as an extreme expression of the male Warrior archetype and the hero myth. To those whose cause he has committed his life, he is a saint; to those he opposes, he is a "demon."

In addition to the spiritual aspect of the Warrior, there is also the carnal aspect, the bloodlust. In some dark corner of the male soul, a corner we keep hidden from our girlfriends and wives, men enjoy the blood and the killing.

In *Dances with Wolves,* when the Native Americans have just killed a buffalo, they remove his hot, steaming liver and devour it with wanton delight. Even the song "Mack the Knife," though sung with a wink and a catchy melody, is about a guy who enjoys sticking his knife into people. People still enjoy the bloodlust. They still have the instinct to kill and take pleasure in the killing, but society no longer acknowledges bloodlust. (Our meat comes to us in Saran Wrap).

Women say they hate war and killing, but they also say they love men in uniform. In truth, on some level, women also enjoy the bloodlust. The Amazonian character in *Basic Instinct* heightened her orgasms by stabbing her male lovers with an ice pick. The maenads, women who participated in the orgiastic Dionysian rites would, in their frenzy, tear live animals to pieces with their teeth and nails, smear themselves with its blood, and cover themselves with its fur. Is a woman wearing a mink coat with bright red lipstick and nails exciting because she is reminiscent of the blood-smeared maenads—literally dressed to kill?

Neumann traces the primal connection between "... warlike ecstasy and fertility":

> The masculine-phallic principle is necessary for the preservation of life as experienced by the matriarchate. The woman is dependent both on the hunting, warring, killing, and sacrificing male—the "knife of the Great Goddess," the phallus that bloodily opens the female—and on the plow that tears open the earth. For she is identical with the thrice-plowed field on which she gives herself for fecundation to the male, of whom she indifferently makes use (Neumann, 1991, p. 303).

The image of the Warrior seems to be a primordial male image grounded in male anatomy, in the same way that the Great Mother image is a primordial female image grounded in female anatomy. This is not to say that men can't nurture or that women can't be warriors. Archetypes transcend gender: Males and females have both a nurturing instinct and a warring instinct. And within the spectrum of males and females, some males are more nurturing than some females, and some females are more aggressive and warlike than some males.

But again, nature conspires against us. Because of the females' childbearing role, we would expect the nurturing instinct would have to be stronger in most females. Though results are inconclusive, some studies suggest that girls have a higher disposition to empathy than boys (Miedzian, 1991, p. 90). Human males may have, by default, inherited a greater propensity for aggression and warring. This is not always true for other species. For example, in predatory animals like lions, the male and female both seem to have an equally strong instinct for killing.

Consider male and female behaviors that occur when we are not trying to be politically correct. Airport bookstores offer an interesting example of basic male and female differences. With their limited space, these stores have, through a kind of natural selection, honed their selection of books down to those that the managers know will sell: The men's books are invariably war and adventure books, "Nazi thrillers," and books that hold the promise of adventure, excitement, and conquest (sometimes there is also a discrete cache of soft-porn paperbacks). The women's books are invariably romances—Sidney Sheldon, Judith Krantz—books that focus on love and human relationships.

Numerous studies have demonstrated a correlation between higher levels of male hormones and aggressive behavior. Camille Paglia picks up this point:

> Nature gives males infusions of hormones for dominance in order to hurl them against the paralyzing mystery of woman, from whom they would otherwise shrink. Lust and aggression are fused in male hormones. Anyone who doubts this has probably never spent much time around horses. Stallions are so dangerous they must be caged in barred stalls; once gelded, they are docile enough to serve as children's mounts (Paglia, 1992, p. 24).

Like the female, the male too is Mother Nature's instrument. If the female is "nature's whore," then the male is her stud, a rutting buck, testicles swollen with sperm, driven to impregnate any available female. Nature infuses the male with testosterone to increase his aggressiveness, to insure that he will chase down the female and copulate with her. Testosterone also increases the male's aggression toward other males. The male must fight and compete with other males for a chance to impregnate receptive females. Mother Nature is a tough task-master; she wants to make sure that only the strongest genes are passed along.

Camille Paglia, the outspoken feminist, states, "Aggression and eroticism are deeply intertwined. Hunt, pursuit, and capture are biologically programmed into male sexuality" (Paglia, 1990, p. 52). There is a violating, violent aspect to male sexuality. Human sexuality incorporates elements of lust and violence, and this is especially true of male sexuality. Nature doesn't take chances. In order to ensure species survival, the male must be hard-wired to fulfill his basic function, which is to impregnate the female. The male's role in coitus is essentially a violating, violent act. Even when the female is a willing participant, the male must literally break into the female; he must rupture her hymen and penetrate her being. This is not always an easy task. The virgin's hymen can sometimes be so tough it must be opened surgically.

The projective/penetrating male character, infused with testosterone, is not only aggressive but predisposed to violence. (Unfortunately, this predisposition to violence is glorified by our culture.) Violent crime is almost invariably committed by males. Burglary, the invasion of someone else's private space, is an inherently male act. Spears, arrows, swords, guns, missiles, and so on, are the phallic artifacts of Warrior cultures whose function is to penetrate another body or country.

The connection between testosterone and male violence is also being debated in the courts. In several cases where athletes and body builders have illegally used steroids (testosterone) to build strength and muscle, the athletes claimed the overuse of male hormones caused them to commit violent crimes—"roid rage." Also, "hypermasculine males," males with two Y chromosomes (XYY) have been shown to exhibit a greater propensity for temper tantrums, violence, and criminal behavior. The number of male prison inmates with a double-Y chromosome is statistically significant— higher than expected as compared to the general population (Manning, 1989, p. 54).

Again, this is not to say that males are incapable of tender, loving relationships with women. The vast majority of men have learned to keep their violent instincts in check—most of the time. But there is a dark side to human sexuality that has been exposed in movies like *Silence of the Lambs* and *Basic Instinct,* which most audiences found shocking and yet somehow strangely compelling. Human sexuality is a daemon, a powerful, animal instinct that surges up from the unconscious psyche. Humans have great difficulty keeping this force under control. Every day people engage in sexual behaviors that jeopardize their marriages and careers; people risk everything they have and are for a rush of feeling.

The connection between the male libido and aggressive, violent behavior has been ritualized in some pretechnological cultures like the North American Plains Native Americans and the African Masai, where a man was not allowed to marry until he had proven himself in combat or taken a scalp.

• • •
The Showdown

Male aggression ultimately leads to combat. Male combativeness is ritualized in the *Showdown,* wherein two males square off in a potentially mortal confrontation. From the Great Plains of Africa to the school yard fight, to six guns at high noon, to Desert Storm, the ritualized male showdown is the male will to power taken to high drama. In the Warrior world, courage is highly prized. Proving he "has the balls" to stand up to other males is another hurdle that the male must scale in order to prove his manhood before other men. Every male has experienced the terror of having to face the bully who says:

"I'll see you in the school yard at three o'clock; I'm, gonna kick your . . ."

Women do not have to fight. There is no shame in a young woman refusing to fight; she can simply say its unladylike. But for a young man, refusing to fight is a humiliating, emasculating experience. He is looked on as "a weakling," "a wimp," by the other boys, as well as by the girls. In an *Esquire* magazine article, John Berendt underscored the connection between masculine honor and "balls":

> The Latin root of the word testicles (testis, meaning "witness"), incidentally is also the origin of *testify* and *testimony,* which suggests a profound link between balls and honor. In ancient times, when a man swore a solemn oath, he would place one hand on his testicles, thereby putting his most prized possession—his virility— on the line (Berendt, 1993, p. 21).

The ultimate male nightmare, in fact a symbolic castration, is to be put down by another male in front of your girlfriend. The original Charles Atlas ad, which seemed to be a fixture in the back of comic books, captured this moment of male humiliation. The ad showed a skinny guy at the beach with his girlfriend while a big muscular guy kicked sand in the skinny guy's face. The Charles Atlas body-building course promised to transform every skinny kid into a powerhouse. It was a powerful ad because it vividly brought to life every young guy's worst nightmare. In his heart, every male knows that he must be constantly on his guard, ready to defend himself and his family/ girlfriend/country from other hostile, violent males. One lesson males learn early on in the streets is that it's okay to be nice guys, but they also had better be prepared to defend themselves, if necessary.

This business of having to prove themselves before other men doesn't go away when men grow up. During the Desert Storm operation, Evan Thomas, a Washington correspondent, commented on how "Some pundits have wondered if the president is still fighting the wimp factor" because he was acting like a tough guy.

The Superbowl, with its gladiatorial combativeness, is one of the most celebrated, ritualized male showdowns. Football, with its phallic character (the object being to penetrate your opponent's defense and score) and endless showdowns, is quintessentially male. Sportscasters like to talk about the strategizing that goes on in football games, and admittedly, the strategic aspect of football is part of its appeal. But it's the violence and the competitiveness that fills the stadium seats and keeps men glued to their TV screens. Men get excited watching big men smash into each other, whether in football, hockey, or boxing. The competitive instinct, the need to win, to beat the other guy, is deeply embedded in the male psyche. Thousands of spermatozoa stream doggedly toward the egg, but only one will score.

Sports were invented to practice and hone warrior skills—as well as to keep males from killing each other between wars. Men have a relationship with sports that women will never understand. Women today take a more serious interest in sports and play much more competitively than they once did. But men *need* sports to keep the wild, hairy beast in them under control.

Male sports figures are popular Warriors that Madison Avenue often employs to appeal to males. One of the most memorable commercials of this type is Coca-Cola's "Mean Joe Green" commercial. In the commercial we see a little boy offer his Coke to a sweaty, battle-weary Mean Joe Green. Joe has evidently just come off the playing field and he looks battered and angry. At first he tries to brush the kid off, but the little boy persists and Mean Joe finally takes the Coke and drinks it down in one long gulp. The little boy, who is obviously a great fan of Mean Joe, watches in silent sadness as Mean Joe turns to walk away. And then there is this wonderful, magic moment, where this fierce, angry warrior shows us his tender, nurturing side by turning to his admiring little fan and giving him his football jersey.

• • •
Has the Warrior Outlived His Usefulness?

During the last decades the image of the Warrior has come under attack, and there has been a shift toward a softer, more sensitive, fatherly male image. (Remember all the hairy-chested guys holding bare-bottom babies?) But the men of the 1990s began complaining that they were losing touch with their masculinity. Men began marching off to attend consciousness-raising sessions in the woods where they could bang drums, "piss on trees," and hug other men. Robert Bly *(Iron John)* blamed the women's movement for emasculating men and making them too soft. Bly felt that men needed to get back in touch with their fierceness, the "Wild Man" inside of them. Sam Keen (author of *Fire in the Belly*) said the problem is that a definition of masculinity based on war and the warrior archetype is no longer useful and must be replaced (Keen, 1991, pp. 113-114). The question is, by what?

Some have begun to question "whether a postpatriarchal understanding of masculinity is a contemporary possibility" (Moore, 1989, p. 159). Others have suggested that our culture's overdeveloped sense of masculinity with its emphasis on androcentric values represents an unhealthy, male ego trip, a form of "masculine inflation." In *The Phallic Quest,* Jungian analyst James Wyly uses the Greek God Priapus, a male god with enormous genitals, as a metaphor for masculine inflation. Priapus is also a urological term that represents a condition (often painful) that occurs in males, wherein the male's penis remains in a constant state of erection. According to Wyly, the American culture is suffering from this same condition; we are a male culture in a constant state of erection. Wyly maintains that a lot of cultural problems can be traced to this condition. U.S. culture's obsession with money and power is a "split off" form of "masculine inflation" that needs to be reunited with, and brought into balance with, the feminine aspects of men's psyche (Wyly, 1989, p. 112).

But the tumescent penis is also the male's source of power and creativity: ". . . the swollen 'inflated' phallus is the physiological instrument of creativity" (Wyly, 1989. p. 11). Indeed, without it, nothing happens in the eternal *pas de deux.* The essence of maleness ultimately comes down to a functioning, erect penis. But Wyly says "phallus must be reintegrated into the male psyche." And "the goal of reintegration of *phallos* is *coniunctio,* creativity, paternity" (Wyly, 1989 p. 113).

In her thoughtful work, *The Chalice and the Blade,* Riane Eisler uses different metaphors but makes essentially the same point as Wyly. Eisler says the "problem" is a social system that overvalues the power of the sword, a system based on "dominance and violence." Eisler draws a contrast between the contemporary, male-dominant, Warrior cultures, and the goddess-worshiping cultures wherein the emphasis was on "the power to give and nurture, which the chalice symbolizes:"

> There were both men and women in the prehistoric societies where the power to give and nurture, which the chalice symbolizes, was supreme. The underlying problem is not men as a sex. The root of the problem lies in a social system in which the power of the Blade is idealized—in which both men and women are taught to equate true masculinity with violence and dominance and to see men who do not conform to this ideal as "too soft" or "effeminate" (Eisler, 1988, p. xviii).

In a similar vein, Robin Morgan asserts that terrorism and violence are the products of a male identity that is tied to violence and killing, and to the fact that the male ultimately perceives himself as a weapon:

> If manhood is perceived as localized in a hardened penis, and if the penis is perceived as a weapon, then manhood itself is the means by which male human beings must (and do) make of themselves weapons . . . [F]rom the droppings of "Little Boy" in an ejaculation of death over Hiroshima to Jean-Paul Sartre's hymn to violence as man's way of recreating himself, the obsession is consistent (Morgan, 1989, p. 176).

Western culture's emphasis on aggression and competitiveness has produced a world full of hostility and violence, and has brought the world to the brink of a nuclear nightmare. The images of marauding, male Somali warrior tribes with machine guns and bandoleers of bullets juxtaposed with images of starving Somali children was an all-too-vivid reminder of the high cost of Warrior worship. The question is, can humanity change? Can men somehow conquer the daemon of war and aggression that has perennially plagued humanity? Eisler is optimistic. She points to the early goddess-worshiping cultures wherein warfare seems to have been nonexistent. Eisler also maintains that males are not inherently violent and warlike, and she cites references that support her view.

On the other hand, many psychology experts believe there is an aspect of maleness that is inherently combative and violent. The daemon of aggression cannot be wished away. Kindness and killing exist side by side in men's souls. For now, the best we can hope for is an uneasy, tenuous balance between the chalice and the sword. People need both. The symbol of America, the bald eagle, is depicted holding the olive branch (a symbol of peace) in one of its talons, and a bunch of arrows (a symbol of war) in its other, just in case. History has taught that peace never comes easily or cheaply. Evil exists, both as a separate entity and within men's souls. People are kidding themselves if they think otherwise, and it will only be a matter of time before they find themselves vulnerable, unprepared, and facing the daemon of male aggression.

On the other hand, humanity must work toward establishing a world that values the chalice at least as much as the sword, a world that values and rewards kindness and compassion as well as aggression and competitiveness. Some try to embrace both the sword and the chalice by compartmentalizing them. In the film *Wiseguys,* Mafia men are portrayed as devoted family men who debate the fine points of getting their pasta sauce just right, but who ruthlessly kill each other because it's "just business." The Mafia has always had an unwritten law that says in effect that a man's family is sacrosanct and should not be harmed. However, it is difficult to be "married to the chalice" when your mistress is murder and mayhem.

Unquestionably, men have to learn to embrace and develop their feminine side (Jung's anima) both individually and culturally. Men have generally failed to embrace, or even acknowledge, their feminine side. Consequently, the lopsided, phallocentric world of today undervalues women and feminine values and overvalues men and aggressive, even violent behavior. People must create an environment that allows men to acknowledge and embrace their feminine side and use it to balance their masculine side.

Men must learn to value kindness, compassion, and caring as much as aggression and competition, and to channel aggressive instincts into more constructive uses. Men are afraid that if they become too life-affirming, too kind or compassionate, they will lose their edge and become vulnerable to other men, armed intruders with a taste for blood who will destroy them and enslave their women and children. It's the old "Catch 22." Men, fearing the aggressive, warring instinct in other men, embrace the Warrior archetype and ideology in order to protect themselves and their family/country, but in doing so, they run the risk of becoming the very thing they are trying to defend against.

On some level, men recognize that the real enemy is not out there, not some unknown, armed invader waiting to swoop down and destroy them. The really dangerous enemy is the powerful warring instinct that lives in men's souls, and that, uncontrolled, may ultimately destroy the world. It won't be easy, but maybe men can one day learn to become spiritual Warriors who, like Jesus, Ghandi, and Martin Luther King, Jr., fight without swords to make the planet a better place for all humankind.

Chapter 5
• • • • • • • • • • •

Brand Mythologies

Chapter 5 provides an overview and historical perspective on some of the more successful, enduring brand mythologies we have all come to know and love. The chapter explores the origins of some of the more familiar brand mythologies and how they have evolved over the years. At the same time, the chapter also analyzes the various brand mythologies. The analysis will focus on the two most important aspects of brand mythologies:

- their mytho-symbolic or archetypal imagery (the images on which most brand mythologies are based are the same archetypal images explored in Chapters 3 and 4)
- their level of functioning (like cultural mythologies, brand mythologies can function on a number of different levels)

The brand mythologies explored in Chapter 5 will be categorized using a simple typology based on the central executional element or focus of the brand mythologies. Based on this typology, brand mythologies are divided into three categories:

- brand mythologies built around mythical *characters*
- brand mythologies built around mythical *places*
- brand mythologies built around mythical *moments/situations/themes*

• • •
Analyzing Brand Mythologies

The chapter employs two levels of analysis to examine the various brand mythologies: an analysis of the mytho-symbolic imagery that forms the basis of the brand mythology, and an analysis of the brand mythology's level of functioning.

Whence Does Mytho-Symbolic/Archetypal Imagery Come?

The same archetypal images discussed in Chapters 3 and 4—those images that have shaped cultural mythologies—are also the basis for most brand mythologies. This should hardly come as a surprise, because advertising generally tries to mirror the mythologies and sensibilities of the culture for which it has been created. Brand mythologies based on mythical characters are often based on archetypal images. In attempting to mirror U.S. cultural mythologies in their brand mythologies, advertisers have generally created brand mythologies that reflect and perpetuate the same images that have traditionally dominated our culture. Female images used in brand mythologies have generally been based on either the Great Mother or some aspect of the Maiden (Virgin, Temptress). Male images used in brand mythologies have been generally based on either the Great Father or Warrior archetype.

However, with the advent of the women's movement and the changing role of women in contemporary society, female images in advertising are being based on other archetypes, especially the Warrior archetype.

In addition to brand mythologies created around mythical characters, brand mythologies are also created around mythical places and moments/ situations/themes. These brand mythologies too are created around mythical, often archetypal places, situations, and so on. For example, Hidden Valley Salad Dressing is a brand that uses a brand mythology created around a mythical place: a lush, fertile valley hidden from humanity. The mythical hidden valley is archetypal, based on a universal image. It is a place that exists in the human psyche—a Garden of Eden, an idyllic place where food is bountiful and we can be completely happy. Or, for example, a brand mythology can be created around mythical moments (birth, first step into the adult world, marriage, death, and so on). Kodak and Hallmark have created wonderful brand mythologies that focus on life's universal (mythic) moments.

Level on Which Brand Mythologies Work

Like cultural mythologies, brand mythologies can function on a number of levels. Many of the earlier brand mythologies functioned on a more basic level; they worked to engage and entertain the consumer while communicating specific brand attributes and benefits. However, in today's more competitive marketing environment, most brand mythologies go beyond product-based attributes and benefits; they also function on a more psychological/emotional level by providing important psychological and emotional benefits.

At the simplest level, brand mythologies work to get consumers' attention by engaging, involving, and entertaining them. On another level, brand mythologies work to inform the consumer by communicating essential product attributes and/or benefits. But brand mythologies can provide important emotional/psychological benefits, too. Brand mythologies often provide a sense of identity, both individually and culturally, by reflecting and reinforcing consumer's values and sensibilities.

Many of the earlier brands used advertising to create brand mythologies that were fairly simplistic and essentially "informational"; they focused single-mindedly on communicating a physical product benefit or attribute. In today's highly competitive markets, however, with their similar competing products, most brand mythologies also include an emotional benefit. In William Wells' terms, they are both "informational" and "transformational." Today's brand mythologies generally work on many levels. They communicate product attributes/benefits and emotional/psychological benefits.

For example, much of Virginia Slims' cigarette mythology works to communicate both product-based benefits (the supposedly feminine taste of the cigarettes) and emotional/psychological benefits (affirmation of femininity and female values).

Brand Mythologies: A Typology

The history behind many of the enduring brand mythologies is fascinating. The basis for many of the early brand mythologies was often the result of some serendipitous combination of instinct and inspiration. There are many ways in which advertising can be used to create brand mythologies, and it is useful to look at the kinds of mythologies that have been created for other brands. If an advertiser sorts through the various brand mythologies, a simple typology emerges—the categories of mythical characters, places, and moments described earlier.

• • •
Brand Mythologies Created Around Mythical Characters

Advertising is peppered with examples of successful, enduring brands that have used mythical characters to capture and convey a product's essential attribute(s) and/or benefit(s) as well as compelling psychological and emotional benefits. Many of these characters have become so recognizable and so strongly linked with their brands that they have come to represent the brand's essential nature in consumers' minds. Such characters have become advertising *icons,* enduring images that contribute to the popular culture.

On the other hand, some brand mythologies do not use specific characters such as Betty Crocker or Aunt Jemima. Instead, these mythologies use many different personas based on the same archetype. For example, there have been more than 200 different Breck Girls, but archetypically they all represent the Maiden. Another example of a mythical brand character that uses many representations is the Budweiser Man. The Bud Man is everyman. We may see many actors portraying him, but archetypically, they are all based on the Warrior.

In keeping with the structure used in Chapters 3 and 4, which divided cultural mythologies into male and female categories, the brand mythologies created around mythical characters are described here by gender, with the female mythologies first.

The Great Mother Archetype: Betty Crocker

Betty Crocker, a corporate symbol of General Mills, is a mythical female character based on the Great Mother archetype. The name Betty Crocker was first used in 1921 in replying to customers who wrote to the company for baking advice. *Betty* was a popular name (think of Betty Grable and Betty Boop) and *Crocker* was the surname of company director, William G. Crocker. Betty Crocker proved to be very popular with consumers, and in 1936 General Mills created an image to go with the name. As you might expect, the first Betty Crocker looked like a typical 1930s homemaker. (See Figure 5.1.)

Although the Betty Crocker character is based on the same Great Mother that spawned the early goddesses, she is clearly a domesticated, declawed figure who does not threaten the existing patriarchal structure. (Recall that goddesses predate the patriarchal male gods, who didn't really come to dominate the deities until Judeo-Christian influence spread.) Still, the Betty Crocker character incorporated enough of the instinctual, archetypal traits of the Great Mother to exert a powerful influence on our psyche.

Over the years Betty Crocker has had thousands of fans and even received a couple of marriage proposals. However, during the early 1970s some feminists criticized advertisers for perpetuating the idea that the role of women was confined to homemaker. The feminists had made their point: The image of woman as a homemaker had become a cultural stereotype that limited women to housework, and advertising had unwittingly perpetuated the stereotype. The Great Mother archetype represents an important aspect of the female soul, but advertisers must be careful that it does not become a stereotype that prevents women from realizing their full human potential. Advertisers, of necessity, have become much more sensitive to social issues and are generally careful not to perpetuate limiting stereotype images.

Nevertheless, the need for a Betty Crocker, for a nurturing, universal mother image, is buried deep in the human psyche. Indeed, Betty Crocker,

Figure 5.1

Betty Crocker

Used with permission of General Mills

the archetypal Great Mother figure and enduring brand icon, has been around for more than 70 years and is still going strong.

Advertising mythologies that create appealing user imagery based on archetypal images like the Great Mother often try to create an *affiliative feeling* in the intended user. For example, Campbell's Soup advertising has traditionally created mythologies whose central theme is nurturance and mother love. The advertising typically depicts a loving mother who is comforting and nurturing her child who has had a bad day (a bad report card, a drenching in the rain). The ad's mom represents the archetypal good mother. Presumably, the target consumer, a woman with young children, can identify with the good mother and the situation. She will see herself in the commercial, and the commercial will evoke her own instinctive, maternal feelings. In this way the consumer comes to identify with the kind of person who uses Campbell's Soup, and to associate the brand with warm, nurturing, maternal feelings.

The Black Great Aunt: Aunt Jemima

Aunt Jemima is everybody's favorite aunt. She has been a familiar face at America's breakfast table for more than 50 years. Obviously, the Aunt Jemima image is an archetypal representation of the universal Great Mother. She is a black Betty Crocker. The appeal of the Aunt Jemima character works on a number of levels. At the product level, she provides reassurance of quality. On a more emotional/psychological level, her character gives the consumer a warm, nurturing feeling. Her visage with its warm, beaming smile exudes a feeling of warmth and motherliness.

Like Betty Crocker, the pictorial image of Aunt Jemima has undergone several transformations to contemporize her, more specifically, to make her look less like a slave or a domestic. Like most of the early black images used in advertising, the original image of Aunt Jemima betrays her servant status. She was originally portrayed as a servant-cook. This is clearly a reflection of American culture—one that until recently did not acknowledge blacks except as domestic help or minstrels.

This point was powerfully driven home in the 1960s and 1970s by black authors like James Baldwin and Ralph Ellison (author of The Invisible Man), who pointed out that the black man (and woman) was essentially "invisible" in mainstream American culture. One of the reasons Alex Haley's televised "Roots" had such an enormous impact on black Americans is it gave them back their own mythology, one that came out of a proud African heritage.

Despite her earlier, negative associations, Aunt Jemima has endured and become a part of America's folklore. The character's universal appeal transcends and overpowers the earlier, negative associations. The Aunt Jemima story is a fascinating case of an image in search of a person and a heritage. Aunt Jemima Pancakes began in 1888, when Chris L. Rutt, a

Figure 5.2

Aunt Jemima Ad

Courtesy of The Quaker Oats Company

newspaper writer, and his friend Charles G. Underwood, who had a milling business, developed a pancake mix. Pancakes have long been a popular food. Their origins are lost in antiquity, but they are associated with Lent, which required abstinence from meat. Pancakes were popular in England, where the ringing of the "pancake bell" was the signal to begin making pancakes.

Rutt and Underwood decided that their new pancake mix needed a catchy package design and trademark. Legend has it they came up with the idea of Aunt Jemima—the image of a traditional southern black cook with a bandanna headband—from a minstrel act that featured the then-popular song "Aunt Jemima":

> My old missus promise me,
>   Old Aunt Jemima, oh, oh, oh
> When she died she'd set me free,
>   Old Aunt Jemima, oh, oh, oh
> She lived so long her head got bald
>   Old Aunt Jemima, oh, oh, oh
> She swore she would not die at all
>   Old Aunt Jemima, oh, oh, oh   (Sacharow, 1982, p. 72)

Rutt and Underwood registered the name Aunt Jemima as a trademark, but, when they became short of money, sold it to the Davis Milling Company. R. T. Davis was the new owner of the trademark, and he decided to find a real black woman who could represent Aunt Jemima and bring the image to life. He found exactly what he was looking for in Nancy Green, an ex-slave who had worked as a cook for a judge for many years and whose specialty was—you got it—pancakes. She is remembered as a wonderful, friendly soul, with a winning personality full of laughter and kindness. She became famous as "Aunt Jemima" when during the 1893 World's Fair in Chicago she reputedly flipped more than one million pancakes.

In 1923 Nancy Green died in a car accident at the age of 89, and Aunt Jemima Mills was purchased by the Quaker Oats Company in 1925. Subsequent versions of Aunt Jemima's familiar face have graced the front of Aunt Jemima's Pancake Mix for almost 70 years, and her representation of the Great Mother/Aunt is still going strong.

The Maiden: The Breck Girl

The Breck Girl, used in Breck shampoo advertising, is a wonderful example of advertising that uses the positive aspect of the Maiden archetype. The Breck Girl has been around for more than 50 years. She has become a brand icon and an enduring symbol of feminine beauty and purity. There have been more than 200 different Breck girls, including Brooke Shields, Kim Basinger,

Jaclyn Smith, and Cybil Shepard. The long line of Breck Girls was interrupted during the early years of the women's movement, because the advertiser feared that they would be impuned for exploiting feminine beauty. Happily, the Breck Girl was brought back to American media in 1988.

● ●

" The Breck Girl, used in Breck shampoo advertising, is a wonderful example of advertising that uses the positive aspect of the Maiden archetype."

● ●

The Maiden: The Coca-Cola Girl

In its early days of advertising, Coca-Cola tried to get the consumer's attention and, at the same time, create an appealing, wholesome brand mythology and identity by associating Coke with beautiful, wholesome, all-American gals. One of the first Coca-Cola Girls was Lillian Nordica, the Metropolitan opera star in the early 1900s. (See Figure 5.3.) A bevy of Coca-Cola Girls followed. The Coca-Cola Girl had to have just the right balance of sex appeal and wholesome, middle American looks. Taken as a whole, the changing Coca-Cola Girls provide a fascinating chronology of the changing views of feminine beauty. Over the years, our definition of beauty may have changed, but one thing remained a constant: the Coca-Cola Girl is someone you can take home to your mother.

The Nymph/Water Maiden: White Rock Girl

The White Rock Girl is another example of a mythical female character based on the primordial maiden archetype. Interestingly, the White Rock Girl is also an example of a mythical advertising character that is based on a mythical figure taken from classical Greek mythology. The White Rock Girl was inspired by a painting of the mythical Greek figure, Psyche. (See Figure 5.4.)

In Greek mythology, Psyche was the young maiden whose beauty rivaled that of Venus, the Goddess of Love. Venus was jealous of Psyche's beauty, and sent her son Cupid, the God of Love, to make Psyche fall in love with the most wretched, vile man he could find. But instead, when Cupid saw Psyche, he was so struck by her beauty that he fell in love with her. Venus plotted against them, but in the end, love won out. Fittingly, Psyche (the Soul) married Cupid (Love) and they lived happily ever after.

In the early 1890s the owners of the White Rock Mineral Springs Company

Figure 5.3

The Maiden: Coca-Cola

Courtesy of the Coca-Cola Company

Figure 5.4

White Rock Girl

Courtesy of White Rock Products Corporation

were inspired by a painting of Psyche looking at her reflection in the water ("Psyche at Nature's Mirror" by the German Artist Paul Thurman). The White Rock Girl is a wonderfully appropriate symbol for a bottled mineral water company, a symbol that works on several different levels. The ethereal, almost translucent White Rock Girl, gazing at her reflection in the water, seems to capture and convey the sense of purity one would like to associate with a bottled mineral water. At the same time, her enchanting, feminine beauty also adds a little borrowed interest.

● ●

"The early Calvin Klein Jeans commercials that featured a comely actress wearing Calvin Klein Jeans. . . . are a terrific if controversial example of advertising based on the Virgin/Harlot dichotomy."

● ●

On another level, the White Rock Girl has an aura of magic and enchantment. In ancient mythology, water creatures (mermaids, pixies, nymphs, and so on) are invariably feminine. Women, with their bodies' cycles, seem to have a natural connection with nature and water.

The image of the winged White Rock Girl takes us back to a time when the world was young and we were still connected to mountains, trees, and streams. Forests were still enchanted by pixies and nymphs in those ancient times, and we might chance upon one of these beguiling creatures admiring herself in a clear pool.

The Harlot: Calvin Klein Jeans

Madison Avenue mythologies based on the Seductress/Harlot flip side of the Maiden archetype have been around as long as advertising. The early Calvin Klein Jeans commercials that featured a comely actress wearing Calvin Klein Jeans and sitting with her legs wide open ("You want to know what gets between me and my Calvins? Nothing!"), are a terrific if controversial example of advertising based on the Virgin/Harlot dichotomy.

Until recently, sex in advertising has been very one-sided; male sexuality had not been exploited as extensively or overtly as female sexuality. This is a reflection of the androcentric values and sensibilities dominant in America's patriarchal society. However, with the emergence of a stronger female sensibility, consumers now witness male sexuality also being exploited:

- Joe Namath wears panty hose.

- Jim Palmer and Marky Mark sport Calvin Klein underwear.

- Frederic's of Hollywood now features a sexy man along side the sexy woman on the cover of their lingerie catalogue.

The changes being brought about by the women's movement have *not* gone unnoticed on Madison Avenue. Advertisers have tried to reflect these changes in their advertising mythologies. In the 1970s and 1980s consumers witnessed the emergence of advertising with female user imagery based more or less on the Warrior archetype, an archetype more closely associated with aspects of masculinity. This was a distinct departure from the female user imagery in the 1950s and 1960s, which revolved around the Great Mother and Maiden/Seductress archetypes.

Charlie Perfume: The New Woman's Debut

The Charlie perfume commercial was one of the first of the "new woman" commercials. Charlie celebrated the debut of the new independent woman: a woman with a man's name. In a white satin jumpsuit that accentuated her thin, mannish figure, Charlie strode confidently across our TV screens while Bobby Short sang "Here's a fragrance that's here to stay." To a world that had grown up with Donna Reed, the new woman seemed more like a man than a woman. Moreover, the Charlie myth turned the male playboy myth on its head. Charlie was depicted as a successful, independent woman with an exciting lifestyle, Rolls Royce, and handsome gents at her beck and call. Coincidentally, it was about this time that Playgirl magazine appeared on the newsstand.

• •
" . . .the Charlie myth turned the male playboy myth
on its head ."
• •

The most fascinating aspect about using perfume advertising to track the changing roles and sensibilities of women is that perfume advertising is pure mythology. There is no product story (what can you say about perfume?). And the Charlie mythology worked like a charm. This myth, created on Madison Avenue, was in synch with the new feminine sensibility that rejected tired feminine roles and stereotypes, and the mythology helped to make Charlie perfume an instant success.

The Sexy Superwoman: Virginia Slims and Enjoli

Virginia Slims advertising created a feminist mythology that tried to ac-knowledge the gains women were making: "You've Come a Long Way, Baby" campaign. And Enjoli perfume created a new feminine mythology that introduced us to the Superwoman, the woman who could do it all: career, mother, and lover. The commercial depicts a confident, sexy woman singing "I can bring home the bacon, fry it up in the pan, and never ever let you forget you're a man." We see the Enjoli woman carrying a briefcase, cooking dinner, reading to her child, and promising her man that she still has enough energy left to make him feel like a man.

Crystal Light's Linda Evans commercials also seemed to connect with the new woman. Linda Evans promised women that if they drank Crystal Light and believed in themselves, they could look terrific and do anything they set their minds to.

At this point, the women's movement seemed to catch fire, and suddenly things really began to change. Women were challenging the old structure on every front. Women began to be hired for "men's jobs." Women became police officers, bus drivers, and construction workers. Women were running for higher political offices. Women were becoming more competitive in sports. Madonna began grabbing her crotch, just like the guys. There were even women body builders with muscles big enough to intimidate most men.

The Woman in Management: MCI and the Evolving Logos

The 1980s inspired advertising mythologies that used female user imagery even more strongly based on the Warrior archetype. We began to see commercials like that for MCI—tough-talking women managers, wearing big-shouldered suits, going toe-to-toe with their male counterparts. The "new woman" looked and acted more and more like a man. Feminity was passe. Again, femininity and feminine beauty had become associated with weakness and traditional feminine stereotypes.

The Amazon: Reebok Tennis Shoes

The female imagery used in advertising, especially for sports equipment, has begun to use very strong, aggressive warrior imagery. Some of this extreme warrior imagery has been coupled with male bashing to create advertising with female imagery that has taken on a decidedly Amazonian tone and character.

The Amazon archetype is associated with strong warrior women who are also man-haters. A recent commercial for Reebok's pump tennis shoes opens with a woman hitting tennis balls. As each of the balls comes at her, it becomes a different male face (her boss, an obnoxious flirt, and so on), which she bashes with increasing relish.

The Great Father Archetype: Quaker Oats Man

Turning to male characters, consider the Quaker Oats Man. He is an excellent example of a mythical character based on the Great Father archetype. His face is an immediately recognizable, enduring brand icon that works primarily at the product level to capture and convey the brand's essence and primary attribute: old-fashioned goodness.

The Quaker Oats Man was created in 1877 by the Quaker Mill company when the company registered as a trademark "the figure of a man in Quaker garb" (Sacharow, 1982, p. 72). Several stories have been handed down to explain how a Quaker was chosen to represent this product. Henry Seymour, one of Quaker Oats's founders, says he came up with the idea while looking through an encyclopedia for "a virtuous identity that would instill buyer confidence." The other story comes from William Heston, another one of Quaker's original founders. He said the Quaker Oats Man was inspired by a picture of William Penn in Quaker clothes.

• •

"The Quaker Oats man . . . communicates an old fashioned goodness that goes beyond the product."

• •

In any case, the Quaker Oats Man is a brand character that works primarily at the product level to convey the idea that the product, oatmeal cereal, represents old-fashioned goodness. However, as was the wish of the founder Henry Seymour, the Quaker Oats Man also communicates a sense of old-fashioned goodness that goes beyond the product. On a subliminal level, the Quaker Oats Man also represents a religious figure, a father figure, and a God figure.

The image of the Quaker Oats Man is rooted in the Senex archetype (*senex* is the Latin word for "old man"), which, as we saw in Chapter 4, ". . . expresses all that is old, ordered, and established" (Hillman, 1990, p. 19). Some common personifications of the Senex archetype are the wise old man, father, king, ruler, and a clergyman. The Senex archetype and images of old men, especially bearded men, are also associated with holy men (Moses) and patriarchal God images of an all-powerful, juridical male god like the Judeo-Christian God or Zeus.

It is also important to understand that the Senex archetype from which the Quaker Oats Man is derived represents not only the image of an old man but a sensibility and an aspect of consciousness that people all share: "The high God of our culture is a senex God; we are created after this image with a consciousness reflecting this structure. One face of our consciousness is inescapably senex" (Hillman, 1990, p. 19).

The Quaker Oats Man has been with us for more than 100 years. In some not-so-subtle ways, the Quaker Oats Man serves not only as a reassuring cultural fixture but also as an enduring Great Father figure.

The Great Car-Repairing Father: Mr. Goodwrench

Mr. Goodwrench is another example of a mythical advertising character

Figure 5.5

Quaker Oats Man

1877

1946

1957

1970

Courtesy Quaker Oats Company

based on the Great Father archetype. The Mr. Goodwrench character represents *logos*, that aspect of the Great Father archetype that represents order and reason. At the same time, Mr. Goodwrench also represents the protective, caring aspects of the Great Father.

The Mr. Goodwrench character works at both the product level and on an emotional/psychological level. At the product level, Mr. Goodwrench communicates important product attributes: competent, knowledgeable service. And he conveys important product benefits: a well-running car.

The Mr. Goodwrench character also works on a more emotional/psychological level. Consumers report their perceptions of the Mr. Goodwrench character as "protective, trustworthy, reassuring, and knowledgeable . . . it's like having a friend in the auto repair business." Thus, the Mr. Goodwrench character embodies and communicates compelling emotional benefits: reassurance and the peace of mind that comes from knowing that your car will not be in the hands of incompetent or unscrupulous service mechanics.

The Great Handyman Father: The Maytag Repairman

The Maytag Repairman who waits by the phone that never rings is another example of a character based on the Great Father archetype. The Maytag Repairman works primarily at the brand level to communicate a general brand attribute: dependability. Like Mr. Goodwrench, the Maytag Repairman represents the protective, caring aspects of the Great Father.

The Western Warrior: The Marlboro Man

The Marlboro Man is a terrific example of a mythical advertising character based on the Warrior-hero archetype, a uniquely American version of the Warrior: the American cowboy.

The image of the Marlboro Man is prefigured in Marduk, the Babylonian male god who overthrew the Great Mother Goddess, and all of the other Warriors that succeeded him.

It doesn't matter that there are very few real cowboys. The cowboy is a mythical figure. Many of us grew up with cowboy heroes like Gene Autry, Roy Rogers, and the Lone Ranger. The image of the lone cowboy riding his faithful steed into the sunset has been emblazoned into the American psyche.

The cowboy is a symbol of America's pioneering spirit and "rugged individualism." But it is not the image of the hard-working, cow-poking cowboy that has made a lasting impression on America's soul; it is the cowboy as Gunslinger. With his unfeeling, unflinching, steely-eyed squint, the

Marlboro Man is reminiscent of the Gunslinger—the Wild West Warrior who haunts our dreams and shapes our sensibilities. Richard Slotnick explores this idea in his book, *Gunfighter Nation* (Slotnick, 1992).

Americans like to think that our cowboy hero is a good guy who rides a white horse, wears a white hat, and kills bad guys (who wear black and ride dark horses) to uphold justice and defend the weak and helpless. The early cowboys represented by Roy Rogers and the Lone Ranger were, indeed, righteous, clean-living men who were as committed as was Superman to "truth, justice, and the American way." They never shot to kill but only to disarm or wound the bad guy.

Then came the later cowboy characters portrayed by Clint Eastwood in the "spaghetti westerns," who embodied another kind of cowboy-hero: a gritty, dirty, unshaven, stogie-chewing cowboy who does not hesitate to blow away the bad guys. And we've enjoyed watching Clint blow away the bad guys, whether he's playing a nineteenth- or twentieth-century cowboy. After all, these bad dudes usually deserved it. (We seconded Clint's gun-toting challenge to these scum: "Go ahead; make my day.") Like the sword, the gun is definitive. Bang! You're dead. It's the American way.

Like all Warriors, the Gunslinger Cowboy is committed to "slaying dragons." Just like the Medieval crusaders or knights of Camelot, Gunslinger Cowboys have undergone a spiritual transformation in which they embraced death—their enemies' and their own. Such a hero is a loner, a saddle tramp, unattached, with no home, no sense of community, and no commitments. He will never grow old and paunchy or have to listen to his wife nag him for not taking out the garbage. He is wedded to his Colt .45 and his horse. He will go out in a blaze of glory, with his six-shooter still smoking in his hand and his boots on. He glories not in life but in death—in the orgasmic ecstasy of his exploding gun.

The gunfighter has no need for women or his feeling side, which women represent. Just as with the older tradition of the loner Lancelot, women will only drag him down, weakening his sense of duty and resolve. In the western film, *High Noon,* we see what happens when a Warrior-Gunslinger gets involved with a woman: She complicates his life with feelings. In this classic, an aging gunfighter, played by Gary Cooper, who is torn between his love for a woman (during his midlife crisis) and honor (his commitment to fight to the death). He wants to put away his gun and join the life-affirming world of the living, but first he must square off at high noon with another Gunslinger in a potentially mortal confrontation.

The Marlboro Man has become an advertising icon. Marlboro has used the Warrior-Hero archetype to transform a brand that originally had a feminine image into a brand with a rugged, masculine image. Marlboro has leveraged the mythic American Cowboy, a "killer image," to create one of the most recognizable brands in the history of advertising.

The Military Warrior: U.S. Marine Corps

The Warrior Archetype in Advertising

One of the best examples of a brand mythology created around the male Warrior archetype is the U.S. Marines. Of course, the Marines bring their own mythology—a mythology built with courage and blood. Madison Avenue simply tries to capture and convey the Marines' mythology.

One of my favorite U.S. Marines commercials is the one which uses the sword as a symbol of the Marine as Warrior. The commercial opens with a blast furnace belching fire, and raw steel being forged and pounded into a gleaming steel sword. In the background a drum pounds and a voice-over says, "We take raw steel and with fire, muscle, and sweat, we polish it to razor-sharp perfection. The Marines are looking for a few good men with the mettle to be a Marine." The commercial is so awe inspiring that many viewers find themselves saying, "I want to be one of the few good men. I want to stand proud and wear that splendid uniform. I want to wear a big, shiny sword. I want to be part of their mythology!"   This commercial, with its powerful archetypal warrior imagery, touches something irrational, some primitive, male craziness deep in a man's soul.

Sword Symbolism

The sword is an an ideal metaphor and symbol for the Warrior. Its raw steel is transformed into a razor-sharp sword, and the young man who wields it is transformed into a Warrior.

The sword is a masculine, phallic symbol (note too that the Latin word for sheath—the sword's resting place—is *vagina*). It is a symbol of dynamic male energy, logos, the penetrating power of the intellect, male virility, and war. The sword represents strength, power, courage, the "white arm" of justice, and the golden power of discrimination:

> The sword represents the golden power of discrimination which
> enables us to pierce through layers of confusion and false images to
> reveal a central truth. In this connection one is reminded of King
> Solomon when he was confronted with two women, each claiming
> to be the mother of the same infant. He suggested cutting the child
> in half, whereupon the true mother was instantly revealed by her
> emotional reaction (Nichols, 1991, p. 155).

Alexander the Great used his sword to cut the Gordian knot. Legend has it that Gordus, who was a simple farmer, became king of Phrygia when it was believed that he was the king promised by the oracle. He tied his wagon outside the temple of the God of the oracle. It was believed that whoever could untie the knot would become the king of Asia. Like everyone else,

Alexander tried to untie the knot, but failed. At which point he drew his sword and decisively ended the matter by cutting the Gordian knot with his sword.

The sword is the masculine counterpart of the cauldron and the chalice: It is the male instrument of transformation. The sword (or the arrow), like a flash from Zeus's lightning bolt, is a solar symbol depicting the sun's rays. It represents responsibility and the solar or higher aspect of phallic consciousness. To take up the sword is "To sever the umbilical cord . . . to cut oneself free from childish dependence" (Nichols, 1991, p. 155). The hero must take up the sword in his solar flight from the world of the Great Mother, the unconscious. He uses the sword to defend humanity's higher ideals and those who cannot defend themselves.

In Arthurian mythology, men are knighted by touching their shoulders with a sword. It is a symbol of the Warrior's highest ideals, the chivalric code with its emphasis on selfless bravery and noble deeds. King Arthur was only a boy (teenager) when he pulled the sword Excalibur from its steadfast position in a large stone. When Arthur performs this mystical act that legend has stated would reveal the future king, Merlin the Magician tells Arthur his true identity: Arthur is the son of King Uther-Pendragon. Merlin then tells Arthur that he must use his magical sword Excalibur, which means "to sever iron and steel," and defend the Castle of Camelot in the Kingdom of Logris.

The sword is often said to have supernatural powers. The sword of fire bars mankind from paradise. A sword also has a personality. It is worn like a garment and becomes an extension of the user. Men frequently were buried with their swords. In *The Book of the Sword,* Richard F. Burton elaborates on the special relationship between a man and his sword:

Uniformly and persistently personal, the Sword became no longer an abstraction but a Personage, endowed with human as well as superhuman qualities . . . To surrender the Sword was submission; to break the Sword was degradation. To kiss the Sword was, and in places still is, the highest form of oath and homage (Burton, 1987, p. xv).

In the Japanese culture the sword is sacred and symbolizes courage. The Samurai's sword is considered the soul of Japan. Ancient Japanese sword makers prayed, fasted, and went through a ritual shower and cleansing before they began the arduous process (by hand) of transforming the raw steel into a sword.

There is something mystical, numinous (psychically charged) about the naked blade of a sword. The ancients believed that a sword should never be left unsheathed among men, because the naked blade of a sword has the power to cast a svengali-like spell over men, to incite them to kill each other.

The Indian Gurkhas carried a large, wickedly curved sword-like weapon, which they believed could not be unsheathed unless it drew human blood.

Even if they just took it out to cut a piece of bread, they would not put it back until it had tasted blood (they would draw their own blood by nicking their skin). In a similar vein, Anton Chekhov often has an exposed dagger or sword casually lying about during the opening scenes of his plays because he believed it set an ominous tone and foreshadowed the violence to come.

In my presentation entitled "Advertising to Men," I tell clients about the Warrior archetype and the sword as its symbol. When I explain that there is something electric and alive about a naked sword, they look at me in disbelief. This is in part because most people have never seen or held a sword. I now bring a large sword to the presentation, which I unsheathe at just the right moment. And I invite people to come up after the presentation and hold the sword. Now their reactions are very different.

•••••••••••••••••••••••••••••••••••

" When I explain that there is something electric and alive about a naked sword, they look at me in disbelief. "

•••••••••••••••••••••••••••••••••••

Some U.S. Marines' commercials have compared the Marines to the Arthurian knights. The commercial opens with a young man dressed in knightly armor riding into a castle on a horse. He dismounts and is knighted by the king's sword. As the sword touches the knight, his image is replaced with a young Marine's face. The sword is again the symbol of making the Warrior what he is, the symbol that ties the Marines' mythology to the Arthurian knights. This commercial works well to capture the spirituality of the Warrior mystique. It also illustrates the pedigree lineage of all Warriors and their timeless values. However, the Marines don't need a borrowed, Arthurian mythology. They have their own mythology, one created in blood in places like Guadalcanal, Mount Suribachi, and Da Nang.

The U.S. Marines commercials represent the pure Warrior arche-type. However, advertising mythologies often use a more subtle warrior image. In the mid-1950s, Ogilvy and Mather Advertising introduced the now-famous Man in the Hathaway Shirt campaign. David Ogilvy had been trying unsuccessfully to come up with a new advertising campaign for Hathaway Shirts. The company has been around since 1837, but few people were familiar with either the company or its products. As Ogilvy tells it, he was on his way to work when he stopped in a drugstore to buy a $1.68 black eye patch to give the model in the ad "story appeal." The idea worked like gangbusters. The Hathaway Shirt Man, with his mysterious black patch and British air, emanated a mystique that struck a chord among American males—and females.

The black eye patch exudes intrigue and suggests that the Hathaway Shirt Man is a man with a past. In Scandinavian mythology, Odin, king of Aesir, trades one of his eyes for a drink from the well of knowledge and wisdom so that he might know the mysteries of the universe. And Austrian and Hungarian-German men have described a secret Prussian society/fraternity whose mark is a "Schmiss," a scar across the member's cheek. The scar is delivered in a ritualized sword duel wherein the young male initiate must prove his courage by not retreating, even one inch. To ensure that he will not retreat, a small glass brimming with cognac is placed against the heel of his foot (he must not spill a single drop!). The wound is crudely stitched to maximize the scarring, which the young male initiate wears proudly, a symbol of his courage. The Schmiss is a status symbol that earns the admiration of other men and enhances the young man's appeal among women.

Did the Hathaway man's eye patch hide a hideous battle scar (or just an eye infection)? Is the Hathaway Shirt Man a British adventurer, a Sir Richard Burton type, just back from his latest expedition in search of the source of the Nile? Note too that blinding is a symbolic form of castration. Is this a man who has looked death in the eye and still managed to hold on to his masculinity? Yes, this campaign was more than intriguing; it also sold a lot of shirts.

In the 1970s, the Street-Smart Cop emerged as the modern replacement for the cowboy. Cop shows like "The Streets of San Francisco" replaced the Westerns that were so popular in the 1960s. And a grim Karl Malden, looking like the cop he played in the television series, subsequently ordered viewers to use American Express Traveler's checks in the famous "Don't Leave Home Without Them" admonition.

The 1980s brought a new breed of Warrior—the Wall Street Warriors, ambitious yuppies aspiring to become Masters of the Universe. Instead of the selfless defenders of truth, justice, and the American way, the new breed of Wall Street Warriors were greedy, self-involved, and power hungry. Actor Michael Douglas portrayed a fictional Wall Street Warrior ("Mr. Geckko") in the movie *Wall Street,* whereas Ivan Boesky enacted a real-life variation. By the late 1980s, Madison Avenue seemed to be glutted with brand mythologies based on high-powered Wall Street Warrior types with their power ties and limousines.

The Magician: Mr. Clean

The Mr. Clean character is based on the Magician archetype. The Magician is related to the Jester/Fool archetype. Whereas the Jester/Fool makes people laugh, the Magician mystifies and renews people's sense of wonder.

Procter and Gamble's Mr. Clean is a mythical advertising character who works primarily at the product level to communicate important product attributes and benefits. When consumers are asked how they feel about housecleaning, they report that it is "drudgery, . . . a thankless job." They also respond that they wish someone would come into their home and do it for them. Enter Mr. Clean. Mr. Clean is every housecleaner's fantasy: a big, strong, friendly guy who comes out of a bottle and cleans the whole house. (Mr. Clean was the original househusband.)

The Mr. Clean character mythologizes the product by humanizing it (sort of) and giving it a distinct identity and personality. It is a character and a mythology borrowed from Arabian mythology. With his shaven head, gold earring, and other-worldly look, the Mr. Clean character is reminiscent of a genie-in-the-bottle character from *A Thousand and One Arabian Nights.*

Arabian mythology is full of magical, wish-granting "genies" and "jinns." A magical, wish-granting genie was also the basis for a popular television series "I Dream of Jeannie." The magical genies and jinns were said to be the offspring of fire, and they frequently appeared to men as serpents and dogs as well as in human form. Some genies were good and some were evil (Mr. Clean is obviously one of the Good Guys—he wears white!).

Despite his imposing physique and nonmainstream looks, most consumers generally perceive the Mr. Clean character as friendly, benign, and nonthreatening. "According to a P&G survey of women, Mr. Clean is muscular and powerful, but not harsh or chauvinistic . . . " (Solomon, 1985). Through the years, the Mr. Clean character has undergone some changes that seem to further reinforce his friendly, nonthreatening character. He has lost his whiskers, black eye, and—to downplay his single gold earring—the earring no longer glints.

Consumers seem to find Mr. Clean nonthreatening because of his friendly persona and otherworldly appearance. Some women also perceive him as nonthreatening because they think of him as nonsexual—a eunuch. And this is probably all to the good because if the Mr. Clean character had retained his sexuality, he may have been too threatening. Some women might have found the idea of having a big, strong, virile guy helping them clean house while their husbands were away, titillating, but he would probably have been too threatening for their husbands and the patriarchal establishment.

In any case, the power of a mythical advertising character like Mr. Clean (or any of the aforementioned advertising characters) goes beyond communicating a product story. Advertising characters like Mr. Clean lend drama and intrigue to a boring activity.

And more importantly to the longevity of this brand mythology, the Mr. Clean character is *appropriate* for the product it represents. Who doesn't want a genie to come do the housecleaning in an instant? The image works to engage and involve the consumer and to communicate the promise of an effortlessly clean house in a way that is at once entertaining, compelling, and memorable.

In a study conducted by *People* magazine, the Mr. Clean character was found to be more familiar than the vice president of the United States, despite the fact that Mr. Clean had not been advertised on television for 10 years (Vamos, 1985, p. 95).

Father Nature: Jolly Green Giant

The Green Giant is counted among the so-called Leo Burnett critters that include Tony the Tiger, Charlie the Tuna, and Morris the Cat. The Green Giant's humble beginnings were the Minnesota Valley Canning Company, founded in 1903. The company chugged along until the early 1920s when it developed a seed that produced peas that were unusually large and tender. The code name for the new peas was "Green Giant," and in 1926 the image of a Green Giant became the trademark for the company's superior peas.

Then, in the early 1930s, a young copywriter named Leo Burnett entered the picture. Burnett changed the image of the Green Giant and made it more friendly and appealing. He also introduced a new descriptor: "Jolly." (A good thing, too, because giants are generally perceived as threatening.) As Leo tells it, the idea came to him out of the blue while he was looking at an ad proof: ". . . a proof of a *Ladies Home Journal* ad came across my desk. Because it was so alliterative and just for the heck of it, I inserted the word *jolly* in an ad that was about to go to press. The client liked this, and it has remained importantly in the Green Giant vocabulary ever since" (Advertising Age, 1969, p. 230).

Through the years both the brand and the company prospered. The Green Giant became one of the most widely recognized trademarks, and in 1950, on the advice of the Leo Burnett Advertising agency, the Minnesota Valley Canning Company changed its name to the "Green Giant Company." This proved to be a wise decision for many reasons, not the least of which is the fact that, when the company went public in the 1960s, the name carried with it instant recognition and respect.

The Green Giant character works on a number of levels:

- It works to engage and entertain the consumer by lending a sense of drama and intrigue to an otherwise unexciting category.

- Once the consumer is engaged, the Green Giant character communicates important product attributes: quality, freshness, and consistency.

- The character also works as a mnemonic, an immediately recognizable brand trademark and symbol.

Interestingly, the Leo Burnett executives were pleasantly surprised to discover that the Green Giant character seemed to have the same appeal all around the world. This raises the question: What is the basis for the Green Giant's universal appeal?

Figure 5.6

Jolly Green Giant

Figure 5.7

The Green Man

The idea of giants seems to be inherently intriguing. Giants crop up in many of the ancient mythologies:

- Odysseus encountered the giant one-eyed Cyclops.

- In Germanic mythology, the giant Baugi tried to obtain the mead of poetry for Odin.

- There is even a biblical reference to a race of giants that existed before the great flood. And of course, there is also the story of David and Goliath.

However, the universal appeal of the Green Giant character may also lie in its symbolic significance, in its ability to tap into the awe (and fear) of the regenerative powers of Mother Nature. One phenomenon that must have impressed early humans was nature's continual cycles of decay and re-newal—nature's ability to constantly renew itself. Recognizing their own mortality and finiteness, humans felt insignificant in the presence of nature's life-giving power. The Egyptians feared decay more than they did death; that's why they developed techniques for preserving their dead.

● ●

" . . .The Leo Burnett executives were pleasantly surprised to discover that the Green Giant character seemed to have the same appeal all around the world."

● ●

The mystery of nature's transformative powers can also be explored in terms of its association with the fertility rituals of the Great Mother and the transformative powers of woman. The seed is placed into the womb of the earth, where it gestates and is transformed into a living plant. The goddess as "Lady of the Plants," is found beginning with the Sumerian Goddesses up through the Greek Goddess Demeter and later in the Madonna as "The Madonna of the Sheaves."

In ancient fertility rituals, the male god, usually represented as the goddess's consort or son-lover, is sacrificed before the Great Mother. Attis (the son-lover of the ancient goddess Cybele) castrated himself before her. Castration and self-flagellation seems to have replaced the earlier ritualized killing of the male high priest. In the Mithraic rites, a bull, which represented the life force of the earth, was sacrificially killed. And Eleusis, the Roman male god who is the equivalent of Attis, was referred to as the "cornstalk" and "ear of wheat."

Vestiges of the vegetative myths with their fertility rites and symbols can also be found in some of the later mythologies. One interpretation of the medieval poem "Sir Gawain and the Green Knight," is that this epic is a vegetation myth, an allegorical representation of the ancient pagan rituals. The poem centers around a mysterious Green Knight who challenges King

Arthur's bravest knights to cut his head off, with the promise that he will return in one year to cut off the knight's head. Sir Gawain steps forward and takes up the Green Knight's challenge. He chops off the Green Knight's head, then looks on in astonishment as the Green Knight picks up his head and rides off saying "I'll see you in one year." The symbolism is fairly obvious: the head-chopping equals harvesting; the fact that the Green Knight doesn't die symbolizes nature's powers of regeneration and renewal; and the Green Knight's promise to return in one year also suggests nature's cyclical nature.

Remnants of the vegetative myths and ancient fertility rites are apparent, in Christianized form, in the May Day festival:

> In 46 B.C., the Julian calendar, established by Julius Caesar, altered the date of the Hilaria festival of Attis from 25 March to 1 May, and so all over Europe until this century the rites that once coincided with the spring equinox in March were advanced to May. May instead of March became the month sacred to the goddess, and May was later to become the month sacred to Mary. On the first of May, in Christian times, the statue of Mary was, and still is, crowned and garlanded with flowers (Baring and Cashford, 1991, p. 410).

May 1st was also celebrated in Europe by the decorating of the Maypole and naming of the May Queen and Green Man. The Green Man, clothed in leaves, represents the goddess's "consort"; he can also be viewed as a male version of Mother Nature—a kind of Father Nature.

There is an obvious similarity among mythical characters like the Green Man (Figure 5.7) the Green Knight, and the Green Giant brand character. Thus, on some level, the universal appeal of the Green Giant character may be rooted in the human instinctive awe of the regenerative powers of nature.

• • •

Brand Mythologies Created Around Mythical Places

Advertising can also be used to mythologize products by creating brand mythologies around imaginary places. And again the mythical worlds created in advertising are often archetypal, derived from universal images.

America's Good Old Days: Maxwell House 1892 Coffee

Maxwell House 1892 Coffee is an example of advertising and packaging working together to create a brand mythology around a mythical place. The Maxwell House 1892 advertising campaign works primarily on an emotional level to create a brand mythology around a mythical location: a place in time and America's cultural past, "the good old days." The

Maxwell House 1892 campaign represents a simpler time when life seemed less harried, and "the coffee somehow tasted better."

It's an appropriate mythology for a coffee product because coffee is generally associated with relaxing—taking a coffee break. By associating Maxwell House 1892 coffee with the slower, more relaxed pace of "the good old days," the advertising may work to subliminally remind the consumer to relax and take a break with Maxwell House 1892 coffee.

A West Liberty Town: Louis Rich Cold Cuts

Louis Rich Cold Cuts recently introduced an advertising campaign that uses a mythical place to support a taste superiority strategy. Not only does it help to create an appropriate, appealing brand identity, it should ultimately help to build a brand mythology for Louis Rich. Advertising is used to create a mythical place, the Louis Rich farm in the mythical American town of West Liberty, as remembered through the eyes of Louis Rich's daughter. The Louis Rich Farm takes us back in time to a more agrarian America, a time when most everyone lived and worked on a farm. It is a simple, honest place where people still believe that working hard and trying your best is important.

The Louis Rich West Liberty farm mythology, together with a new product attribute, "slow roasted," communicates the idea that Louis Rich Cold Cuts taste best because they're slow roasted and still made with the same commitment and dedication to quality. At the same time, the Louis Rich farm mythology also works on an emotional/psychological level to create an appealing brand identity and to leave the consumer with a good feeling about Louis Rich.

The powerful appeal of the Louis Rich farm mythology stems from the fact that it already exists in the American psyche. The Louis Rich farm is a place in America's heart . . . where Dorothy and Toto live—the mythical farm Americans wish they had grown up on.

Today's Brigadoon: Hidden Valley Salad Dressing

Hidden Valley salad dressing is another example of a brand mythology in which the brand name, packaging, and advertising all work together to create a brand mythology around a mythical place. Hidden Valley is a lush, green, fertile valley where the salad ingredients are the freshest and where only the best salad dressing will do.

This mythical place appeals both on the product level and emotional/psychological level. At the product level, it communicates the idea that Hidden Valley salad dressings offer superior taste and freshness (the freshest salad ingredients demand the best salad dressing.) On the emotional/psychological level, the mythical Hidden Valley is the archetypal familiar, rural, comforting place. The valley exists in the human psyche as the cradle of creation, the garden of Eden, a safe, peaceful place, a place without strife or stress, where people can enjoy nature's bounty.

Fertile valleys, farms, gardens, cornucopia, and so on, are all archetypally similar. On a symbolic level, they represent the eternal womb of the Great Mother. (See Figure 5.8.) The earth is our first mother; her bounty nourishes and sustains all of her creatures.

The All-American Town for Kentucky Fried Chicken

Kentucky Fried Chicken (KFC), the fast food franchise that now goes by the name KFC, recently introduced a new advertising campaign based on a mythical place: Lake Edna. This mythical town is an appealing middle-American community of likeable, down-to-earth folks whom everyone would like to have as neighbors. Lake Edna is a lot like the Louis Rich town of West Liberty; it is the quintessential American town.

Colin Moore, the senior vice president of marketing at KFC, described Lake Edna as "a fictitious place that is simultaneously nowhere and everywhere. This notion of a small town is as much a state of mind as a physical location."

In some sense, KFC's mythical Lake Edna tries, on a symbolic level, to capture the essence of small-town America. It is a microcosm of everything America is supposed to be. McDonald's advertising creates the same feeling but without resorting to a mythical, symbolic place. However, McDonald's too created a mythical place, "McDonaldland," which the company uses in some of its children-oriented Saturday morning advertising. In any case, like McDonald's advertising, the Lake Edna brand mythology works on an emotional/psychological level to give the consumer a good feeling about KFC and the kind of people who eat there.

A Chocaholic's Paradise: Bounty Candy Bars

M&M / Mars' Bounty Candy Bars has created a brand mythology around the ultimate mythical place: paradise. The Bounty advertising created by D'arcy, Masius Benton & Bowles New York mythologizes the product by associating it with exotic, South Seas island imagery. The idyllic island imagery, together with the product attribute "made from kalapuno coconuts," is used to communicate and support the promise that Bounty Candy Bars deliver the exotic taste and pleasures of paradise. At the same time, the images of a mythical paradise island also work on an emotional/psychological level to create a sense of excitement, the exotic, and feelings of escape and bliss.

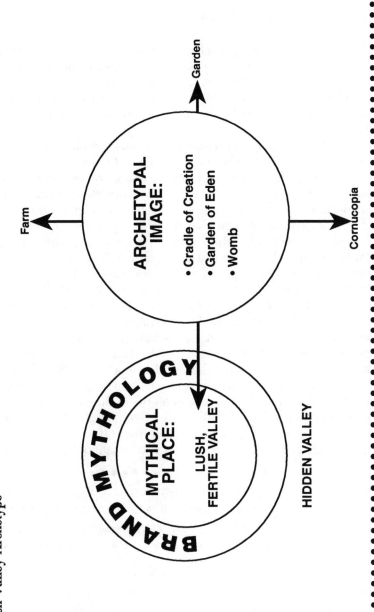

Figure 5.8
Hidden Valley Archetype

• • •

Brand Mythologies Created Around Mythical Moments and Themes

The First Day of School: Kodak

Advertisers can also mythologize products around mythical moments associated with the products. Kodak provides a great example of a brand mythology using this strategy. Kodak has used an advertising approach that communicates the high quality of its products, but like Hallmark Cards, the emphasis of its advertising has been on the emotional benefits provided by its products.

Kodak advertising focuses on the precious, mythical moments captured on its film and by its other products. One of the more memorable Kodak commercials was one that captured the drama and emotions surrounding a child's first day of school. Like the baby's first steps, a child's first day of school is a momentous, mythical moment. (See Figure 5.9.) Symbolically, it represents the child's entry into the world. Every culture creates rituals for a similar moment in a child's life. The rituals take different forms—an initiation into tribal customs, a bar mitzvah or first communion, or a heroic quest—but the meaning is the same: the child is leaving the protective sphere of its parents and taking his or her first step into the world.

The Kodak first day of school commercial is a wonderful example of an *individual* advertising mythology (a single commercial) created around a mythical moment. It re-creates a mythology that captures and evokes the powerful feelings (both the parent's and child's) that arise when the child must for the first time enter the world without his or her parents.

The child must find the courage to take an important first step, and the parents must have the courage to let the child go. Of course the Kodak camera saves the day (after all, this is advertising!) when the teacher uses the Kodak instant camera to take pictures of the children, which makes them smile and reassures them that maybe school isn't so scary after all.

• •
"Advertising mythologies that evoke feelings are
especially effective because the feelings serve to
validate the emotional/psychological benefits . . ."
• •

Advertising mythologies that evoke feelings are especially effective because the feelings serve to validate the emotional/psychological benefits that advertisers wish to associate with their product. They make an emotional appeal, *not* a rational selling proposition. The feelings evoked by the advertising work to disarm the consumer and create a product appeal that is based on emotions and feelings rather than logic and reason. When the advertising mythologies are appropriate and credible, the feelings serve as their own validation of the claimed emotional/psychological benefits.

Softening Up the Teacher: Hallmark Cards

The advertising campaigns created for Hallmark Cards are a wonderful example of a brand mythology that works primarily on an emotional level to associate feelings and emotions with a product: greeting cards. Hallmark understands that greeting cards are really about feelings. The company has developed a powerful brand mythology focused on the emotions that greeting cards evoke. And Hallmark clinches the sale with a tagline that communicates product superiority: "When you care enough to give the very best."

One memorable Hallmark commercial features a little girl and her piano teacher (an older man who is having a birthday). The piano teacher seems to be a stern taskmaster and a bit of a curmudgeon, but as the story/commercial unfolds, the little girl leaves him a birthday card, and viewers see that he is really a big softee who is deeply moved by her thoughtfulness. As viewers watch the commercial, they too are moved.

• •

"Mythology helps people to deal with life's universal themes and struggles. People draw wisdom and comfort from mythological stories that tell how others have struggled and coped with these same mythic moments."

• •

The fact that the commercial evokes these same feelings in the viewer proves that the little advertising mythology is both appropriate and credible. The commercial ultimately leaves the viewer with a good feeling that spills over to Hallmark and their products.

Becoming a Big Brother: McDonald's

Like Kodak and Hallmark, McDonald's has become adept at commercials that create a brand mythology dealing with truly mythic moments. One example is the McDonald's commercial that centers around the birth of a new baby girl and the impact of this momentous event on the baby's three-year-old brother. The whole commercial is seen through the eyes of the little boy. The commercial opens with mom and dad bringing the new baby girl into the family's home. Naturally, the parents, grandparents, and everyone else make a big fuss over the new baby. We also see her brother in the background, feeling forgotten and left out. This is his first realization that he is no longer the center of his parents' universe. He must now share his parents' love with his new baby sister.

Luckily, his dad sees that the boy is a little sad and bewildered. So the dad takes him to McDonald's, where they have a "man-to-man talk" about how his little sister will "need someone to show her the ropes."

Again, McDonald's captures a universally felt, mythical moment and its powerful emotions. What parent, at the birth of the second child, doesn't experience the mixed emotions of joy at having another child as well as the feeling of somehow betraying the first born?

Mythology helps people to deal with life's universal themes and struggles. People draw wisdom and comfort from mythological stories that tell how others have struggled and coped with these same mythic moments.

Note: Although most of the advertising and brand mythologies explored in Chapter 5 focused on single-image advertisements that employ a mythical character, a mythical place, or a mythical moment/theme, advertisers often create advertising and brand mythologies by *mixing* the three.

• • •
Beyond Brand Mythologies

Up to now, the focus of this chapter has been various brand mythologies. However, the mythologization process has many broader applications. For example, corporations and companies can be mythologized. In other words, advertisers can create *company* or *corporate* mythologies in the same way that they create brand mythologies. Advertisers can also extend or broaden the definition of "brand." For example, presidential candidates can, in a real sense, be thought of as brands. Like brands, presidential candidates can be— and today usually are—mythologized, and advertising can be used to communicate their personal mythology just as advertising conveys brand mythologies. In any case, the following examples appear in this chapter to help advertisers appreciate the mythologization process on a broader scale.

Ben & Jerry's Homemade, Inc.: The Mythologization of a Corporation

Like brands, companies and corporations have mythologies. Corporate and company mythologies communicate the company's or corporation's ethos, that is, the beliefs, values, and sensibilities that shape and guide the company. A company's mythology works both inside the company and outside; it is important both to consumers and company employees. The mythology works internally to give the employees a sense of the company's identity, personality, and culture. When people are part of an organization, they need to have a sense of what the company stands for. A company can seem like a cold, impersonal, uncaring entity. When employees have a clear understanding of the company's mythology, it gives them a sense of what their priorities should be and what they can expect from the company.

A company's mythology also works externally. The proliferation of mass media has made this more true than ever. In a mass media world, a world of instant communications, there are no secrets. The electronic media have empowered the consumer by making them more informed, not only about products but also about the companies and corporations that manufacture those products. Consumers have become increasingly circumspect about the companies behind the products. If corporations are not paying their fair share of taxes, are using unfair hiring practices, or are polluting the environment, consumers will find out about it. Consumers increasingly "buy" the corporation or company as well as the product.

Consumers are demanding that companies and corporations be more responsive and responsible socially, ethically, and environmentally. Companies whose mythologies, values, and practices are out of synch with the values and sensibilities of today's consumers increasingly come under fire from various consumer groups. Companies can no longer afford to maintain a "fat cat," bottom-line attitude while they ignore social and environmental issues. Thus, it's no longer enough for a company to sell its *products,* it must also sell the *company.*

Ben & Jerry's Homemade, Inc. exemplifies a company that has done a terrific job of creating an appealing corporate mythology that seems to work for both its employees and its consumers. The story of how Vermont entrepreneurs Ben Cohen and Jerry Greenfield parlayed $12,000 and an old rock salt ice cream-making machine into a multimillion-dollar company is itself the stuff of legend and mythology. Ben & Jerry, two self-described ex-hippies, began their ice cream business by selling crepes and ice cream out of an old Vermont garage back in 1978.

Right from the start, Ben and Jerry were committed to making very high-quality, premium product, and this undoubtedly is an important factor behind their success. But the appeal of Ben & Jerry's Ice Cream clearly goes beyond the product. Ben & Jerry's created a corporate philosophy and mythology that maintained that social responsibility is more important than profits. This was no smokescreen. The company put its money where its mouth was. For example, when a weakened federal dairy purchase program caused milk prices to drop, the company continued to pay Vermont dairy producers the original, higher prices. The two owners said they felt it would not be fair for them to profit from the misfortune of the milk producers. In a similar vein, they sell products like Peace Pops and Rainforest Crunch (the profits from Rainforest Crunch are used to help preserve the Amazon rainforest).

● ●
" . . . Socially responsible corporate mythology
seems to be working."
● ●

The Ben & Jerry's socially responsible philosophy is also evident in its corporate culture, which has taken great pains to make sure that women and minorities are fairly represented in staffing all levels of the company. At the company's annual meeting, managers hold an open forum in which partici-pants discuss not only earnings and profits but also the corporate policies affecting women, minorities, gays and lesbians, and so on. Ben & Jerry's recently confounded corporate America by instituting a policy that says that no company employee can earn more than five times the lowest paid employee. Recycling and waste management are top priorities at Ben & Jerry's, where managers even make it a point to print the annual report on recycled paper.

Ben & Jerry's socially responsible corporate mythology seems to be working. In 1991 the company reported sales of more than $77 million.

Ronald Reagan: The Mythologization of a Presidential Candidate

A president can be "packaged" and advertised (mythologized and lionized) in much the same manner as a product or company by creating a personal mythology. A personal mythology serves the same function as a brand mythology: It tells the voter what the presidential candidate stands for, and, at the same time, helps to establish and communicate his or her identity and persona.

Everyone has a personal mythology, but politicians and other public figures are generally more conscious of their personal mythology and take greater pains to cultivate and nurture it. As with brand mythologies, personal mythologies can be drawn from different sources:

- latent personal mythology—facts and folklore about a person's back-ground, heritage, personal history, and life experience.

- cultural mythology—personal mythologies that reflect the values and sensibilities of the people's history and culture.

Electing a president can be seen, on a symbolic level, as a mythic quest, a search for the Great Father, a King (and, when we begin to elect women as presidents, a search for the Great Mother, a Queen).

Like Telemachus, we are trying to find our father, someone who represents our cultural destiny, someone to lead our country. We can see reflected in each of the recent presidents (Nixon, Ford, Carter, Reagan, Bush, and now Clinton) our own shifting cultural and spiritual values. On October 10, 1992, the *New York Times* quoted folklorist Alan Dundes as saying, "There is an unconscious aspect in politics, where we are looking for a hero who will turn out to be a father figure for the country" (Dowd, 1992, p.A1). And Robin Lakeoff, a linguistics professor at Berkeley, added: "We act modern, cool, and sophisticated. . . . But underneath, we want a daddy, a king, a god, a hero. We'll take the heel if we can get Achilles, a champion who will carry that lance and that sword into the field and fight for us. It's sort of scary" (Dowd, 1922, p.A1).

In describing the president and his cabinet at the White House, the press often draws on mythological images such as "Camelot." A *New York Times* cover story, "Of Knights and Presidents: Race of Mythic Proportions," described the presidential campaign as a modern-day version of the knightly tryst. The article stated that because of the generational differences between George Bush and Bill Clinton, the campaign battle resembled the "epic imagery of a battle between a son and a father."

Political candidates intuitively understand that in order to get elected, they must be perceived as appropriate Great Fathers and at the same time espouse political views that are in synch with the country's current values and sensibilities. The image makers who help the president to develop an appropriate, appealing mythology generally draw from the candidates' history and experience. The mythologization of presidential candidates generally begins with facts drawn from the candidates' personal history and builds on them to create an appropriate, appealing personal mythology. It is not surprising, given the fact that western cultures are Warrior cultures, that presidential candidates—the people chosen to lead our country—are often male war heroes. Pointing up the candidate's courage and heroic deeds in battle is generally a surefire way to convince the populace that he has what it takes to lead the country.

One of the first presidential candidates to use this strategy was Andrew Jackson, in the 1828 election. Jackson's "handlers" hit on the idea of using the name "Old Hickory," a name given to Jackson because of his toughness and perseverance in battle. The "Old Hickory" name helped to build the Jackson legend, the cornerstone of the Jackson mythology. "Old Hickory" became a recognizable symbol of the candidate's courage. Indeed, like brands, presidential candidates often try to come up with a symbol or a slogan that captures and conveys what they stand for. In *Packaging the*

Presidency, Kathleen Hall Jamieson referred to the "hickory branches and hickory poles [which] were powerful symbols in the Jackson campaign" (Jamieson, 1992, p. 6).

● ●

" The power of a symbol or a single compelling image is nothing short of astonishing. "

● ●

And in the 1840 presidential campaign, the "log cabin and cider" became powerful symbols for Harrison. Van Buren's supporters made the mistake of associating these symbols with the Harrison campaign because they thought their effect would be negative, but instead the symbols held a powerful appeal for the common man.

The importance of finding appropriate symbolism to capture and convey a person's personal mythology cannot be overemphasized. Prominent people often develop their own mythology and symbolism without the help of handlers. For example, in his excellent biography of General MacArthur, *American Caesar,* William Manchester described MacArthur's instinct for image making. He recounts a specific incident that occurred during World War II. MacArthur had made good on his "I Will Return" promise to return to free the Philippines. It was a historic moment, and MacArthur was getting ready to come ashore. Manchester noted:

> The General, impatient and annoyed, wouldn't wait for Egeberg to test the depth of the water. He ordered the barge ramp lowered, stepped off into knee-deep brine, and splashed forty wet strides to the beach, destroying the neat creases of his trousers. A newspaper photographer snapped the famous picture of this. His scowl, which millions of readers interpreted as a reflection of his steely determination, was actually a wrathful glare at the impertinent naval officer. When MacArthur saw a print of it, however, he instantly grasped its dramatic value and the next day he deliberately waded ashore for cameramen on the 1st Cavalry Division's White Beach (Manchester, 1979, p. 450).

The power of a symbol or a single compelling image is nothing short of astonishing. During the 1964 presidential campaign, Tony Schwartz created the now infamous "daisy" ad for Doyle Dane Bernbach. The ad shows a little girl counting "1, 2, 3, 4," while pulling petals off a daisy. When she reaches nine we hear a male voice in a countdown, "9, 8, 7, 6." As he is counting down the camera closes in on the girl's face, focusing on the pupil of her eye. On zero the camera dissolves from her eye to the mushroom cloud of an atomic explosion. The ad never actually mentions the presidential candidate, Barry Goldwater, and it was only aired once. But the impact of the image on

America's psyche was so powerful that it essentially destroyed Goldwater's bid for the presidency.

Ronald Reagan's "Morning in America" theme exemplifies a presidential campaign that used powerful symbolism to create and communicate an appropriate, appealing presidential mythology. The campaign used television commercials to communicate its compelling mythology.

The illustrious advertising group that created the commercials was called the "Tuesday Team" and included advertising giants like Phil Dusenbery of BBD&O, Kenneth Roman of Ogilvy and Mather, and Ed Ney of Young and Rubicam. And on the creative side, it included Hal Riney of Ogilvy and Mather and Jim Weller and Ron Travisano of Della Femina Travisano and Partners.

The spiritual center of the Ronald Reagan mythologization was not built around the candidate's personal mythology but rather around feelings of patriotism and hope. The Tuesday Team created "warm and fuzzy" advertising that worked on an emotional level to evoke feelings of patriotism and hope, and to associate those feelings with Ronald Reagan. The "Morning in America" commercial created by the Tuesday Team is a masterfully crafted personal mythology. The commercial opens with a new day dawning—a symbol of hope and new beginnings. There were at least 14 flags in the commercial—usually in the process of being raised. The commercial also used an appealing song by Lee Greenwood that sings America's praises.

• •

" The spiritual center of the Ronald Reagan mythologization was not built around the candidate's personal mythology but rather around feelings of patriotism and hope. "

• •

Reagan's personal mythology is an advertising mythology created solely around feelings and emotional/psychological benefits. The Reagan mythology is a borrowed mythology, a reflection of the values, sensibilities, and lifestyles that are near and dear to most Americans. The Reagan mythology used the flag and appealing imagery to evoke feelings of patriotism and pride, and to associate those feelings with Ronald Reagan. Reagan's image makers paid close attention to the imagery and symbols that surrounded Reagan. Rumor had it that Reagan was only to be shown in three-quarter portraits (usually with the flag as a backdrop) in order to show off his broad shoulders.

In all fairness, the Republicans also deserve credit for running a good campaign. They did a good job of telling voters what's good about America, while the Democrats spent most of their time wringing their hands and explaining all the things that were wrong with the country. When Ronald Reagan wisely asked: "Are you better off today than you were four years ago?" most Americans had to admit that things *did* seem to be better. In Ronald Reagan, we had finally found the Cowboy hero of our dreams.

Down Home with the Clinton Campaign

In the most recent presidential election, Bill Clinton defeated incumbent George Bush by embracing an ideology and a mythology that represent the "new America" that is emerging and rapidly replacing the older America. Yes, America is changing—again. Just as the influx of different immigrant groups changed the face of America in the early 1900s, new waves of immigrants are once again changing the face of America. The face of America is increasingly diverse, multicultural, and multiracial. By the year 2020, census projections indicate that "minorities" (African-Americans, Hispanics, Asians, and so on) will become the new majority. In cities like Los Angeles, Anglo-Caucasians are already a minority.

The new America brings with it a new world view and sensibility that is more tolerant and pluralistic, more accepting of diverse values and lifestyles. The new America is an America where, as Mario Cuomo says, "Everyone comes to the table." America's diversity is unique in all the world. It is the source of our strength.

On some level, Bill Clinton's campaign and inaugural festivities were clearly a way of communicating the fact that Bill Clinton represents a new American mythology (which is actually an old, recycled mythology—the one on which America was built). The bus that Clinton and Gore used in their campaigning, as well as Clinton's publicized visits to McDonald's for a fast food hit and a chance to mingle with the people, were some of the more obvious symbols that communicated the idea that Bill Clinton did not place himself above his constituents, that he would be a president who would be sensitive to the needs of everyday people. But more importantly, Clinton captured and reflected the cultural and racial diversity of the new America.

Part I I I
• • • • • • • • •

Building and Maintaining Brand Mythologies

Part III focuses on helping the practitioner understand how advertising can be used to build and maintain successful, enduring brand mythologies. It explains the key steps in the process of creating advertising that builds and maintains successful brands.

Chapters 6, 7, and 8 comprise Part III. Chapter 6 explains that the first step in creating brand-building advertising is to uncover a critical consumer insight or key idea that can be leveraged to create a powerful brand positioning (how the brand will be positioned in the marketplace and in the consumer's mind) and a compelling advertising message (what the advertiser wishes to communicate). The chapter further explains the importance of consumer research, and how the advertiser must be able to go beyond information and facts—to make the leap to insights and ideas.

Finally, Chapter 6 focuses on understanding the brand. In addition to understanding the consumer and looking to the consumer for key insights, the advertiser must also understand the brand. If the advertiser is working with an established brand, consumers will have some existing perceptions, feelings, and product experiences that they associate with that brand. An established brand will most likely have an existing brand mythology, image, personality, and essence or soul. The advertiser is introduced to a number of different techniques like the BIP (brand identity profile) that allow the advertiser to assess the brand's perceptual inventory, brand mythology, image, personality, and essence, which grow out of its perceptual inventory.

Chapter 7 explains how the critical consumer insights derived from consumer research become the basis for the brand positioning and the advertising message. And the brand positioning and advertising message are, in turn, translated into an advertising execution. The concepts of both brand positioning and advertising message are explained and explored under varying circumstances. The focus is on helping the reader to understand how the brand positioning and advertising message are determined. In order to give the reader a better perspective, the history and evolution of some of the most commonly used message strategies are also presented and explored in Chapter 7.

The chapter further explains how the creative teams (art director, copy writer, and production people) translate the brand positioning and advertising message into an execution (commercial or advertisement) by helping the reader understand how to create advertising executions that go beyond short-term selling and help to build brand mythologies. As explained in Chapter 7, the creative team must begin by coming up with a core executional idea that not only becomes the basis for the commercial at hand, but also has the potential to become the core of the brand mythology. The chapter explores a number of key sources (latent product mythology, brand heritage, and so on.) from which the creative team can draw ideas for a core executional idea. At the same time, Chapter 7 underscores the power of archetypes in creating advertising that endures and can help to build brand mythologies.

Chapter 8 concludes this study of advertising archetypes by presenting methods of maintaining brand mythologies. The chapter uses a number of case studies to explain how the advertising practitioner can assess existing brand mythologies. It underscores the importance of evaluating a brand mythology, not only in terms of how well it is working in the marketplace (market share, profitability) but also in terms of how well it is working in the consumer's mind (share of heart—creating a brand image and personality that help the consumer to form an emotional bond with your brand). Chapter 8 also emphasizes the importance of keeping your brand mythology in sync with the values, sensibilities, and lifestyles of the target consumer.

All three of these chapters provide shortcuts and ways to enhance your brand's mythology that are presented in "tip boxes". These tips, called from my experiences in advertising campaigns are geared toward constructing the brand mythology (Chapter 6), positioning the brand (Chapter 7), and maintaing the brand's mythology (Chapter 8).

Chapter 6
• • • • • • • • • •

Building Your Brand's Mythology: Information, Insight, and Ideas

Before beginning the actual process of creating advertising, the advertiser must state his or her objectives. Advertising objectives should be communication objectives, not marketing objectives. Marketers often make the mistake of stating that the objective of the advertising is to build market share. "Building market share" is a marketing objective, not an advertising objective. A typical advertising objective is to persuade Brand X users to use your brand. Once you have established the advertising objective, you must then develop an advertising strategy, that is, you need to specify how you are going to persuade Brand X users to use your Brand.

Figure 6.1 summarizes the process of building brand mythologies. The advertising practitioner must look to the consumer for information, insights, and ideas about the product and the target consumer. Out of this understanding of the product and the consumer, the practitioner must select one (sometimes two) critical consumer insight(s), which will become the basis for the brand positioning (what the client wants the brand to stand for in the consumer's mind) and the advertising message (what the client wishes to communicate). The brand positioning and advertising message go hand-in-hand. What the advertisement communicates ultimately establishes the brand positioning in the consumer's mind. At the same time, advertising plays a key role in building a brand's overall brand mythology.

A brand's mythology—along with its identity, personality, and unique perceptual inventory of imagery, feelings, and associations—is the result of many factors. However, advertising generally plays a dominant role in building strong, enduring brand mythologies. Every commercial and/or advertisement should be thought of as an *individual advertising mythology* that ultimately helps to create the overall brand mythology.

Advertising enables the practitioner to access the consumer's mind and

● ●

Figure 6.1

The Process of Building a Brand Mythology

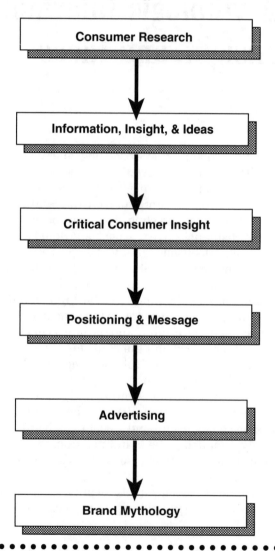

● ●

to establish a perceptual space for the product—a brand space—wherein advertisements can create appealing, mythical characters, places, moments, and worlds. The mythical characters, places, and situations created in individual advertising mythologies communicate product attributes and benefits, and position the brand in the consumer's mind. At the same time, the mythical worlds created in our individual advertising mythologies transform generic products into brands by mythologizing them—giving them distinct personalities and sensibilities. Carefully consider every image, feeling, and association communicated in advertising, because it will ultimately impact the brand's overall mythology, identity, and personality. You can create a unique, appealing brand mythology by choosing the kind of imagery, feelings, and associations that will ultimately define your brand.

• • •
The Importance of Insight

The first step in developing advertising and building brand mythologies is to gather information. Accurate, reliable information is vital. The advertising practitioner "must look to knowledge generated by consumer research to guide him in understanding consumer wants, needs, and desires and their relation to the product, service, or institution for which he must prepare advertising" (Weilbacher, 1979, p. 152).

Indeed, the new technologies have created an abundance of information. Some clients would literally need a tractor-trailer to deliver the files of information they have on their brand. But information alone is not enough. The key to developing effective, well-founded brand mythologies lies in your ability to go beyond information and make the leap to insight and ideas. Insights and ideas, which give a new understanding of the product and consumer, are critical in developing the individual advertising mythologies (commercials and advertisements) that help to build the brand mythology.

Insights and ideas can occur at any point in the information-gathering process. You may come to an insight about the product/brand, how consumers perceive the product/brand, their motivations for using it, or how they use it. The insight can come from anywhere and is important because it usually leads to a deeper understanding of the product/brand and the consumer, which, in turn, usually leads to more effective advertising.

Hurry, Watson, the Game Is Afoot

Trying to find the critical consumer insight(s) that will become the basis for your brand mythology is a lot like detective work. Practitioners have to collect and sort through a lot of facts in order to find the clue (critical consumer insight) that will finally solve the case. Columbo, the TV detective incarnated by Peter Falk, and Jessica Fletcher, the writer/sleuth character played by Angela Lansbury, are ideal role models for the advertising researcher. Both characters are relentless in their pursuit of truth. They have restless minds that are always trying to fit things together. There is always "just one more question" or "one more loose end."

• • • • •

Construction Tip:

To underscore the importance of insight (especially with new clients), I arrange a "little briefing" at the beginning of a new project. I tell clients that we are going to take a little trip together, both literally (such as travel to different cities to conduct focus groups) and figuratively (traveling in psychic space—a trip through the consumer's mind).

I explain that "it is likely to be tough sledding through unknown terrain," that "our mission is not simply to gather facts and information, but also to uncover new insights about the product/brand and the consumer. We mustn't be afraid to turn over rocks. A lot of weird stuff may come crawling out, but that's also where we will most likely find the new insights." During focus group exploratories, I keep an "insight board" hanging on the wall in the focus group viewing room so that, if anyone has a flash of insight while watching the focus groups, he or she can record it on the board before it gets lost.

• • • • •

It is always exciting when you come to an insight: They are like precious little gems, flashes of light against the vast, dark unknown. Sometimes, neophyte researchers ask how do you know when you come across an insight. My reply invariably is, "Experience helps a lot. Through experience, you learn to recognize what's truly important." When a researcher experiences an "aha!" reaction, he or she has hit on an insight.

Scope Mouthwash has run an advertising campaign that seems to be based on a gem-quality consumer insight. The advertising depicts different people (average folks) being caught in the act of denying that they have bad breath. The insight inferred from the advertising is that people do not like to admit to their inadequacies or foibles. More to the point, people don't like to admit that they have bad breath. The quality and multiple dimensions of the insight stem from the fact that they touch on a universal truth and reveal the consumer's innermost feelings about bad breath.

Denying that one has bad breath is a wonderfully human behavior. Humans do not like to admit that they have bad breath or body odor, or that they snore. The reasons for this denial are actually quite complex. The most obvious is that they want others to accept them, like them, and (ultimately) love them. People deny that they have bad breath because they fear rejection by other people. This fear is not unfounded. Consumers associate bad breath with lots of nasty things, including rotten teeth, mental illness, homeless people, and sickness. Bad breath and poor hygiene, in general, are usually taken as signs that the person is either mentally ill, sick, or "just a slob."

On another level, a denial of bad breath (or any body odor) is also a way of denying that people are animals. Humans do not like to think of themselves as animals. Because of their "superior intellect," people like to think they are distinct from, and superior to, other animals. But human bodies, and the odors they produce, are a constant reminder of the animal nature of humans.

Ultimately, a denial of bad breath is also a denial of death. The connection between bad breath and death is not a conscious one for consumers. However, consumers do associate bad breath with illness. Illness is associated with death—the ultimate illness. And death is associated with a dead body or a rotting corpse—the ultimate body odor. Thus, a denial of bad breath (and all body odors) is, on some level, also a denial of death.

● ●

"Consumers laugh because they see themselves."

● ●

Another interesting aspect to the "denial insight" occurs when consumers see someone caught in the act of denial of having bad breath; they laugh because the frailty of the human condition has been laid bare. Consumers laugh because they see themselves.

The laughter is particularly effective in the Scope commercials, because it makes it easier to deal with an otherwise awkward subject. And, at the same time, this glimpse of human frailty makes the advertising characters more human, more appealing, and more endearing to the viewer.

● ● ●
Understanding the Consumer

In order to uncover the one or two critical consumer insights that will form the basis for our brand positioning and advertising message, we begin with a thorough understanding of the consumer: the who, why, and how.

Who: Defining the Target Consumer

Demographics

Demographics are a logical place to begin defining the target consumer. Demographics are the consumers' vital statistics. Are your consumers male or female? Married or single? What is their average age, education, and income level? Demographic information is generally straightforward and provides a basic definition of your target consumers. You might find, for example, that your target consumer, the person you wish to reach with your advertising, is a male teen. Or you might find that your target audience is predominantly age 25 to 34, college educated, female professionals.

Demographic information provides a basic definition of the target consumer. The advertising practitioner can try to "flesh out" the target consumer with psychographic information.

Psychographics

Psychographic information defines your target audience in terms of its values, attitudes, and lifestyles. Psychographic information also helps you to understand your target consumer's sensibilities or ways of thinking. It tells what's important to them and how they spend their time. In short, it helps you to understand "what makes the audience tick."

The luxury car category offers an interesting example of how psychographic information helps you to gain a deeper understanding of the consumer. Luxury car buyers have at least one similar demographic— they can all afford to spend a lot of money on a car. However, their psychographics—their values, sensibilities, lifestyles, and how they think about cars—are often radically different.

For example, the person who buys a Lincoln or a Cadillac is generally looking for traditional luxury car features—creature comforts. That person sees the car as an extension of his or her living room. The person who buys a Porsche, however, is generally looking for performance and excitement. He or she sees the car as something exciting, something to be experienced.

Psychographics are fascinating, but they can also get complicated. For experienced researchers, psychographic information can be a treasure trove of insights and ideas. But neophyte researchers can quickly find themselves in over their heads.

For example, if you do psychographic research on male teens, you will quickly discover that they are a skittish group. No longer boys, but not yet secure in their manhood, they are extremely insecure. Psychologist Erik Erikson, in *Identity, Youth & Crisis*, describes adolescence as a period of crisis and "identity confusion," wherein the adolescent is trying to discover his identity and his place in the world (Erikson, 1968).

Erikson offers Hamlet as the adolescent archetype— "an exalted example" of identity confusion. Erikson states that one of the most important areas of identity confusion in young people is their struggle for an occupational identity. During this period of identity confusion, peer pressure, and the need to identify with and belong to a peer group becomes extremely important.

We can learn a lot about male teens from experts like Erik Erikson. He uncovered a universal truth about adolescence. It is a time when young people are involved in an intense struggle to understand who they are and to define their place in the world. This is an invaluable insight that you can use to help develop more compelling advertising.

For example, one project targeted male teens with a new deodorant. Using a series of focus groups with 14- to 15-year-old male teens, advertising were exploring the idea of using an attractive teenage girl as a spokeswoman for a new deodorant. The strategy was based on an obvious, but nonetheless important, piece of information—teenage boys are intensely interested in girls. Advertisers reasoned that, by using a pretty spokeswoman, they could get the boys' attention and sell more deodorant.

The advertisers scheduled focus groups with teenage boys to help determine the ideal spokeswoman. The advertising account team intuitively felt that Brooke Shields (at that time still in her teens) would be perfect. Before revealing who they thought would be the best spokeswoman, the advertisers wanted to find out who the teen boys would suggest. After a few minutes the boys came up with the group's unanimous choice: Raquel Welch! The account team was shocked. "Raquel Welch is old enough to be their mother!"

The advertisers decided to tip their hand and see how the boys would react to the idea of Brooke Shields. They hooted, hollered, and yelled, "Oh, no! Not her!" The account team commented, "Well I guess the boys don't like her."

● ●

"Psychographic information also helps you to understand your target consumer's sensibilities or ways of thinking."

● ●

The brand mythologist, however, responded, "On the contrary. Their reaction suggests that Brooke Shields or someone like her would be very appropriate." He explained that the boys' intense reaction and discomfort suggested that we were on target. He further explained that the groups' choice, Raquel Welch, was an obvious "safe choice."

The group had agreed to a woman that is a well-recognized sex symbol, the kind of woman that should appeal to every red-blooded boy. Choosing Raquel Welch was "what a real man would do." Brooke Shields hit a little too close to home. The boys clearly felt uncomfortable admitting that they liked Brooke Shields in front of the other guys.

Additionally, you can also use consumer research to help understand what is important to male teens. What are their values? How do they spend their time? How do they dress? What kind of music do they like? What are their interests and hobbies?

There is no substitute for getting out and talking to consumers, usually through focus groups or one-on-one interviews. If you see a group of male teens talking and interacting in a group situation, you can actually observe the intense peer pressure. Male teens in a group situation, for example, constantly look around nervously at other members of the group to make sure they are not saying anything "uncool."

An Ethnographic Approach

Ethnography is a term borrowed from cultural anthropology. It describes a way of coming to know a people and a culture by immersing oneself in the culture, by living with the people, and observing them up close. Ethnography is a lot like the photojournalistic approach in that it combines on-location interviewing and photos of consumers in their homes using the product. When used as a market research technique, ethnography takes you into the consumers' homes and enables you to observe in great detail how consumers use the product. This often leads to new insights about your consumers and the product.

• • • • •

Construction Tip:

Ethnographic research can be especially useful in uncovering new insights about the target consumer. For example, I used an ethnographic approach to help the creative teams "get a handle on the blue-collar beer drinker." Most of the creative people had grown up in middle-class, white-collar neighborhoods and attended Ivy League schools, so they had no sense of the blue-collar target consumer. The challenge was how to communicate a sense of the blue-collar guy to the creatives.

I immersed myself in the blue-collar culture, drank beer in the local bars with the guys, shot pool with them, and so on. (This is work?) I also spent time with the guys at work, in their homes, and at their gun club. I conducted extensive interviews covering their life values as well as their views on everything from beer and sports to politics. To bring back a sense of the texture of their lives, I also took lots of pictures everywhere we talked.

To shoot some photos of some really hard-core blue-collar guys I went to a place that's as blue collar as it gets—the Fulton Fish Market. It's still much as it was depicted in the film *On the Waterfront*. It was exactly the imagery I wanted.

The final, successful presentation on the blue-collar beer drinker included lots of pictures that captured the blue-collar beer drinker. I also included some scenes from movies like *The Deer Hunter*, which did a wonderful job of capturing blue-collar guys.

• • • • •

For example, the ethnographic approach revealied that the world of the blue-collar male is a very physical world. Unlike the white-collar world, which often deals in ideas and abstractions, the blue-collar guy deals with physical things: he loads and unloads dead fish; he digs ditches; he fixes and maintains the machinery that keeps our world going. His work is often dirty and backbreaking. But perhaps the cruelest cut of all is that his work generally goes unrecognized, unappreciated, and uncelebrated. Like all human beings, he wants to be recognized, respected, and appreciated. The great appeal of the Budweiser and Miller advertising campaigns created in the 1970s and 1980s was that they celebrated the unsung efforts of blue-collar workers.

Macrosegmentation Models

Whenever you identify and define consumers, you are also, in effect, segmenting them demographically, psychographically, and in other ways. There are, in fact, a number of popular, syndicated segmentation models that advertising strategists can use to help define the target audience. Most of the popular macrosegmentation models combine demographic, attitudinal, and lifestyle information to segment consumers. Basically, what macrosegmentation models do is this:

1. Collect demographic, attitudinal, and lifestyle information on a large, national sample.

2. Segment the sample based on demographic, attitudinal, and lifestyle similarities and differences.

3. Project these findings to the population at large. The better models also try to marry the demographic, attitudinal, and lifestyle information to product usage.

For example, the Stanford Research Institute's *VALS model* describes a population segment based on psychologist Abraham Maslow's Hierarchy of Human Needs. According to the original VALS model, the population can be divided into three major subsegments:

• need-driven

• outer-driven

• inner-driven

Within each of these three subsegments are specific segments. For example, within the outer-driven segment, VALS identifies and defines three segments: belongers, emulators, and achievers. Each of the segments is defined in terms of some outer-directed need. For example, belongers are driven by their need to belong, whereas achievers are driven by their need to achieve.

VALS 2, the latest version of the VALS model, segments people into eight

groups depending on their psychological makeup and their "resources"—
which include not only income but education, intelligence, energy level,
health status, and eagerness to buy as well. VALS 2 seems to have broader
marketing applications than the original model, in that it combines consumers' social and psychological motivations with their ability to buy.

At the top of the VALS hierarchy are the *actualizers*—successful,
sophisticated people with lots of resources. Actualizers are concerned with
self-image as well as social issues, and they are more open to change than
consumers at the lower levels (belongers, strivers, and so on).

The next three groups are also affluent and have relatively great
resources—a rung below the actualizers. *Fulfillers* are mature, satisfied, and
comfortable, but open to new ideas and change. *Achievers* are career
oriented, and image is important to them. *Experiencers* are young and
impulsive—they seek new and different experiences.

On the next rung down on the ladder are three more groups. *Believers*
are conservative consumers with strong principles; they favor established brands. *Strivers* are achievers with fewer resources and are concerned
with self-image and gaining approval of others. And, finally, *experiencers*
are into self-sufficiency, gardening, canning, and repairing their own cars.

At the bottom of the VALS hierarchy are the *strugglers*—they are
concerned with taking care of their survival needs for day-to-day living.

Prizm is another macrosegmentation technique that uses a different
approach. Instead of Maslow's Hierarchy of Human Needs, the Prizm
model is based on the idea that "birds of a feather flock together." In other
words, people with similar values and lifestyles tend to cluster together; they
live in the same general area. Prizm uses postal zip codes and census block
clusters to geographically segment the U.S. population, then identifies
and defines 40 different lifestyle-type clusters based on demographic
and psychographic lifestyle information, as well as on buying behavior.
The names of the Prizm clusters seem to capture the essence of what kinds
of things are important to each of the different clusters. Some examples
of Prizm clusters are "furs and station wagons;" "shotguns and pick-
ups;" "God's country."

Advertisers often rely on macrosegmentation models. Some of the
larger advertising agencies have even developed their own models. The
usefulness of the models is a matter of personal judgment. Use
macrosegmentation models heuristically, as a supplement, rather than a
substitute, to your judgment.

Why: Motivational Research

At Backer & Spielvogel Advertising, Bill Backer's standard marching orders
on any new account were, "Find out how the heavy user sells himself/herself

on using the product/brand." Backer intuitively understood that one of the most important first steps in creating advertising is to find out "where the rubber meets the road"—to understand the consumer's motivations for choosing a product/brand.

There are many reasons consumers choose a product. Some reasons are product related: "This hair conditioner seems to give my hair more body." Some reasons are emotional/psychological: "I want to look like the woman in the commercial. . . . I want to use the product used by that glamorous movie star so that I, too, can feel glamorous."

Consumers' reasons for choosing a product are often a complex mix of product-related and emotional/psychological/sociological reasons. It remains for the astute advertising researcher to uncover and understand these reasons. In some ways, the "why" question is the hardest question to answer, but it can also be the most interesting question. It inevitably takes you on an endlessly fascinating journey through the labyrinth of the human mind, through convoluted by-ways and "locked attics" where consumers have hidden (even to themselves) the motivations for using a product.

The process of uncovering hidden motivations is similar to the psychoanalytic process. Consumers, like the analysand, often resist any efforts to probe or uncover their hidden motivations. Consumers will lie to protect their egos. They will offer many plausible, rational reasons for using the product, but hide the more emotional reasons that might reveal their vulnerabilities and insecurities.

Ernest Dichter, the Viennese psychiatrist, pioneered many of the ideas and sensibilities used in "motivational research." Dichter's psychoanalytic approach had its heyday in the 1950s, but it is currently enjoying a comeback. Motivational Research has become fashionable once again, and there has been a commensurate spate of articles, including a cover story in *New York Magazine*, about researchers using drawings and other psychoanalytic techniques to uncover hidden consumer motivations.

If you ask consumers about their motivations for using a product, they generally talk about tangible benefits related to the product's physical attributes. For example, in the soup category, consumers who use canned soup generally respond to questions about why they use soup by saying

- "I cook it because it's warm and nutritious."

- "It's easy to prepare and the kids like it."

- "It's tasty and nourishing."

Consumers are often unaware of their hidden emotional reasons for using a product. For example, the consumer may not be conscious of the fact that soup provides an emotional benefit but, in the course of the interview, the consumers may discover that they associate soup with their childhood and warm feelings of being loved and nurtured. It is often as much a surprise to the consumer as it is to the researcher. But even when consumers are aware, they often will *not* readily admit to such reasons. Consumers won't admit to their hidden product motivations because such motivations are often socially unacceptable and/or because they expose consumers' vulnerabilities and insecurities. For example, vanity, or the need to feel important and successful, is a hidden product motivation consumers will resist revealing. Consumers do not like to admit to motivations such as, "I drive a BMW because it makes me feel important and successful" or "I drink this beer because I want to feel like one of the guys."

The "why" question can sometimes be answered quantitatively, using survey techniques (questionnaires, telephone polls, and so on). However, the quantitative techniques usually fall short of uncovering the deeper, hidden motivations for using a product. Quantitative techniques generally uncover the rational, "socially acceptable," product-related reasons for using a product, and it remains for qualitative techniques to uncover the deeper, hidden emotional reasons.

Belief Dynamics

Belief dynamics is a proprietary technique developed by D'Arcy, Masius, Benton & Bowles. The technique helps the advertising strategist to understand the dynamics of the consumers' beliefs about the brand, themselves, and the significant others in their lives. The technique is based on the idea that "all behavior is mediated by beliefs." Thus, to understand consumer behavior, you must understand the beliefs that cause the behavior. Once you understand these beliefs, you can use advertising to change or reinforce the consumer's beliefs to benefit your brand.

Belief dynamics is basically a brainstorming technique. The brand group (the client and agency people working on the brand) is used to generate a *belief structure* or *belief map* roughly drawn by the interviewer on a large chart (see Figure 6.2).

The belief map enables the strategist to visualize the consumers' beliefs about themselves, the product, and the significant others who affect their purchase of the product. The consumers' beliefs result in a *summary belief* that tells you whether the consumers are positively predisposed toward your brand. If consumers' beliefs about your brand are positive, they need to be reinforced. If consumers' beliefs are negative, they need to be changed.

Regardless of the technique employed, you must ultimately understand why the consumer uses a product on two levels:

- the product level—rational, product-related reasons for using the product

- the emotional/psychological level—hidden, emotional, and psychological reasons for using the product

Figure 6.2

Sample of a Belief Map

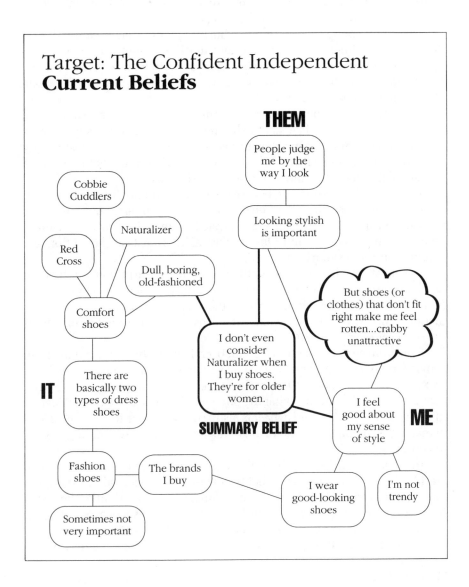

Courtesy of D'Arcy Masius, Benton & Bowles, Inc. / Worldwide Communications

Beer Example

If you ask beer drinkers why they drink a particular brand of beer, they invariably say that they prefer the taste. They will immediately begin to talk in terms of product attributes: "It's smoother"; "It's richer." Taste enjoyment is a product-level motivation for drinking beer.

But if you snoop around the beer business long enough, you will also discover that, although breweries might not like to admit it, most mainstream, American beers are fairly similar in taste. Breweries have learned to produce beers within a fairly narrow taste range, which appeals to the palate of the American beer drinker.

In other words, whereas there are some real taste differences between mainstream American beers, the differences are generally small. Most American beer drinkers can probably become accustomed to the taste of any one of the mainstream American beers. And, over time, the beer they become accustomed to then becomes their preferred brand of beer.

In fact, in blind taste tests, beer drinkers have unknowingly been given the same beer twice, and they often have completely different taste reactions the second time. Moreover, in a blind taste test, most beer drinkers cannot identify their preferred brand. One quickly realizes that taste perceptions are complex and often spurious.

Yet, most beer drinkers adamantly maintain that the primary motivation for choosing one brand of beer over another is taste preference. How can this opinion be reconciled with the fact that taste perceptions are, at best, inconsistent? Are there hidden emotional/psychological reasons for choosing one beer over another?

Times are changing somewhat, but beer drinking has traditionally been a male form of refreshment. When males get together to discuss "sports and women," they drink beer. Do you think they glance over at the other guy's beer bottle? Do you notice what the other guy is drinking? Here's a deeper, hidden truth: A guy's brand of beer is also a source of identity, a badge, a way of making a statement, an extension of his male ego, a way of fitting in with his buddies.

In other words, for most beer drinkers, the motivation for choosing one brand of beer over another is probably not taste preferences alone. It is more likely some combination of taste acceptability and, importantly, the beer's image. Can you imagine what would happen if Budweiser began portraying the "Bud Man" as a wimpy, ineffectual character? Guys who say they drink Budweiser because they prefer the taste might be looking for a new beer.

Magazine Example

As part of a new business pitch involving *Time* magazine, consumer research uncovered some basic but vital missing information that led to a new insight, positioning, and message strategy. *Time* subscribers were letting their subscriptions lapse rather than renewing them. The advertising objective was to convince current users (subscribers) that they should continue to subscribe.

Creative teams had already developed storyboards (rough advertising). The message strategy focused on the product's benefits, a product-benefits strategy: "*Time* brings you the best news coverage because *Time* has more news correspondents on location around the world than any other news weekly." The product benefit was "better news coverage," supported by a unique product attribute, "*Time* has more news correspondents located around the world than any other news weekly."

• •
"Make time for *Time*."
• •

The agency had decided that the most effective message strategy for convincing consumers to continue to subscribe was that *Time* reported the news best. The creative teams who worked on the project were among the best, and the storyboards were, indeed, first rate. Advertising teams decided to use focus groups to explore consumer reactions to the storyboards and to the message. The focus groups reactions quickly revealed that something was wrong with the strategy. Group members readily accepted the idea that *Time* had more correspondents around the world, and they believed that *Time* was an excellent product. The publisher didn't need to convince them that *Time* was the best news weekly. So what was the problem? People were letting their subscriptions lapse because they simply didn't have time to read *Time*!

The irony was that *Time* had recently run a cover story, "America Is Running Out of Time." The article begins by saying, "If you have time to read this article, congratulations, you are in the minority." With both parents working, American parents barely have time to talk to their children, let alone read magazines.

The team had only a week or so before the new business presentation to *Time*, but the team made an impassioned plea for changing the strategy. The focus groups had shown that the current brand positioning, which pitted *Time* against other news magazines, completely missed the mark. *Time*'s real competition was "time" with a lowercase *t*.

In other words, the advertiser did not need a strategy that convinced consumers that *Time* was the best news magazine, but a strategy to convince consumers that they had to *"Make time for Time."* The implied consumer benefit was that the consumer would be smarter and better informed and, therefore, better able to compete in today's world.

Unfortunately, agency politics prevailed and the team went with the original, ill-founded product benefits strategy. The agency didn't get the business, but the agency that won the *Time* account won it with—you guessed it—"Make time for *Time*."

"The Bermuda Triangle" Negative Motivation Example

In a project in which the team was trying to find the motivations for *not* using a product, the assignment was to develop a new business pitch for the Bermuda Tourism Board. The agency was asked to develop some rough advertising that would get American vacationers to consider Bermuda as a vacation spot. The problem was that many American vacationers were not even considering Bermuda, despite the fact that the island is located only a few hundred miles off the eastern U.S. coast.

The tourism people and advertising team needed to understand why many American vacationers generally failed to consider Bermuda as a vacation spot. The advertiser needed to understand vacationers' lack of motivation and interest—why Bermuda was not even a part of their consideration set.

Focus group interviews with frequent vacation travelers and travel agents revealed that many vacationers loved Bermuda's brand mythology—which combined its British heritage and its own island culture—but they complained about the perceived higher costs of travel there and the fact that the island is not warm enough for sunbathing during the winter season. There were also some aspects of the Bermudan mythology that, depending on your point of view, might be less appealing. For example, some vacationers said they found Bermuda's staid, old Republicans and honeymooners image boring. All of this information had the ring of truth.

The account group watching the research from behind the one-way mirror was encouraged and excited by the findings. They were already racing ahead to rough out some advertising ideas. Obviously, the advertiser couldn't do anything about Bermuda's weather. If vacationers were looking for a warm beach in the winter, Bermuda would not do. But the team could develop advertising that addressed some of the more "boring" aspects of Bermuda's image and its perceived priciness. In fact, the account team was already moving toward a message strategy that leveraged the appealing aspects of the Bermudan mythology (its British heritage coupled with its proximity to the states).

The creative teams were delighted. They didn't need to *create* an advertising mythology for Bermuda. All they had to do was to capture and convey Bermuda's *existing* cultural mythology.

But something seemed to be missing. There was something else going on that had not yet surfaced. And, suddenly, there it was. In the middle of her interview, a young woman said, "We considered Bermuda, but we lead very hectic lives and, when we go on vacation, *we like to relax*." When the interviewer stammered out, "You mean you feel you can't relax on this island?" she replied, "Not really. You know how the British are.... You have to dress up and stuff."

This was the missing piece—the hidden emotional reason for not considering Bermuda. Although Americans are almost anglophilic in their admiration of the British, they are, at the same time, a little intimidated by them.

Indeed, most of the American vacationers subsequently interviewed said they felt a sense of inadequacy around the British, a feeling that "we're still the colonists."

This consumer insight, revealing a hidden negative motivation, was the key to helping the team to develop more effective advertising. It clarified the idea that, if the advertising tried to attract American vacationers by playing up the appeal of the British heritage, it also ran the risk of scaring them away.

Bermuda's brand mythology, with its dominant British heritage, turns out to be a double-edged sword for U.S. vacationers. It creates what psychologists call an *approach/avoidance situation.* The positive aspects of the British culture have a positive effect and attract the consumer in an approach behavior. But the perceived negative aspects of the British culture (feelings of intimidation and inadequacy) have, on some level (probably subliminal), a negative effect; they repel the consumer (create an avoidance behavior).

The approach/avoidance situation can create a conflict of feelings and leave the potential vacationer psychologically uncomfortable. So, the team's task was to overcome this psychological barrier through advertising that captured and conveyed the rich, British-Bermudan mythology in a way that did not leave the American vacationer feeling intimidated or inadequate. (Who said advertising was easy?)

You usually have to work a little harder to get consumers to reveal their emotional reasons for using a product but, again, it is important to understand both the *rational* product level motivations and the *emotional/psychological* level motivations. As any good salesperson knows, consumers often rationalize their purchases, but their emotions are what close the sale.

How: Product Usage

Understanding how the product is used is perhaps the most straightforward of the three areas (who, why, and how) of inquiry. Market researchers often cover the question of how the product is used in attitude and usage questionnaires that simply ask the consumer: How do you use the product? For example, if you conducted an attitude and usage survey among consumers who purchase ice cream, you might find that ice cream is used most often as a dessert, a between-meals snack, or a treat.

But even a question as seemingly straightforward as this can be approached more creatively and can yield rich insights about the consumer and/or the product. For example, you can use an ethnographic approach to help reveal more insightful reactions. Often, when you actually observe someone using a product, you pick up behaviors that do not show up in the attitude and usage surveys. The attitude and usage survey provides a statistical base. It tells, for example, what percentage of people use the product as a dessert versus as a snack. The ethnographic approach enables you to talk directly to consumers and to observe them in their homes using the product.

For example, researchers at Young and Rubicam Advertising reported using an ethnographic approach to help them understand how ice cream lovers eat ice cream. When the researchers observed ice cream lovers eating ice cream at home, the team learned that many ice cream lovers made a ritual out of eating ice cream: eating ice cream alone, during their quiet time, after all the chores were done, and the children in bed. And they often used a special bowl and spoon to eat the ice cream. This revelation about how ice cream lovers ritualized the treat's consumption is the kind of insight that can lead to a more effective message strategy and a more compelling advertising mythology.

In another situation, an ethnographic approach was used to help gain a better understanding of how potato chip lovers use potato chips. Again, the ethnographic approach revealed a new insight about how consumers use the product: It is impossible to eat potato chips and be a snob or be pretentious. These consumers explained that the taste of really great potato chips is so compelling that you simply cannot eat potato chips gracefully. You might start out eating them gracefully, one at a time, but pretty soon you'll find yourself "stuffing them in your face." Potato chips force you to get real—to let your hair down.

Champagne Example

Champagne is like perfume: consumers are buying a fantasy (an appealing product mythology) as much as they are buying a bubbly wine. In product categories like perfume and champagne, the consumer is conscious of the product mythology. The product's mythology dominates consumers' perceptions and drives their motivations for using the product.

If you ask consumers how they use champagne, the two most often-cited usage occasions are

- celebrations—birthdays, holidays, weddings, bar mitzvahs
- romance—to enhance or set the mood for a romantic evening

But what happens when you probe more deeply and you really push consumers to reveal their less obvious reasons for selecting champagne on these usage occasions? For example, *how* does champagne enhance a romantic situation? What role does the champagne play? And what are the underlying psychodynamics?

The consumer's use of champagne to enhance a romantic evening seems to be rooted in our cultural mythology. Consumers point back to the old Hollywood movies, where the leading man bought/brought the champagne for/to the leading lady—the woman he was trying to "woo." Now, look at this scenario a little more closely. Typically, it was the male who *controlled* the champagne. He used it to lower the woman's inhibitions ("get her a little tipsy") so that he could seduce her.

On another level, the man uses champagne to impress the woman and make her feel special. Champagne is perceived as expensive and special. Therefore, when a leading man presents a bottle of champagne to his leading lady, he is saying "I think you're special." At the same time, he is also making a statement about himself, "I'm a successful, thoughtful suitor." Symbolically, a bottle of champagne can be viewed as feminine or masculine. A container that holds fluid is feminine. But its masculine, phallic shape is much more obvious and dominant. Thus on a more symbolic level, the male presenting the bottle of champagne is presenting a phallic symbol (a power symbol) with which he hopes to seduce the woman. Note, too, that it is the male who usually pops the cork. The popping of the cork and the foaming champagne spilling out of the bottle can be symbolic as well.

Thus on some level, the traditional, romantic, champagne fantasy can also be seen as a power play—a struggle for control between the male and female. Traditionally, the male assumed the dominant role. The female was generally expected to play the subordinate role. She was not supposed to use and display power openly. A woman's power came from her ability to control and manipulate a strong male from behind the scenes (as in Lady Macbeth).

However, the role of women is changing. Most women no longer think or behave like the women in the old Hollywood movies. Women are no longer willing to play passive, subordinate roles to men. In surveys that ask women what *they* want or what is most important to them, the most frequent answer is independence—including financial independence. Independence is another way of expressing a desire for power and control. Today's women have and use real power—openly, just like their male counterparts. Today's women are no longer satisfied with the idea of expressing power, behind the scenes, through the control and manipulation of a strong male. Today's woman might call a guy up for a date, bring the champagne, pop the cork, and seduce him.

"South of the Border" Example

Consumer research is an important source of new insights. However, clients—the people who have the most experience with the brand—are also an important source for new insights. After all, they have been exposed to a lot of consumer research on the brand and the category. They usually just need someone to help them bring their insights to the surface.

Sometimes the insights which come out of a brainstorming session with a brand group are truly extraordinary. One of the consumer insights uncovered by a Mexican restaurant chain's food brand group was that consumers perceive the restaurant as feminine and maternal. (This was surprising to people who associate Mexican with a macho-masculine personality.) The brand group explained that consumers perceive its restaurants as having a "warm and inviting ambiance . . . like being inside your mother's kitchen."

This Mexican restaurant chain competes with other family restaurant chains, as well as restaurant chains like Bennigan's and The Olive Garden, which attract a lot of young, single people who live alone. It occurred to the team to use the restaurant's unique ambiance, along with its delicious Mexican food, to attract more young people who, from time to time, may enjoy the emotional benefits associated with eating in an environment that feels like "mom's kitchen."

During the brainstorming session, the group came up with another gem. They discussed the fact that many Americans have a negative perception of Mexico and Mexican food. They perceive Mexico as "a poor country, with dirty, lazy people," and Mexican food as "a cheap, starchy belly-filler." The question was raised: is this an opportunity to use advertising to change this perception? People in the group began talking about the richness of the Mexican culture, its Mayan heritage, and so on. This led to a discussion of how Mexican food is a true cuisine, rich in different flavors, textures, and colors. Then one of the marketing managers said, "Mexican food is very involving. . . . You touch it with your hands. . . . There's a lot of dipping and rolling and scooping." Others agreed that touching the food and being involved in it by hand somehow adds to its enjoyment. People are not as involved with the preparation of other foods—food is cooked by someone else in stainless steel vats and eaten out of a Styrofoam box. The group was onto something: Mexican food gives diners the chance to get involved with their food once again.

An additional insight resulting from the brainstorming session was that "Mexican food is a feast for the eyes as well as the stomach; it's very exciting and colorful; it sizzles and pops."

Subsequently, the restaurant chain ran advertising that stressed value but, simultaneously, did a terrific job of creating appetite appeal by celebrating the color and excitement of Mexican culture and food.

• • • • •

> **Construction Tip:**
> The critical insight uncovered through consumer research should lead to a leverageable brand positioning (what you want the brand to stand for in the consumer's mind), and advertising message (what you wish to communicate in your advertising).

• • • • •

Trends

An understanding of consumer motivations must include some understanding of trends, which can serve as macro-motivators: "Everyone else is trying to stay young and fit—I guess I should too." We will consider two types of trends: social trends and product trends.

Social Trends

Social trends are the pervasive, general ones adopted by a large segment of the population. The health-and-fitness craze exemplifies a social trend. For many Americans, the desire to have a healthy, beautiful body and "to look good for as long as you can" has become an obsession. Social trends are important because they reflect a society's values and have a real impact on behavior—including consumer behavior. The advertiser who wishes to understand consumer motivations must maintain a constant awareness of social trends. He or she must be a sociologist as well as a psychologist.

Savvy marketers understand the importance of social trends and their impact on consumer behavior. Witness the rush to market "lite" versions of everything from potato chips to dairy products. Manufacturers of exercise, sports, and fitness-related products have also benefited from the health-and-fitness trend.

Once advertisers and marketers become aware of the importance of social trends and their impact on consumer behavior, the advertising teams move quickly to query, "What if we could anticipate or predict social trends?" And, in fact, there are people who make a living from tracking and predicting social trends. Yankelovich, one of the more prominent social forecasters, tracks 30 different values in these areas: the family, status of women, pluralism, morality, and so on.

John Naisbitt (author of *Megatrends* and *Megatrends 2000*) also tracks trends, but his group uses a different technique—*content analysis.* Content analysis has its roots in World War II, where intelligence experts used the technique to gather information about enemy nations. Basically, Naisbitt's group tallies the amount of printed lineage devoted to various issues—the more space devoted to an issue, the greater its importance. The system is based on two beliefs:

- The news reporting process is a forced choice or closed system.
- Societies can only handle so many concerns at one time.

Naisbitt explains that, using content analysis, he can predict trends accurately. For example, he noted that during the 1960s almost all of the newspaper space was devoted to what he called, "concerns about discrimination." However, beginning in 1969, that space began to be shared with material about sexism. Thus, Naisbitt too claims he was able to predict the dramatic changes in women's thinking and behavior.

Futurist Jeff Halett ("The Present-Futures Group" based in Washington, D.C.) is representative of the new breed of gurus who help marketers understand how to manage a business and market products in today's rapidly changing world. Halett pulls together information, insights, and ideas about how technological, cultural, political, and economic forces are reshaping our world. He makes predictions and projections based on this data, which help the marketer see what's ahead and plan accordingly.

Product Trends

Product trends generally occur within the larger framework of an overall societal trend. Product trends generally reflect a society's sensibilities, values, and lifestyles. In fact, the endurance of a product trend can be attributed, in large part, to its ability to continue to reflect the society's values and lifestyles.

Simply defined, a *product trend* is a means of tracking shifts in popularity of a specific type of product. Running shoes are an example of a recent product trend that grew out of a larger societal trend, the trend toward greater health and fitness. The health-and-fitness trend can be traced back to a core value or belief that it's important to have a beautiful, healthy body. This core belief or value is, in turn, driven by primary and secondary basic human desires and needs, such as the sex drive and the need for self-esteem/self-worth (see Figure 6.3).

Sometimes product trends seem to occur outside of the framework of a larger, societal trend. Product popularity shifts tend to be short-lived fads, rather than enduring trends. They seem to crop up out of nowhere and, suddenly, they're everywhere. Product fads and crazes are generally products with uniquely appealing characteristics that almost immediately capture the consumer's fancy. Hula hoops and pet rocks are an example of product trends that seemed to come out of nowhere.

• • •

Understanding the Brand: Tools and Techniques

An appropriate, appealing brand mythology, identity, and essence are a

Figure 6.3

Drives-Values-Trends Hierarchy

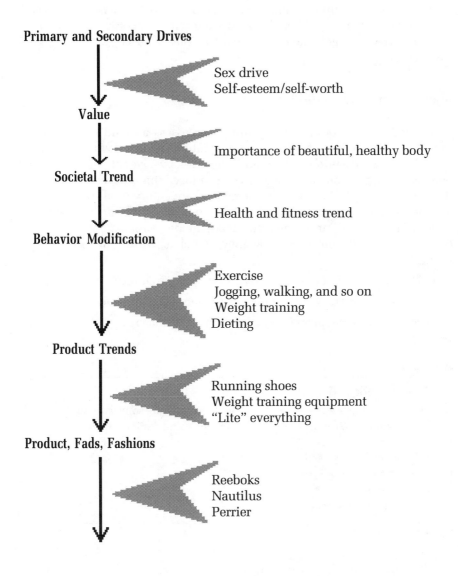

Primary and Secondary Drives

Sex drive
Self-esteem/self-worth

Value

Importance of beautiful, healthy body

Societal Trend

Health and fitness trend

Behavior Modification

Exercise
Jogging, walking, and so on
Weight training
Dieting

Product Trends

Running shoes
Weight training equipment
"Lite" everything

Product, Fads, Fashions

Reeboks
Nautilus
Perrier

brand's most valuable assets, and advertisers must take great care to maintain and cultivate them. When you are working with established brands, you must first identify and understand your existing brand mythology, identity, personality, and soul—core value(s). It's easy enough to find out about your brand's physical qualities; simply ask consumers what they perceive to be the brand's attributes and benefits compared with the competition's. The hard part is trying to get a handle on the intangibles: "the halo of psychological meanings."

Brand Identity Profile (BIP)

The *brand identity profile* is a technique to assess a brand's perceptual inventory—the imagery, feelings, and associations affiliated with the brand in the consumer's mind. The brand's mythology, overall identity, and personality all grow out of its perceptive inventory. This is how it works. The first step is to collect a complete perceptual inventory of all the images, associations, and feelings associated with your brand. These data are best handled qualitatively, in a series of in-depth interviews or focus groups. Ask consumers to tell you everything they associate with your brand. For example:

- "When you think of Budweiser, what comes to mind?"
- "What images or feelings do you associate with Budweiser?"

Have consumers generate an exhaustive list of images, associations, and feelings.

• • • • •

Construction Tip:
To facilitate the interviewing process and also provide some structure, ask consumers to think of images, associations, and feelings in terms of four areas:
- product/service itself
- product usage
- product users
- product values/benefits

• • • • •

The exhaustive list of images, associations, and feelings consumers generate at this time represents the brand's *unique perceptual inventory* shown in Figure 6.4.

Once you have developed an exhaustive list of the brand's images,

Figure 6.4

Hypothetical Perceptual Inventory: Budweiser

Product

Clydesdales

Thirst quenching

Relaxing

Alcohol

Smooth

Refreshing

Satisfying

Eagle

Cold

Red, white and
blue label

Beechwood aging

Spotted Dog

User

Manly

Everyman

Regular Joe

Macho

Blue collar

Tough

A man's man

Ed McMahon

Usage

Relax

Socialize with friends

Thirst quenching

With food

After playing sports

Cool down

Unwind

Value/Benefits

Sociability

Affirm male identity

Male bonding

A sense of belonging to
a distinct male group

Clean crisp taste

associations, and feelings, ask consumers to rank them in terms of the *degree to which each of these various elements connotes "Budweiserness"* or somehow captures the essence of Budweiser. This can be handled qualitatively or quantitatively. If your budget allows, use a quantitative approach; it involves a larger, more reliable sample.

What you ultimately wind up with is a rank-ordered list of images, attributes, feelings, and things that are most strongly associated with your brand

For example, Budweiser's BIP might look something like this:

- Clydesdales

- Blue Collar

- Macho

- Beechwood Aged

- Red-and-White Can

- Eagle

- Spokesperson Ed McMahon

- Crisp, Clean Taste

- Spotted Dog

The BIP is useful in and of itself because it reveals what elements of the brand's perceptual inventory are most representative of the brand. But you can also compare your brand's BIP with that of competitive brands. How does your brand stack up against the competition in terms of rich imagery, feelings, and associations? You might wish to see how your BIP varies among different consumer groups.

The final step toward understanding your brand's image is to take elements from the rank-ordered list that most connote "Budweiserness" (Clydesdales, blue-collar values, and so on) and qualitatively probe them for insights and a deeper understanding of what these elements mean in the consumer's psyche. For example, what do the Clydesdales represent to consumers? Consumers might respond that the Clydesdales represent "power," "strength," and "tradition." "They're workhorses—they work hard. . . that's the way they used to deliver beer. . . . Bud has been around a long time."

Probing further, we might discover that the Clydesdales symbolize the working-class male. Some interpolation is required, but these kind of insights and a deeper understanding of the key elements in the BIP should help you to get a handle on your brand's overall mythology, image, and essence.

Projective Techniques for Assessing Brand Image and Personality

In addition to understanding the brand's core essence and mythology, you can also use projective techniques to help flesh out a brand's personality. Projective techniques are easy to use and fairly straightforward.

Begin by asking target consumers to personify the brand:

- What would the brand be like if it were a person?
- Would it be male or female? Young or old?
- What would its occupation be?
- How would the personified brand be dressed?
- How does it spend its time?
- What are its hobbies and interests?
- What kind of car does it drive?
- What kind of music does it listen to?
- Where would it most likely go on vacation?

You can also ask what would the brand be like if:

- it was a vacation;
- it was a fabric;
- it was a restaurant;
- it was a movie star; or
- it was a car?

In this way, you can develop an understanding of the brand's personality—what the brand would be like if it were a person.

Together with the brand personality, the brand's overall image and essence are the key elements that compose the brand concept. For example, look at the brand image, personality, and essence of IBM. Prior to the recent upheaval and restructuring of 1993, IBM had a clear image and personality. Some of these perceptions are probably changing, but they still work as an example.

Brand Image: The brand image of IBM shows consumers' overall perception of the brand: "IBM is one of America's preeminent corporations, a leading manufacturer of business computers known for quality products and professional service."

Brand Personality: The brand personality reveals what IBM would be like if it were a person. The IBM brand personality has both positive and negative elements:

Big Blue	Conservative/Corporate
Solid/Established	Bureaucratic
Trustworthy	Insensitive
Professional	Unresponsive
Republican	Nerdy/Stuffy
Paternal/Fatherly	Stodgy
Dependable	Staid
Conservative	Boring
Capable	Workaholic
Professional, fatherly businessman	nerdy accountant type

What Would IBM Be Like If It Was:

Car	**Fabric**	**Color**	**Music**
Mercedes	Wool	Blue Pin-stripe	Classical

IBM Brand Personality Statement: Drawing from the information and insights culled from projective personality techniques, you can formalize a brand's personality by writing a *brand personality statement*—a distillation of the brand personality, which generally captures and conveys a brand's personality in the form of a written paragraph. This statement is for IBM: IBM is a 40-year-old successful businessman. He is a conservative Republican who drives a Mercedes Benz sedan and listens to classical music. He is dedicated, hard working, dependable, and conscientious. At the same time he is also a little stodgy and boring. . . .

IBM Brand Essence: IBM's brand essence is determined by interpolating IBM's BIP, overall image, and personality. So, for example, we might, after studying all of the brand information, conclude that IBM's enduring core or brand essence is best summed up by one word: professionalism.

IBM Brand Mythology: IBM's overall brand mythology is also determined through interpolation, by examining the BIP, brand image, personality, and brand essence or soul. Looking at the various brand elements, it is clear that IBM has built a brand mythology based on the image of a professional, conservative businessman. The message and positioning communicated by the IBM mythology are: IBM is the thoroughly professional, preeminent computer company.

Having determined IBM's overall brand mythology, image, personality, and essence or core value, the advertising practitioner must then decide whether these brand elements are appropriate for the target consumer. In IBM's case, the brand image, personality, and core value were indeed wonderfully appropriate for its core target—business professionals. However, IBM is currently going through a difficult restructuring. IBM will have to redefine its business, and it may also have to alter elements of its brand image and personality.

Figure 6.5

Perceptual Map

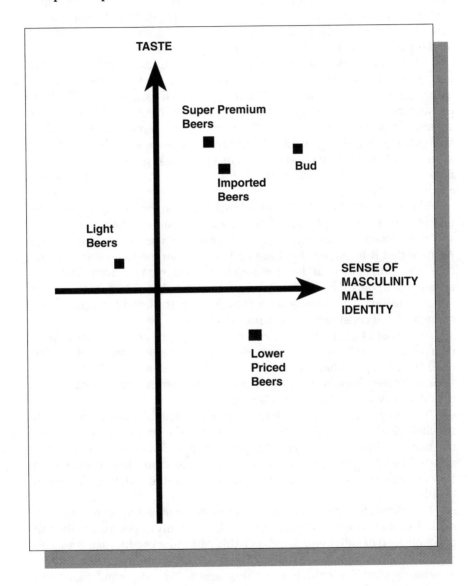

Brand Mapping

Brand mapping is used to help you understand how the consumer perceives your brand compared with competitive brands. This useful technique enables you to summarize and visualize the brand positioning—how each of the brands in a product category is perceived relative to the others in the marketplace and in the consumer's mind.

A brand map is drawn in psychological space—mindspace. It shows you how the consumer perceives different brands, and their relative positions along various key dimensions. The key dimensions are determined by consumers, and they generally represent product attributes and benefits that are most important to consumers. The hypothetical perceptual map shown in Figure 6.5 would be generated by asking consumers what they see as the most important attributes and benefits in a particular product category and then having consumers rank the various brands in terms of these key attributes or benefits.

The "category attributes/benefits" are the reason the consumer comes to the category. For example, if you were mapping brands in the beer category, you would begin by asking consumers what they want most from a beer. Assume that it turns out that taste and quality are the two most relevant consumer dimensions in the premium beer category. You would then ask consumers to rank the various brands of beer in terms of each of these two key dimensions. The important point here is that the key dimensions must come from the consumer, *not* the manufacturer.

You would then plot the consumers' perceptions of each of the brands on a perceptual map in terms of its ability to deliver taste and quality. The resulting perceptual map would illustrate the consumers' relative perceptions of different brands in the premium beer category in terms of their ability to deliver key product attributes/benefits.

It is important to understand that a perceptual map is drawn in psychological space, and the distances between the brands (represented on the map by dots) approximate the perceptual differences in consumers' minds. The map gives you a view of the consumers' mindscape and shows how the brands are positioned with respect to each other in terms of taste and health.

In addition to mapping brands in terms of the most important product-related attributes/benefits, you can also determine any important emotional/psychological benefits associated with this particular product category, and map the competing brands in terms of their perceived ability to deliver these emotional/psychological benefits. And, again, it is important that these emotional/psychological benefits come from consumers.

For example, using motivational research, you might discover that one of the hidden emotional benefits derived from drinking beer is that it serves to reinforce the beer drinker's sense of masculinity. By asking consumers to rank the various brands of premium beers in terms of masculinity, and other emotional/psychological benefits/dimensions associated with, or relevant to, beer drinking, you could generate a perceptual map to show how consumers perceive each of the brands in terms of these emotional/psychological benefits/dimensions. For example, you could hypothesize that because beer drinkers use beer brands as a badge, they also feel that "a sense of contemporariness" (modern, up to the times) is another key psychological dimension that is important to premium beer drinkers. The hypothetical perceptual map would show how the various premium beer brands are perceived, relative to each other, in terms of masculinity and contemporariness.

Chapter 7
• • • • • • • • • •

Building the Brand's Mythology: Positioning, Message, and Execution

• • •
Brand Positioning

Brand positioning is really a marketing concept, a crucial first step in developing and marketing a brand. However, the brand positioning also plays a critical role in shaping a brand's overall mythology. The brand positioning is what advertisers (and clients) want the brand to stand for both in the marketplace and in the consumer's mind. Brand positioning and brand mythology go hand in hand. The brand mythology, which is mostly created and communicated through advertising, establishes the brand's positioning, both in the marketplace and in the consumer's mind.

Sandage and Fryburger's text, *Advertising Theory and Practice*, distinguishes between the brand's positioning in the marketplace and the brand's positioning in the consumer's mind: "Positioning can be viewed in different ways . . . one way is to literally position the product on the supermarket shelf" by changing the ingredients, packaging, and so on. The other way, "the ultimate positioning," is to position the product in the consumer's mind (Sandage and Fryburger, 1975, p. 195).

Positioning the Brand in the Marketplace

Positioning the brand among its competitors in the marketplace is a complex marketing decision based on a number of different considerations, including the physical product, its attributes (form, size, and so on) and the market conditions. Ultimately, however, the brand positioning must define the

product and the competitive set—the products/brands you will be competing against. For example, an ice cream manufacturer may decide to introduce
a new brand of "premium low-fat ice cream." Based on the product's
physical characteristics, the marketplace positioning for the new brand will
most likely be against other brands of premium low-fat ice creams.

However, advertising also enables you to perceptually position your
brand in consumers' minds. You can use advertising to define the competitive set in which the brand will be competing. You can use advertising to
position your brand against a more narrowly defined competitive set, such
as other brands of premium low-fat ice cream. Or, you can use advertising
to position your brand against a broader competitive set, such as regular ice
cream products.

A more narrowly focused positioning taken against other similar competing brands in a particular category—in this case, other brands of premium
low-fat ice cream—is generally an easier sell. This is because it is easier to
sell a product to consumers (the target consumer would be people who use
premium low-fat ice cream) who are already sold on using premium low-fat
ice cream. The trade-off is that the potential sales volume will be smaller.

On the other hand, if you position your brand against a broader competitive set, the potential sales volume will be larger, but it will generally be a
harder sell. For example, if you use advertising to position premium low-fat
ice cream brand against regular ice cream, the potential sales volume will be
much larger. However, your target audience will include nonusers (consumers who are using regular ice cream instead of low-fat ice cream), and it is
generally more difficult to convert nonusers. Of course, if you were introducing a brand that was launching the low-fat ice cream category, you would
have to position it against regular ice cream brands, with the hope of
converting regular ice cream users to low-fat ice cream users. But once the
low-fat category is established, and most regular ice cream users have tried
or are aware of low-fat ice cream but have not switched from regular ice
cream, it becomes increasingly difficult to convert them.

Positioning the Brand in the Consumer's Mind

Manufacturers who are used to thinking in terms of marketing products
sometimes make the mistake of thinking only in terms of positioning the
brand in the marketplace. But again, a brand is more than a product sitting
on a store shelf; a brand is a perceptual entity that exists in psychological
space, in the consumer's mind. Therefore, it is equally important to consider
how the brand is positioned in psychological space, in the consumer's mind
and heart.

In order to try to differentiate your premium low-fat ice cream from other
premium low-fat ice creams, you need to develop a brand positioning that

also differentiates your brand from the others. The perceptual positioning, or how the brand is positioned in the consumer's mind, includes, but is not limited to, the marketplace positioning. For example, you could use advertising to position your premium low-fat ice cream brand as the best-tasting premium low-fat ice cream. Of course, you would need to support this claim ("made with the finest natural ingredients," and so forth). But the perceptual positioning created through advertising can also be an emotional/psychological positioning. For example, you might position the brand as "the premium low-fat ice cream that tastes so good it will make you feel like a kid again." In this case, the brand positioning tries to differentiate the brand from other brands by communicating taste superiority as well as the emotional and psychological benefits that go with feeling like a kid again. In other words, because the perceptual positioning is created in psychological space (in the consumer's mind), you can go beyond the physical product attributes and benefits to create a perceptual positioning that also promises the consumer emotional and psychological benefits.

● ●

" . . .if you position your brand against a broader competitive set, the potential sales volume will be larger, but it will generally be a harder sell. "

● ●

● ● ●
Introducing a New Brand That Represents a New Product Category

Developing a brand positioning for a new brand that is also introducing a new category is different than developing a brand positioning for a new brand in an established category. When a brand is introducing a new product category, the brand positioning generally functions as a product positioning. In other words, for new product introductions, the first brand out there tries to sell the brand by selling the attributes and/or benefits of the new product category. The brand that launches the category tries to make the consumer aware of the new products' attributes and/or benefits—ones related to the generic product.

Pizza

For example, the first home-delivery pizza franchise most likely emphasized the "deliciousness of pizza" and the convenience of having the pizza delivered right to the door. The "deliciousness of pizza" and the conve-

● ●
Figure 7.1

Brand Positioning: Introducing a New Brand

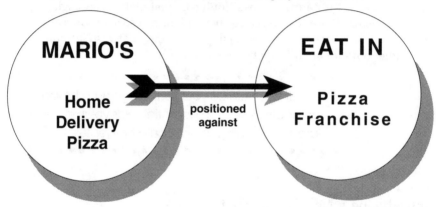

BRAND POSITIONING

Introducing a New Brand
That Represents a New Product Category

When positioning a new brand that is also a new product
category, the brand positioning generally functions as a
product positioning, i.e., it sells the category benefits.

MARIO'S   **EAT IN**

Home   *positioned*   **Pizza**
Delivery   *against*   **Franchise**
Pizza

Brand Positioning: Convenience/Taste (Category Benefits)

Positioning: Mario's Home Delivery Pizza is a more
                    convenient way to enjoy delicious pizza right
                    in your own home.

● ●

nience of home delivery would be the category benefits that the consumer
would hope to derive from any home-delivery pizza. However, as the home-
delivery pizza category became established and other brands began to
compete for a share of the consumer's wallet, the brand that introduced the
new product category no longer had a unique position as the sole supplier
and thus had to switch to positioning that emphasized the new brand's
superiority over other brands.

In positioning a new product in the consumer's mind, Jack Trout and Al
Reis stress the importance of linking the new product to an existing category.
According to Trout and Reis, developing a positioning that will get your

• •

Figure 7.2

Brand Positioning: Introducing a New Brand in
an Established Product Catergory

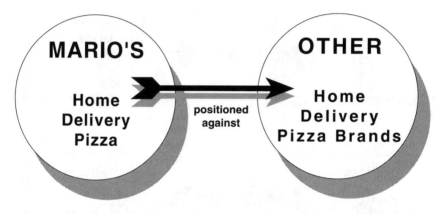

BRAND POSITIONING

Introducing a New Brand in an
Established Product Category

When positioning a brand in an extablished product
category, the brand is generally positioned against other
brands, i.e., the brand positioning emphasizes the brand's
superiority over other brands.

Brand Positioning: "Taste Superiority"

Positioning: Mario's Home-Delivery Pizza is the
                     best tasting home-delivered pizza.

• •

product a foothold in the consumer's mind is particularly difficult if it is a
new product. Consumers' minds are already busy holding on to lots of
existing brands and products, and consumers will resist committing new
products to memory unless the product is somehow related or connected to
the purchasers' existing product perceptions. In other words, new products
or product categories have a better chance of creating awareness and being
remembered if they are presented to the consumer in a way that allows them
to become connected to the consumer's existing cognitive framework. This
is often accomplished by defining the new product in terms of how it is
different or better than the existing category. The cordless phone, sugarfree

Consumer Framework

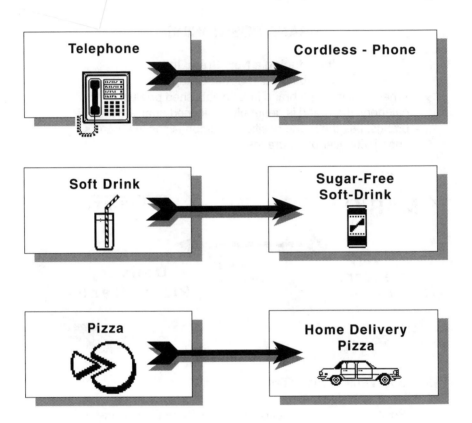

soft drinks, and home-delivery pizza are examples of new products positioned against product categories that are already firmly established in consumers' minds.

In a discussion of product positioning, Sandage and Fryburger make this point even more strongly: "In a sense, there is no such thing as a new product. Whatever the new entry may be, the consumer immediately relates it to existing products. . . . Perceptual positioning, this process of fitting into an existing scheme of things, epitomizes the principle that learning is a matter of relating to prior learning."

O'Doul's

Anheuser Busch's recent introduction of O'Doul's Brew, a "nonalcoholic beer," is a great example of a new product positioning that links the new product to an existing product: beer. The ideal positioning for the new product would have been that of being a nonalcoholic beer. In that way, the product would have been linked to beer, a product that is well established in the beer drinker's mind.

The problem was that the new product could not legally be called beer or use the term beer in its label or advertising. In other words, Anheuser Busch could not refer to or position the product as a nonalcoholic beer. And yet, Anheuser Busch realized that in order for this product to be successful, the advertisements had to establish its link to beer.

The advertisers developed a terrific strategy to get around the fact that the developer could not refer to the product as beer: that O'Doul's is "what beer drinkers drink when they're not drinking beer." In order to fully appreciate the power and subtleties of this positioning, recall that beer is an emblematic product. Beer drinkers wear their brand of beer as if it were a badge.

By positioning O'Doul's as "what beer drinkers drink when they're not drinking beer," Anheuser Busch simultaneously achieved three positioning goals:

- linking the product back to beer
- establishing the product's "beer credentials" by pointing out that it is what beer drinkers drink
- helping beer drinkers save face because it establishes the fact that the person who drinks this product is really a beer drinker (and not a teetotaling wimp!) who happens at the moment not to be drinking beer

• • •

Introducing a New Brand in an Existing Product Category

When introducing a new brand in an existing product category, you must first consider how the other brands are positioned both in the marketplace and in the consumer's mind. The marketer must then decide whether to try to compete by using an existing brand positioning or to find an as yet undiscovered, powerful, new brand positioning. Bovee and Arens say: "Companies usually have two choices in selecting a position. One is to pick a similar position next to a competitor and battle it out for the same customers. Another is to find a position that is not held by a competitor, a hole in the market ... a differentiation strategy" (Bovee and Arens, 1986, pp. 229-230).

• • • • •

> **Positioning Tip:**
> I find it helpful to identify and list the brand positioning for each of the brands in the product category, along with its market share. This makes it easier to compare the various brand positionings in terms of their compelling reason(s) or benefit(s) and success in the marketplace. It is also helpful to know which brands are using a positioning based solely on physical product attributes/benefits and which brands are using a positioning based on emotional/psychological benefits or a positioning that combines both.
>
> I derive the brand positionings for each of the brands in the product category by asking consumers how they perceive each of the brands: what do each of the brands stand for in the consumer's mind? I also infer or interpolate the brand positioning from the advertising. Both approaches can be useful, but the consumer's perceptions are usually critical. Sometimes it's also helpful to perceptually map how the consumer perceives the various brands in terms of key category dimensions. A comparison of the various brand positionings and their respective market shares, as well as a perceptual mapping of the consumer's perceptions of the various brands, gives me a better perspective and may help me to discover a new positioning opportunity that has been overlooked by the competitors.
>
> • • • • •
>
> | | Brand A | Brand B | Brand C |
> |---|---|---|---|
> | **Market Share:** | 34% | 20% | 18% |
> | **Product Level Positioning:** | Taste Superiority | Taste Superiority | Taste Superiority |
> | **Support:** | Unique Process | Better Ingredients | Heritage Commitment to Quality |
> | **Emotional/ Psychological- Level Positioning:** | A Man's beer Identity, reinforces sense of masculinity | None | A cool beer Feel Contemporary hip |

• • • •

One obvious strategy would be to choose the same brand positioning as the category leader—the brand with the largest market share. (Presumably, the positioning must be effective, or the brand would not be the category leader.) However, going toe-to-toe with the category leader is usually a difficult strategy. In order to successfully compete against an established brand, the new brand must come up with a compelling point of difference, as well as a sizable advertising budget. Nevertheless, there have been brands that have successfully taken the same brand positioning as the category leader. For example, when Crest toothpaste was introduced, the brand took the same positioning as the category leader (Colgate): superior cavity prevention. Crest was eventually able to overthrow the existing category leader because it offered the consumer compelling evidence (doctor recommendations and its unique ingredient, stannous fluoride), that Crest was indeed a better cavity fighter.

In some categories, such as food and beverages, it is not uncommon to find many brands using the same brand positioning. For example, food and beverage brands frequently use some kind of taste superiority positioning (taste is, after all, one of the primary reasons why consumers eat and drink). However, brands using the same taste superiority positioning will try to differentiate themselves by using different (and ideally, unique) supporting attributes and/or dimensionalizing taste superiority in different ways. For example, Miller Genuine Draft Beer uses a taste superiority positioning that emphasizes its unique "cold filtering process." And Budweiser uses a taste superiority positioning that emphasizes its unique "beechwood aging." Budweiser also dimensionalizes its taste superiority positioning: "crisp, clean taste."

Instead of using the same brand positioning as other brands in the category, new brands entering an existing product category often try to develop a new brand positioning. In order to find it, the marketer must conduct consumer research with the hope of uncovering a new consumer insight that will point the way to a powerful new brand positioning. For example, Procter and Gamble developed a new brand positioning when the company introduced a new brand of dishwashing detergent (Dawn) into an existing category with established brands. Looking at the advertising, it is clear that among the existing brands of dishwashing detergent, Ivory and Palmolive were using a "gentle on your hands" positioning, and Joy was using an "efficacy" positioning ("cleans down to the shine"). There were also some other lesser brands using a value positioning. Instead of trying to compete by taking one of the existing brand positionings, P&G successfully created an entirely new brand positioning that emphasized Dawn's grease-cutting superiority. Evidently P&G did its homework; the new positioning seemed to offer the consumer an important benefit that eventually helped to make Dawn the new category leader.

• • •
The Role of Advertising in Positioning the Brand in the Consumer's Mind

Advertising is the vehicle that enables you to access the consumer's mind, and to argue and establish the brand's position by communicating a compelling point of difference (product-based and/or emotional/psychological). Advertising does this by creating a brand mythology that communicates important product-based and/or emotional/psychological benefits, which in turn work to position the brand both in the marketplace and in the consumer's mind.

Although brand positionings can sometimes be communicated or reinforced by packaging, pricing, promotions, and so on, advertising generally plays a dominant role in establishing brand positionings. Moreover, advertising enables you to go beyond marketplace positionings in order to create powerful emotional/psychological positionings that tap into the consumer's feelings and emotions.

For example, Oscar Mayer Hot Dogs uses advertising to create a brand positioning that works on two levels: the positioning works at the product level to position Oscar Mayer Hot Dogs as a higher-quality (made with the best ingredients), superior-tasting brand of hot dogs. At the same time, the Oscar Mayer advertising also creates an emotional/psychological brand positioning: Oscar Mayer Hot Dogs are positioned as the hot dogs that kids love. Oscar Mayer's product-level positioning has created the perception that Oscar Mayer Hot Dogs are a premium, higher-quality brand of hot dogs. But Oscar Mayer's emotional/psychological positioning has helped to create the perception that Oscar Mayer Hot Dogs are a favorite among children and American families. This emotional positioning has helped to create a brand mythology, image, and personality that has at its center the goodness of children and family. Oscar Mayer has built a wonderfully appealing, enduring brand mythology around children, the all-American family, Boy/Girl Scouts, summer barbecues, picnics, and the Fourth of July.

Most of the more successful, enduring brands have brand positionings and brand mythologies that exceed the physical product. They balance physical product attributes/benefits and emotional/psychological benefits. For example, the McDonald's brand mythology helps to position McDonald's as a great-tasting, all-American, family-oriented fast-food restaurant. The McDonald's brand mythology promises the consumer a great fast-food experience: taste enjoyment plus the emotional satisfaction of being part of a family-oriented, uniquely American experience.

The Budweiser brand mythology positions Budweiser as the superior tasting, quality beer for the all-American male. The Budweiser brand mythology communicates product attributes and benefits (beechwood aging and taste enjoyment) plus compelling emotional/psychological benefits (patriotism and a sense of male identity/bonding).

• • •

Factors in Conveying a Brand Mythology in Your Advertising Message

The advertising message is what you wish to communicate in your advertising. The advertising message has both verbal and nonverbal components. Advertisers often make the mistake of focusing on the verbal component. Keep in mind that it is not only what you say that is important but also what you show. Every image is significant and must be carefully considered. The nonverbal or visual component of your advertising should work together with the verbal message, and if you are creating advertising for an established brand, the visual imagery should be consistent with the brand's overall mythology, image, personality, and soul/essence.

The brand positioning and advertising message go hand-in-hand. In fact they are generally created together because what you communicate in the advertising ultimately establishes the brand positioning in the consumer's mind. In other words, if you repeatedly communicate the idea that children love Oscar Mayer Hot Dogs, the brand will eventually be positioned in the consumer's mind as the "the hot dog that kids love." At the same time, advertising plays a key role in building a brand's overall brand mythology. The brand mythology is what the brand stands for in the consumer's mind. It includes the product attributes and/or benefits and core value(s), but also its unique imagery and symbolism. The brand mythology refers to those loosely held ideas, values, images, and symbolism that perceptually define the brand. Again, a brand is a perceptual entity that exists in psychological space: in the consumer's mind.

A brand's mythology—along with its identity, personality, and unique perceptual inventory of imagery, feelings, and associations—is the result of many factors. However, advertising generally plays a dominant role in building strong, enduring brand mythologies. Every commercial and/or advertisement should be thought of as an individual advertising mythology that ultimately helps to create the overall brand mythology. Advertising is the vehicle you use to access the consumer's mind, wherein you can create mythical worlds that, over time, become associated with and ultimately come to define your brand.

Consistency

In order for advertising to work its magic (that is, to create a brand mythology), the advertising message must be presented repeatedly, and it must be consistent. McDonald's advertising is a great example of advertising

●●●

Figure 7.4

Using Ads to Build and Maintain Brand Mythologies

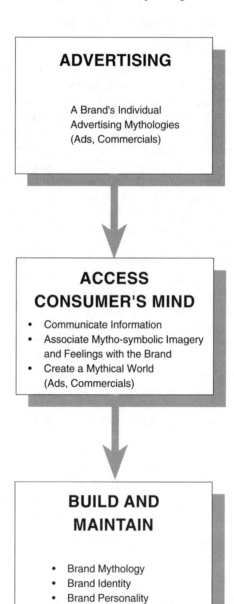

●●●

that has created a powerful, appropriate brand mythology by maintaining a consistent message and tone. The individual commercials may vary, but the message and tone of all McDonald's advertising are very similar: they communicate the idea that McDonald's is the wholesome, all-American, family fast-food restaurant with great-tasting food.

Imagery and Symbolism

Like the brand positioning, the brand mythology is ultimately what the brand stands for in the consumer's mind. The difference is that the brand mythology includes not only the brand's attributes/benefits and values but also its imagery and symbolism.

For example, the Oscar Mayer brand mythology helps to position Oscar Mayer as America's favorite, superior-tasting, higher-quality hot dog. The Oscar Mayer brand mythology creates this brand positioning by associating the Oscar Mayer brand with the goodness of children and family, endearing images of children biting into an Oscar Mayer hot dog, and images drawn from America's cultural mythology, such as Fourth of July family picnics and barbecues.

The imagery of the Budweiser brand mythology serves as another example. It positions Budweiser as a superior-tasting, quality beer for the all-American male. This representative imagery and symbolism consists of the Bud Man, Clydesdales, and the Anheuser Busch eagle. Again, the brand mythology includes not only the ideas conveyed about the brand through advertising but also the images and symbols (mytho-symbolic icons that evoke the mythology).

• • •
The Unique Power of Advertising

The unique power of advertising is that it can be used, to varying degrees, to transform products that are essentially generic (such as salt or baking soda) into brands by mythologizing them. Some advertising makes no attempt to mythologize products. There is little mythologization in "talking-head advertising," the advertising that uses an unknown spokesperson talking at the camera to give consumers information about the product. At the other end of the spectrum, some advertising consists totally of mythology. Perfume commercials are often pure mythology (after all, you can't smell the scent from a broadcast advertisement), with the brand name added on at the end. Calvin Klein perfume commercials focus almost entirely on sexy people consumed by passion. If you were flipping through the channels and stumbled across one of these commercials, you might think it was the tale end of a breathless soap opera scene. It is only at the end that you are made to realize that it is a perfume commercial.

Generally, some degree of mythologizing is preferable to none. Mythologizing the product by creating mythical characters, places, or situations generally makes the commercial more engaging and entertaining. Mythologizing also helps to distinguish your brand from other brands and at the same time helps to establish a bond between the consumer and your brand, by using an appropriate, appealing product identity and personality.

• • •
Advertising Mythologies That Build Brand Mythologies

Every commercial or advertisement should be thought of as an individual advertising mythology that ultimately helps to shape the brand's overall mythology. Again, your advertising team should carefully plan and consider the effects of every image, character, symbol, or feeling that becomes associated with your brand, because they will affect the brand's overall mythology, identity, and personality. The individual advertising mythologies that help to shape the brand mythology are essentially a storied form of communication, a narrative fiction that uses fictitious characters, places, and situations to engage and entertain the consumer, communicate product attributes and benefits, and perceptually position the brand in the consumer's mind.

In developing the individual advertising mythologies (commercials and print advertisements) that will ultimately help to shape the brand's overall mythology, identity, and personality, the advertising team must decide what they wish to communicate, both at the product level (the product's physical attributes and/or benefits) and at the emotional/psychological level (the product's emotionally gratifying side-effects). You can choose to create advertising that focuses solely on communicating physical, product-based attributes and/or benefits, or you can choose to create advertising that emphasizes appealing user imagery and emotional/psychological benefits, or you can choose to create advertising that communicates both physical and emotional/psychological benefits. The first building task is coming up with an effective message strategy.

Learning to "See the Board"

There are no shortcuts or easy formulas for coming up with effective, well-founded message strategies. Strategizing requires experience and a lot of hard thinking. It's a lot like playing chess. Chess is a game of strategy. When you become an experienced chess player, you learn to "see the board" in ways that elude the novice. Experienced players have developed the ability to see the strengths and weaknesses in their opponents' positions as well as their own positions and to use these insights to formulate a strategy, a plan of attack.

Likewise, the advertising practitioner must develop an ability to see the marketplace, and to uncover insights, the hidden truths about the product and/or consumer that can lead to new opportunities and advertising ideas. The seasoned researcher has learned to recognize when something is truly important, whereas the novice often fails to grasp its significance.

• • •
The Most Commonly Used Message Strategies

Over the years, advertising strategies have generally evolved from a focus on communicating physical product attributes and/or benefits to advertising strategies that include or focus exclusively on communicating appealing user imagery and/or emotional and psychological benefits. Moreover, in the life cycle of individual brands, this same evolution occurs. Generally, when a new brand is introduced, the advertising focuses on the brand's physical attributes and/or benefits. But as the brand matures, the advertising usually begins to include or emphasize user imagery and/or emotional/psychological benefits. Typically, this happens as a product category matures and it becomes increasingly difficult for brands to differentiate themselves solely in terms of physical, product-based attributes and/or benefits. Let us look at the most commonly used message strategies.

Product Benefits Strategy

The focus of the benefits approach is clearly on the product: the "sales message" or the "selling proposition." Rosser Reeves developed the concept of the "unique selling proposition" (USP) while he worked at Ted Bates Advertising. According to Reeves, the USP has three components:

- Each advertisement must make a proposition to the consumer that is not just words, not just product puffery, and not just show-window advertising. Each advertisement must say to each purchaser: "Buy this product and you will get this specific benefit."

- The proposition must be one that the competitor either cannot or does not offer. It must be unique—either a uniqueness of the brand or a claim not otherwise made.

- The proposition must be so strong that it can move the mass millions (Reeves, 1968, pp. 47-48).

Because it was one of the first popular message strategies, the product benefits approach is often described as a more traditional message strategy. The benefits strategy seems to have reached its peak in the 1950s, the product era, where, according to Trout and Ries, all you needed was "a better mousetrap and some money to promote it" (Trout and Ries, 1972, p. 35). The focus was clearly on specific product features and consumer benefits.

Detractors such as Trout and Ries feel that the benefits approach is passe, and no longer as effective in our "overcommunicated society . . . where . . . your mousetrap is quickly followed by two more just like it" (Trout and Ries, 1972, p. 35).

• • • • •

> ### Positioning Tip:
> I agree that because of the proliferation of me-too products and advertising clutter, finding USPs is not as easy as it used to be, but I do not agree with the idea that the product benefits strategy is passe. The product benefits approach represents a tried and true strategy that you can still use effectively.

• • • • •

The benefits approach is a message strategy that is essentially directed at the consumer's needs or wants. Understanding the consumer's motivations and the concomitant needs or wants that spring from their motivations is at the heart of the benefits strategy. The benefits strategy, then, is a direct assault on the consumer's needs or wants. The benefits strategy focuses on delivering an advertising message that provides a product benefit, supported by a unique product attribute, which will fulfill the consumer's needs or wants.

The benefits/USP strategy is often described as a "hard sell" in that the selling message is explicitly stated, as opposed to other strategies like the image strategy, where the selling message is usually nonverbal and implied rather than stated explicitly. The Ted Bates Advertising Agency built memorable, enduring campaigns using the product benefits approach, such as the Wonder Bread campaign that promised that, "Wonder Bread helps build strong bodies 12 ways," and the M&M campaign, "M&M's melt in your mouth, not in your hands."

Image Advertising

By the end of the 1950s, consumers seemed to have reached a saturation point. They were being inundated with products and advertising. Many of the products were increasingly similar and so were their claimed benefits or USPs. This set the stage of a new kind of creative strategy, a creative strategy that focused on the product's image.

The 1960s have been described as the era of "image advertising." However, the roots of image advertising go back to the beginning of the twentieth century. Ernest Calkens of the Bates Agency created a new style of advertising when he began producing beautiful magazine ads that resembled original art. Shortly afterward, Theodore F. MacManus developed the idea of the "soft sell." He used an image style of advertising similar to Calkens and a soft-sell copy style that he felt would create a better long-term relationship between the manufacturer and the consumer. He tried to create a positive image through a slow accumulation of positive images. Indeed, his new style of advertising helped establish Buick and Cadillac (Printer's Ink, 1918).

David Ogilvy, with his Rolls Royce and Hathaway Shirts campaigns, is one of the more renowned practitioners of image advertising. In his image advertising, Ogilvy stressed the importance of brand image, which he also viewed as a "long-term investment."

The Leo Burnett Agency's Marlboro Man campaign is probably the most successful example of a creative strategy that focuses on creating an appealing, appropriate brand image. Marlboro was initially introduced in Europe as a pink-tipped woman's cigarette. The fact that it was virtually unknown in America made the image transformation that much easier. The brand was repackaged and introduced as a man's cigarette. The American Marlboro advertising created an entirely new user image. It depicted rugged men with tattoos on their hands, and this evolved into the Marlboro Cowboy campaign that is still running today.

● ●

" Image advertising tries to indirectly persuade consumers to use products or services by creating awareness and presenting a user image or brand image that will appeal to the target audience."

● ●

The Marlboro campaign represented a distinct departure from the benefits or USP approach of the 1940s and 1950s. It used a different message strategy, one that emphasized the product's image rather than its attributes and benefits. In image advertising, the selling message is usually much less obvious, less explicit, or seemingly nonexistent. Image advertising tries to indirectly persuade consumers to use products or services by creating awareness and by presenting a user image or brand image that will appeal to the target audience.

McDonald's does a lot of "feel good" image advertising. Actually, the McDonald's strategy combines appealing imagery with compelling emotional/psychological benefits. The commercials feature wonderful, heartfelt views of senior citizens and how Ronald McDonald House is helping children. The commercials create a positive brand image and leave consumers with a warm and fuzzy feeling about McDonald's. When consumers are asked to describe McDonald's based on its advertising, they respond that it's a "wonderful place where everybody is happy." Never mind that when you go to a McDonald's, it sometimes resembles a cafeteria food fight. The positive perception created by McDonald's advertising has its own reality. For marketers it is a reality that exists in the most important place of all—the consumer's mind. This kind of advertising, in effect, presells the consumer by creating a positive feeling about the brand and the type of person who uses the brand. It makes consumers more receptive to the idea of eating at McDonald's.

Similarly, most corporate advertising aims to establish or maintain a corporate identity or image, normally using no explicit selling message. A strong, positive corporate identity may make it easier for the corporation to attract shareholders. A strong, positive corporate identity may also have a halo effect, which works to leave consumers with a good feeling about the company. This good feeling, in turn, can make consumers more receptive to the company's products or services. (Ultimately, all advertising is in some way beneficial to its sponsors.)

Some image advertising omits product attributes and benefits entirely. Fashion and cosmetic advertising is often pure image advertising without any product or benefit claims. Some jeans commercials offer good examples of pure image advertising. They have no product story and no overt selling message. The jeans ads offer an image with a sense of style and youthful insouciance, which presumably appeals to young people. The product is simply identified. However, the implied selling message is, "If you want to be like these people, wear these jeans."

The Charlie perfume commercials described earlier are another good example of pure image advertising. The commercials say nothing about the product (what can you say about perfume?). Instead, they present the consumer with an appealing image. The implied message is if you want to be like the Charlie woman, wear Charlie perfume.

Advertisers experience a lot of confusion about whether it is necessary for advertising to have a product story (attributes and benefits). In one meeting, an account manager got into a heated argument with the creative teams over whether the advertising should offer a product benefit.

In question was a line of hairstyling products with a chic, high-style, salon heritage. Because of its heritage, the creatives viewed the product as a fashion product and were using an image strategy to generate ads that were pure image advertising—that is, the advertisements contained no product story, no benefits, and no attributes. The team wanted to use the advertising to make a fashion statement, to present a chic, avant-garde image. There was no overt selling message, but the implied selling message was "to be as cool and chic as these people, use these hair styling products."

Arguing on the other side, the account manager viewed the product as a hair care product. Consequently, he argued that the advertising should present some kind of tangible consumer benefit with a supporting product attribute. The account manager was thinking in terms of a benefits' strategy. The account manager and the creatives were both right. The problem was they were using different strategies. An image strategy does not require a product story, but a benefits strategy does.

Unlike the benefits strategy, which is a direct assault on the consumer's motivations and concomitant needs or wants, an image strategy is a direct attack on the consumer's perceptions. If the advertising objective is to create an image or change an existing image, image advertising is the appropriate strategy.

User Image Versus Brand Image Strategy

In contrast to a user image strategy that tries to present an appealing user image, the focus of the brand image strategy is on creating a positive appealing brand image. As stated earlier, the brand image is a nonspecific, transcendent message element. There are many factors (packaging, price, labels, logos, and so on) that contribute to a brand's overall image. And advertising is certainly one of those factors. Advertising can be used to enhance or reinforce a brand's image.

• •

" Another way of looking at brand image strategies
is to think of them as strategies that "romance" the
product, or present the product as 'hero.' "

• •

Russell Haley identifies and defines brand image strategies as those strategies that have a "noncognitive emphasis." According to Haley, "Product performance is translated into hedonistic and sensory benefits. The product looks wonderful, feels wonderful, smells wonderful, sounds wonderful, or tastes wonderful—sometimes all five. . . . other imagery characteristics that may be stressed include newness, modernity, and feelings that the product is fun to buy, to own, or to use. The main thrust of this model is providing sensory benefits" (Haley, 1984, p. 10).

Another way of looking at brand image strategies is to think of them as strategies that "romance" the product, or present the product as "hero." You must consider a brand's image in any advertising strategy in order to nurture and maintain, or at least not detract from, a strong, positive brand image. However, when you use a brand image strategy, the primary focus of your communication is on developing or reinforcing a positive brand image. This type of strategy is particularly important for new brands that require a brand image to be established, or ailing brands, whose image needs to be dusted off and polished.

One factor that strongly contributes to the brand image is the brand personality, which is largely a function of the advertising and user images. Thus, in developing a brand image strategy, you often combine appealing brand imagery with appealing, appropriate user imagery.

Rejuvenation and Contemporization (R&C) for Older, Established Brands

Many of the older, well-established products and brands that peaked in the post-war era often suffer from a tired image. The brand often still has a quality image, but it needs to be rejuvenated and contemporized. The "little, old ladies drink Lipton Tea," and some of the new 1990s advertising for kids' cereals are examples of R&C image strategies being used to revitalize and contemporize otherwise healthy brands.

Emotional/Psychological Benefits Strategy

The emotional/psychological benefits strategy is a message strategy directed against consumers' feelings. The primary emphasis of this strategy is on providing consumers with an emotional or psychological benefit. To accomplish this, you associate brand usage with an emotional/psychological benefit. For example, some of the traditional Campbell's Soup advertising clearly leaves consumers with a warm, wholesome, nurturing feeling. Therefore, along with the product benefits (nutrition and so on) the advertising communicates an emotional benefit (warm, wholesome, nurturing feelings) with using Campbell's Soup.

Emotional or psychological benefits are often overlooked in favor of product-related benefits. Barry Feig points up the importance of emotional or psychological benefits in an Advertising Age article that describes "share of heart." Feig says that along with share of market and share of mind, advertisers need to create advertising that "speaks to the consumer on a personal, emotional gut level—a product that will win the hearts of consumers" (Feig, 1986, p. 18).

• •
" Emotional or psychological benefits are often
overlooked in favor of product-related benefits."
• •

Many advertisers have indeed used the end benefit strategy to capture a share of the consumer's heart, to create a strong emotional bond between the consumer and the client's products. Hallmark and Kodak advertising immediately come to mind. The focus of their advertising is clearly on the emotional or psychological benefits derived from using their products rather than on the products themselves. Through advertising, consumers have come to associate warm, positive feelings with Hallmark and Kodak products.

Russell Haley describes emotional/psychological advertising as an attempt to "make people affiliate with the brand by engaging their emotions in some manner and forging an emotional link with the consumer." Haley's definition of emotional benefits again includes what he calls "affiliation benefits." He cites the Miller Lite commercials and the Garner & Hartley Polaroid commercials as examples of advertising whose "main thrust is to provide affiliation benefits" (Haley, 1984, p. 10).

"Positioning" Strategy

The "positioning" strategy is a marked departure from the other message strategies, in that its focus is not on any of the elements of advertising (product benefits, user image, and so on) but rather on the product's perceptual positioning in the consumer's mind. The product attributes, benefits, user imagery, and other features are generally used to support the product's perceptual positioning, which again is the primary thrust of the positioning strategy.

Trout and Ries downplay the importance of creativity because they say it obscures the positioning. They say that the key to success in the positioning era is "to run the naked positioning statement, unadorned by so-called creativity" (Trout and Ries, 1972, p. 116). Trout and Ries go on to advocate comparative advertising as the best way to position products against the competition. The Avis, "We're Number 2"campaign and the "7-Up Uncola" campaign were two of the more memorable examples of comparative advertising campaigns that seemed to dominate the 1970s.

Problem-Solution Strategy

The problem-solution strategy is really a new twist on the old benefits (USP) strategy. The primary thrust or emphasis of the problem-solution approach is on solving a consumer problem. The main proponents of this approach are the people at the BBD&O Advertising Agency, who believe that "solving the prime prospect's problem is the very heart of an effective advertising strategy." BBD&O uses a research technique called "problem detection," which E. E. Norris describes as "180 degrees opposite" from the benefits approach. Norris explains that the problem-solution approach is superior to the benefits approach because, "the benefits approach will only tell us what we already know." In other words, consumers will essentially play back what you have already told them:

> Benefits or attribute research simply ask consumers what they want. The presumption is that they will tell you something you don't already know. They won't. Because consumers are not creative. What they will tell you is what you have already told them. For instance, if you ask consumers what they want in a dandruff-remover shampoo, they will say they want a shampoo that removes dandruff (Norris, 1975, p. 43).

According to Norris, the first step in the problem-solution approach is to develop a "very long list of possible problems."

The list of problems is developed by "interviewing prime prospects, reviewing secondary data, consulting experts, and relying on pure insight." The second step is to have a large sample of prime prospects rank the problems in three different ways:

- importance
- frequency of occurrence
- the degree to which the problem may have been solved by some existing product or service

From this information, they calculate a problem score: "the bigger the score, the bigger the opportunity" (Norris, 1975, p. 43).

Norris uses the dog food category to compare the benefits approach with the problem-solution approach. Using the benefits approach, Norris found that the three most-wanted attributes in the dog food category were:

1. Balanced Diet
2. Good Nutrition
3. Contains Vitamins

Norris explains that this information was not really useful:

> (1) It summarizes what every other dog food manufacturer on earth was saying at the time. In other words, this particular piece of research got consumers to tell us what we had already told them. (2) The attributes of "balanced diet, good nutrition, and contains vitamins," are all benefits for the dog, rather than for the purchaser. We believe it is silly to advertise to the dog, since no dog—not even Rin Tin Tin—has ever bought a can of dog food (Norris, 1975, pp. 43-44).

Norris then goes on to contrast the benefits approach with the problem-solution approach. Using the problem detection technique, Norris found that the top three problems in the dog food category were these:

1. It smells bad.

2. It costs too much.

3. It does not come in different sizes for different dogs.

Norris points out that time has proven him right, because since that study, a dog food company has come out with a dog food that "smells so good it is called stew rather than dog food;" a second product, called "mixing chunks," was introduced, which helps cut costs because it is mixed with dry food. And several manufacturers have introduced different sizes of cans.

Norris offers Viva towels as another illustration of how the problem-solution strategy is superior to the benefits strategy.

Using the benefits strategy, we found that the most important product attribute is absorbancy. However, using the problem-solution strategy, we found that the number one problem was "durability." By concentrating on durability in our Viva Towel commercials, we helped make Viva the number one towel in the U.S. (Norris, 1975, p. 44).

• • •

Advertising Execution

The process of creating advertising that builds and maintains brand mythologies starts with a "big idea," a key consumer insight, which becomes the basis for the brand positioning and advertising message. The final step in the process of creating advertising is to translate the brand positioning and advertising message into an advertising execution. The advertising execution is the actual commercial or advertisement. The crafting of the individual advertising mythologies (commercials and advertisements) that ultimately shape the brand mythology is done by the art director, copy writer, and production people.

Once you decide what you wish to communicate, both in terms of the physical product as well as emotional and psychological benefits, a creative team is given the task of developing the advertising. The advertising strategist determines what the client wishes to communicate, but it is the art director and copy writer who must determine how you get the message across. Like all artists, the people who create advertising must rely on their creative instincts; they must look to their unconscious psyche for inspiration and ideas about how to best execute the advertising strategy. For example, the Marlboro marketing people made a strategic decision to portray the Marlboro user as rugged and masculine, but it was the creative team that translated this advertising strategy into a commercial that used a cowboy to communicate this idea. By using advertising to repeatedly associate the image of the cowboy with Marlboro cigarettes, the cowboy (Marlboro Man) eventually became the core of the Marlboro brand mythology.

Step 1: Developing the Creative Platform

The creative platform serves as a blueprint to guide the creative team in developing advertising. It summarizes all the pertinent facts and information. In summary fashion, the creative platform contains the advertising objective, key consumer insight, brand positioning, and main message, as well as all relevant information about the brand, the target audience, the marketplace, and the competition. For established brands, the creative platform should define the brand's existing image, personality, mythology, and so on. Generally, unless you are trying to change the brand's overall character, your advertising should be consistent with the brand's existing identity, personality, and overall mythology. When you are introducing new brands that do not yet have a mythology, image, or personality, you must tell the creative teams what kind of brand image and personality you would ultimately like to create.

The creative platform should provide an overview of the brand's previous advertising as well as the competitive advertising. And finally, the creative platform should list the advertising budget. Figure 7.5 is a sample creative platform summary form.

Advertising is in the idea business. Great advertising, the kind that sells products and builds brands, is built on great ideas. The advertising strategist conducts consumer research with the hope of coming up with a critical consumer insight or idea that will become the basis for the brand positioning and advertising message. In a similar manner, the people who create the advertising (art directors, copy writers, production people, and so on), must also come up with a "big idea," a core executional idea around which the commercial or advertisement is created.

Step 2: Finding the Center

Finding the "best" way to translate the advertising message and positioning into advertising is the purview of the creative team. It comes down to the creative instincts and artistry of the people who must create the advertising. However, in order to create the kind of advertising that, over time, builds brands (as opposed to short-term, one-shot advertising), the creative team

●●

Figure 7.5

The Creative Platform Summary

1. **Advertising Objectives**

2. **Target Audience**
   - Demographics
   - Geographics
   - Psychographics
   - Usage Behavior

3. **Key Consumer Insight**

4. **Brand Positioning**

   How Will the Brand Be Positioned
   - In the Marketplace?
   - In the Consumer's Mind?

5. **Main Message**

   What Do You Wish to Communicate as the
   - Product Attributes and Benefits?
   - Emotional/Psychological Benefits?
   - User Image?

6. **Transcendent Message Elements**

   Your Other Considerations:
   - Brand Image
   - Brand Personality
   - Brand Soul/Essence
   - Brand Mythology

7. **Advertising**

   Survey Existing Advertising for
   - Brand Advertising
   - Competitive Advertising

8. **Advertising Budget**

●●

must use a different perspective. The creative team must take the long view. It must be conscious of the fact that it is creating advertising that must work to build an overall brand mythology. The creative team must come up with a core executional idea that is campaignable, big enough to go beyond the specific commercial or advertisement at hand to build a brand.

The core executional idea is the recurrent central advertising idea or executional element that will be repeated in all of the future advertising and that will eventually become the core of the brand mythology. It can be a specific mytho-symbolic image like the Marlboro Man, Mr. Clean, or Lake Edna. Or it can be an advertising idea that is not tied to a specific, continuing character or image. For example, the core executional idea that is at the center of Kodak's advertising ("a Kodak moment"), is to show how Kodak film captures the important moments in our lives. The advertising and the brand mythology it helps to create are based on a recurrent advertising idea rather than a specific executional element.

The core executional idea should work to communicate the advertising message and establish the brand positioning. For example, Procter and Gamble's Mr. Clean character exemplifies a core executional idea that communicates that the product is a strong, effective cleaner that will make housecleaning easy. At the same time, the Mr. Clean character works to position the brand as a superior cleaning product that can be used to clean your whole house.

The core executional idea around which the advertising is created can obviously take many different forms (mythical characters, places, situations, moments, or themes). How can you recognize and select a core executional idea that has the potential to build a brand mythology? Again, this comes down to hiring good creative people. But at the same time, there are a number of ways in which you can guide and help the creative team and maximize their chances of coming up with a compelling core executional idea.

Step 3: Secure Appropriate Creative Input

There are four important sources of input that can be helpful to the creative team at this point: consumer research, latent product mythology, brand heritage, and cultural mythology.

Exploratory Consumer Research (Learning Who, Why, and How)

Exploratory consumer research was covered fairly extensively in Chapter 6. The important point to be made here is that exploratory consumer research basically serves two functions:

- It helps the advertising practitioner formulate a strategy (a positioning and message).

- It provides input for the creative team, helping the team to devise an executional strategy or core executional idea.

Great executional ideas often come out of exploratory consumer research. For example, the "tastes great; less filling" idea that was the basis for Miller Lite's enduring advertising campaign came out of listening to some beer drinkers in focus groups. Miller was looking for an advertising idea that did not position Miller Lite as a diet beer. Gablinger's had introduced the first light beer as a diet beer, and it didn't work. The Miller group wanted a "beery idea" that would appeal to real beer drinkers. During one of the focus groups, some of the beer drinkers said they liked drinking Miller Lite because it didn't make them feel full or bloated. The creative teams picked up the idea and it became a core executional idea in the Miller Lite advertising. The rest is history.

Latent Product Mythology

The advertising practitioner must also understand the generic, unbranded product. An understanding of the generic product is important, because it is often an important source of insights that you can use to create advertising and build brand mythologies.

●●●●●●●●●●●●●●●●●●●●●●●●●●●●●●●●●●

" The latent product mythology can also help you to understand the soul or essence of the generic product. "

●●●●●●●●●●●●●●●●●●●●●●●●●●●●●●●●●●

The latent product mythology refers to the history, facts, folklore, perceptions, beliefs, experiences, and feelings that are associated with that product. As explained in Chapter 1, every product has its own mythology, but the consumer's awareness of the product's mythology is generally limited and not top of mind. If the consumer has any awareness of the generic product's mythology, it is generally latent, that is, it exists below the threshold of awareness. The latent product mythology can be evoked from consumers by coaxing it into consciousness. It can also be derived from secondary sources—books, periodicals, magazines, and so on. For example, if you were exploring the latent product mythology of wine, you could begin by uncovering all of the associations consumers have of wine: perceptions, facts, images, feelings, and experiences. At the same time, you would also use secondary sources to learn about the history of wine, as well as any beliefs, folklore, and legends about it. The latent product mythology culled from the consumer's perceptions and secondary sources is usually a treasure trove of insights and ideas about the product and/or consumer. This mythology often holds the key to building and maintaining a strong enduring brand mythology. It provides an in-depth understanding of the product category, its raison d'etre, and the consumer's hidden (unconscious) emotional motivations for using the product.

An exploration of the generic product's existing latent mythology will usually reveal the attributes and benefits, both product-based and emotional, that are associated with the product (the category attributes and benefits). The latent product mythology can also help you to understand the soul or essence of the generic product. These insights often become the basis for creating advertising that builds brand mythologies. In other words, the generic product's existing latent mythology often becomes the basis for the brand mythology.

For example, in exploring the latent mythology of beer, you might find that beer has long been associated with men, and it is generally perceived as a masculine drink. Drawing from the latent product mythology, the advertiser may try to create a brand mythology that revolves around masculinity. In fact, Budweiser has created a powerful, enduring brand mythology around male identity.

Sometimes the latent product mythology has several different aspects. For example, if you were exploring the latent product mythology of Italian wine, you would have to explore both aspects of Italian wine: the wine aspect as well as the Italian aspect. In other words, you would examine the perceptions, facts, beliefs, folklore, and feelings surrounding both wine and Italy. The mythology that comes out of the wine's Italian-ness will undoubtedly be associated with the cultural mythology of Italy and Italians: Rome, the eternal city, piazzas, outdoor cafes, amore, the land of love, friendly people, and fine food. In exploring the product mythology for Italian wine, you might discover that wine is an important part of the Italian's love of life. In any case, you can again draw from different aspects of the latent product mythology in creating advertising and building brand mythologies.

All products (unless they are in entirely new product categories) have an existing latent product mythology. And even with new product categories, you can usually go back to the product category that preceded the new product category on which to found your new brand mythology. For example, Xerox launched an entirely new product category: copying machines. The machines did not yet have a product mythology, but copying machines had been long preceded by typewriters and carbon paper, and before them, by scribes—monks who copied books and documents by hand. In fact, one of Xerox's more successful advertising campaigns drew from this earliest copier mythology: beatific monks using Xerox machines.

Brand Heritage

Most established brands have some kind of brand heritage: the history, folklore, and myth surrounding the brand and/or company and/or its founder. Even when you are dealing with a new brand, you may find that the company introducing the brand has an existing heritage. The mix of fact, folklore, and fiction surrounding the company and/or its founder(s) and how the product came to be can serve as the basis for an effective message strategy and brand mythology. For example, Breakstone Cottage Cheese has created advertising and built a brand mythology based on its persnickety founder, Sam Breakstone. The advertising portrays him as a demanding individual who is not satisfied with anything but the best quality. Thus, the Breakstone brand mythology works to communicate the idea that Breakstone brand cottage cheese is the best.

Cultural Mythologies

Enduring brand mythologies are often created by mirroring various aspects of our cultural mythologies. For example, McDonald's advertising has helped to build an appropriate, appealing brand mythology that reflects the American culture, values, sensibilities, and lifestyles. Through advertising, McDonald's has created the perception that it is a part of our culture, a microcosm of everything that is good about America.

The Marlboro cowboy is another obvious example of a brand mythology based on an aspect of our cultural mythology. Some of the more recent advertising for various sportswear products like Reebok have begun to portray women as Warrior-athletes. Again, this is a reflection of the changes occurring in our cultural mythologies.

Creating brand mythologies that reflect our cultural mythologies can be an effective strategy for building strong, enduring brands. Manufacturers whose products are a ubiquitous part of our culture often use this approach. For example, soft drink manufacturers for sodas such as Coke and Pepsi often use this approach. So do political candidates. Cultural mythologies offer a powerful means to build a brand mythology. However, advertisers who use this approach must be careful to continually monitor changes occurring in our cultural mythologies and reflect these changes in their brand mythologies to keep them relevant and contemporary.

Step 4: Monitor the Effects of Changing Values on the Brand Mythology

Creative teams should be made aware of our cultural mythologies and the ways in which they are continually evolving and changing. Most good creative people do such monitoring on their own. One of the ways they track our cultural mythologies is by culling through books, magazines, movies, and television shows. Hollywood continually tries to reflect our changing cultural mythologies, because films often represent new ideas and areas of opportunity. For example, the film *Mr. Mom* tried to humorously reflect the more nurturing, child-involved male emerging in the 1980s. And in the recent film, *Point of No Return*, Bridget Fonda represents an attempt to to portray women in the kind of excessively violent role we normally associate with males like Bruce Willis and Arnold Schwartzenegger.

• •

" Creating brand mythologies that reflect our cultural mythologies can be an effective strategy for building strong, enduring brands. "

• •

• • •

Positioning Tools

Archetypes

An understanding of archetypes can help creative teams understand why some advertising ideas and images have a greater impact and are more enduring than others. Ideas and images that are archetypal are universally recognizable ideas and images. According to Jung, such images are universally recognizable because they emanate from the archetypes that exist in the human psyche (the unconscious psyche). The archetypes that exist in the human psyche represent universal feelings and patterns of thinking. These universal phenomena seem to function somewhat like instincts. We all have an instinct for aggression, a warring instinct, that is universally represented by the Warrior archetype. And all people have an instinct to be kind and caring, a nurturing instinct, universally represented by the Great Mother archetype.

There are mnay different archetypes. Life is full of archetypal moments and situations. We all recognize the universal moment a child takes its first steps alone or enters the adult world without its parents. The power of an archetypal image is that it affects us not only on a conscious level but also on an unconscious, feeling level. When used appropriately, advertising ideas and images that are archetypal generally have a greater impact on the consumer and are more enduring.

Symbols

Symbols represent a powerful, underutilized way of capturing and communicating the essence of your brand mythology. Ask your creative team to think about a symbol or a single mytho-symbolic image (like the little boy biting into an Oscar Mayer Hot dog) which captures and communicates the essence of your brand mythology. Symbols are a powerful form of communication.

Jung believed that all symbolic material emanates from the deeper layers of the collective unconscious that "speak to us" in archetypal images. They are not the product of our consciousness, that aspect of our psyche that is logical and ordered. Rather, symbols are a product of our intuitive, soul-felt unconscious psyche. Bachofen points out the unique power of the symbol:

> The symbol awakens intimations; speech can only explain. The symbol plucks all the strings of the human spirit at once; speech is compelled to take up a single thought at a time. The symbol strikes its roots in the most secret depths of the soul; language skims the surface of understanding like a soft breeze. The symbol aims inward; language outward (Bachofen, 1992, p. 50).

A symbol breaks through our conscious psyche and evokes imagery and feelings that touch our souls. According to Jung, "Symbols are always grounded in the unconscious archetype, but their manifest forms are moulded by the ideas acquired by the conscious mind, those contents which are best suited to themselves. The symbols act as transformers, their function being to convert libido from a 'lower' into a 'higher' form" (Jung, 1992, p. 232).

Because symbols are ultimately grounded in the soul, they have a profound effect on the human psyche. Jung used the word geist ("spirit") for symbols that he believed had their origin in the human psyche or soul. The Crucifix is an example of a complex symbol that can break through our consciousness and evoke a response in our unconscious psyche. The power of a symbol like the Crucifix arises from these associations:

- It is immediately recognizable.
- It instantly communicates the essence of Christianity.
- It evokes the mythology of Christianity.
- It evokes the ritual/experience of Christianity.
- It evokes the imagery and history of Christianity.
- It evokes the feelings associated with Christianity.

Consistency and Repetition

The key to creating the kind of advertising that goes beyond short-term selling, that builds and maintains brand mythologies, is consistency and repetition. As mentioned earlier, advertising builds and maintains brand mythologies through associative learning, by associating specific ideas, images, symbols, and feelings with a particular brand. By consistently and repeatedly associating specific ideas, images, and feelings with a particular brand, the consumer comes to associate them with that brand; they become part of the brand's mythology and unique perceptual inventory. Those ideas and executional elements of the advertising that are most often associated with the brand will become most strongly associated with the brand. For example, the Kool Aid pitcher is always shown in Kool Aid advertising. Consequently, when you ask children what they think of when they think of Kool Aid, the smiling, arm-waving pitcher is invariably a primary association. That pitcher has served as a brand symbol across multiple generations of Kool Aid drinkers, an advertising icon and an important part of the Kool Aid brand mythology.

There are two areas in which the advertiser must strive for consistency: the positioning and message, and the brand mythology and execution.

Commercials may change, but the brand positioning and advertising message, as well as the overall brand image and personality, should be consistent. For example, Barbie dolls have had scores of commercials, but the overall positioning, message, image, and personality of the Barbie product line has remained essentially the same. When the positioning, message, image, and personality are consistent, the consumer is left with a clear image of the brand and what it stands for.

Advertising that changes a brand's message too often or that changes its image or personality generally wind up with a mythology, image, and personality that are unclear and unfocused. Imagine what would happen to the clear image consumers have of McDonald's if the advertiser kept changing the message or brand image.

Clients who continually change their advertising agency must ensure that the new agency treats the images of the client's products consistently. The positioning and message must be consistently repeated. Successive advertisers must be consistent in crafting better appeals to the established brand mythology. Maintaining brand mythologies is the subject of Chapter 8.

• • • • •

Positioning Tip:

In these times of frequent "agency hopping" by clients and job hopping by advertising professionals, it's crucial to create a formal document that defines for the record your brand mythology and simultaneously identifies and catalogs the core executional idea, supporting imagery, and symbols that you want to become a permanent part of the brand mythology. It's also a good idea to document the overall brand image, positioning, and personality.

Building an effective brand mythology takes time, work, and money. Documenting all of the enduring features of the brand's mythology, positioning, and personality will help to ensure that whoever works with the brand's advertising—on either the client or advertiser's side—will understand the brand mythology and what the brand stands for in the consumer's mind. The "brand mythological history" document will help to prevent people who later inherit the brand or product from creating communications that are inconsistent with or undermine the brand mythology.

Think of the brand mythological history as the equivalent of a "corporate identity program" or of a film's "continuity consultant" for your brand.

• • • • •

• • •
Case Studies: Using Advertising to Build Brand Mythologies

The case studies presented here are meant to illustrate some ways advertising can be used to build successful brand mythologies.

Dannon Yogurt: Brand Mythology Based on the Latent Product Mythology

The core executional idea for Dannon Yogurt's advertising strategy came right out of its latent product mythology. The yogurt category was well established in Europe, where consumers were familiar with yogurt's product mythology. But when Dannon launched its products in the United States, yogurt was generally unknown, and consumers were not at all familiar with yogurt's product mythology. When Dannon Yogurt decided to mass-market its yogurt in the United States, the company used yogurt's appealing, latent product mythology to create advertising that emphasized the product's health benefits.

Much lore and legend exist regarding yogurt's almost miraculous ability to help people live long, healthy lives. One legend has it that an angel told Abraham, the Biblical figure, that eating yogurt is the secret to living a long, healthy life. Abraham was supposed to have lived until the ripe, old age of 175! And the French king Francois I, who was in poor health, was said to have been cured by a Turkish doctor who prescribed a diet of fermented milk:

yogurt. The French were duly impressed and hailed yogurt as *le lait de la vie eternelle* (the milk of eternal life).

For years rumors circulated about yogurt-eating Bulgarian peasants who lived more than 100 years and were still virile. In the 1900s the French bacteriologist and Nobel prize winner, Elie Metchnikoff, discovered several strains of live bacteria in Bulgarian yogurt that produced vitamin B and reduced toxins in the large intestine, which speeded up aging.

In 1929 Isaac Carasso founded the Danone Yogurt company in France. Carasso found a ready market for his product in Europe. However, when he began marketing his product in the United States under the name Dannon Yogurt, he found that most consumers were unfamiliar with yogurt. Initially, his product attracted only "ethnic types" and "health fanatics," but by the 1960s, Dannon was ready to go mainstream.

The original Dannon Yogurt advertising, which featured people from Soviet Georgia who were more than 100 years old, launched the yogurt category in the United States and helped build the Dannon Yogurt brand mythology, whose spiritual center is health and longevity. Interestingly, the yogurt category is an example of a successful new product introduction that did not try to position the product by defining it in terms of an existing product. In other words, the Dannon Yogurt advertiser could have introduced yogurt as a "fermented milk," but the benefits of yogurt would not have been immediately apparent to the consumer, and fermented milk probably has a negative connotation.

Motel 6: Brand Mythology Based on a Key Consumer Insight

Very often an advertising strategy comes out of an in-depth understanding of the consumer's motivations for using the product, both at the physical product level and also on a deeper emotional/psychological level. Motel 6's series of radio commercials evolved from a keen understanding of its target consumer.

In 1988, The Richardson Group, a Dallas-based advertising agency, won a Gold Effie for its Motel 6 radio campaign. The advertising, which helped Motel 6 turn its decline around, used radio and the folksy, down-home persona of Tom Bodett to create an appealing brand mythology. It is a terrific example of a successful brand mythology conveyed using mostly radio. The brand mythology is down-to-earth, unpretentious, and geared to the budget-minded "road warrior," not to upscale business travelers looking for five-star accommodations.

The advertising strategy behind the mythology is well founded and well conceived. It is a "smart choice/value" strategy that diffuses the negative perceptions associated with budget lodgings, celebrating the "virtues of frugality." The key consumer insight is that budget-minded consumers often feel embarrassed about staying in "cheap hotels." Further digging uncovered the fact that the people who use budget lodgings are generally sensible, down-to-earth people who are saving money—not because they're cheap but for much more noble reasons, like saving for their children's education.

The Motel 6 brand mythology works on both a rational and an emotional level. At the rational level, the advertising promises weary travelers clean, comfortable accommodations at very reasonable prices; it's a smart choice. But its product story is hardly unique. The genius of this campaign lies in its emotional appeal: It helps the traveler who is on a tight budget to save face. Tom Bodett provides emotional reassurance (which we all need to calm our insecurities) by acknowledging that choosing Motel 6 rather than the more expensive motels and hotels is indeed a smart thing to do. Tom Bodett works as a spokesperson because he comes across like the typical target consumer, a no-nonsense, unpretentious, sensible guy who doesn't have a lot of money to spend on a motel.

The other insight that drives the Motel 6 brand mythology arises from an understanding of the product's latent mythology: People who travel a lot and spend a lot of time alone in motel rooms away from home and family are lonely. Tom Bodett's folksy, friendly manner is reassuring. It helps to create an appropriate, appealing brand personality that works to make weary, lonely travelers feel welcome, as if they will be among friends.

As the Motel 6 advertising campaign evolved, the creators came up with a terrific line that captures the down-home appeal of the Motel 6 advertising "We'll leave the light on for you." What a wonderfully appropriate, appealing image for a motel! This line became the core executional element that captures and conveys the brand's appealing character or personality. The line has great emotional appeal. We've all had the experience of coming home late, tired, and weary, happy to find that someone has left the light on for us. What a comforting feeling it is to know that someone is expecting you, cares about you, and is thoughtful enough to leave a light on for you.

All motels and hotels promise physical comfort for the weary traveler, but they are often impersonal, cheerless places. The folksy appeal of Tom Bodett and the "We'll leave the light on for you" line distinguish Motel 6 from all the others that also promise value. It grants Motel 6 a unique identity and personality, which in turn help to create an emotional bond between the brand and the consumer.

Consumers asked what they are looking for in hotel and motel accommodations generally respond that they are looking for clean, comfortable lodgings. Of course, some are looking for more luxurious accommodations and service. But underneath the more obvious, product-related attributes, they are really looking for a safe, comfortable haven.

The powerful emotional appeal of Motel 6's brand mythology speaks to this hidden emotional need. Thus, the spiritual center or brand essence and brand mythology for Motel 6 combine both a rational, product-based benefit (a clean, comfortable room for not a lot of money) and a compelling emotional/psychological benefit (being in a place where we feel welcome and safe).

Symbolically, all motels, hotels, and inns are feminine: They represent the womb, a place where we can feel safe and secure. But remember, the womb also represents the primordial darkness and the unconscious. We have an instinctive fear of darkness. Darkness is associated with death. Our metawomb, the earth, is not only our place of origin, it is also our final resting place, our tomb. And darkness is also associated with evil. Satan is the Prince of Darkness, and the dual aspect of the Great Mother (creator and destroyer) is represented by light and darkness, yin and yang. The Black Virgin (Madonna) is a manifestation of the dark, shadow side of the Great Mother.

In contrast, the idea of "leaving the light on" works on a symbolic level to counteract the negative, dark, depressing aspect of the womblike character of a motel. The sun is a masculine symbol that represents the Universal Father, Brahma, reason, the direct, penetrating ray of logos— the light of day, which illuminates the darkness of the night. "The visible father of the world is the sun, the heavenly fire, for which reason father, God, sun, and fire are mythologically synonymous" (Jung, 1990, p. 89).

The appearance of light represents the emergence of consciousness, the separation of the ego from the chaos of darkness—the human victory over the dark forces of nature and the unconscious.

On another level light also symbolizes divinity, the force of goodness against the darkness of the night that represents evil. God is often represented as the Light; for Christians, Christ is "The Light of the world." For Buddhists, light represents truth, the ultimate reality that transcends the world of opposites. And for Muslims, Allah is the "Light of the Heavens" and of the earth.

Summing up, the line "We'll leave the light on for you" works on many levels: It is a cheery, uplifting image that is reminiscent of home, of being loved, of someone waiting for us. It is like a ship's beacon, a ray of hope guiding us and welcoming us home through a dark stormy night. Light is associated with divinity and goodness as opposed to darkness, which represents evil. Light also symbolizes civilization, the light of the human soul against the darkness and uncertainty of the night.

Purdue Chickens: Brand Mythology Based on Heritage

The advertising for Purdue Chickens and the brand mythology it helped to build evolved from the brand's heritage, and the history, facts, and folklore surrounding the brand's founder, Frank Purdue.

In 1920, Frank Purdue's father, Arthur, quit his job as a Railway Express agent and began raising chickens in Maryland. As Frank tells it, he literally grew up with chickens. Early on young Frank became involved in aspects of chicken farming. Eventually, the Purdues produced high-quality chickens that won top prizes at auctions. Encouraged by this success, Frank believed that he could convince the world that his chickens were superior to all other chickens.

In 1971 Frank Purdue hired an advertising agency (Scali, McCabe, Sloves, Inc.) to help him revolutionize the poultry business by branding what had been a commodity product. The agency created television commercials that introduced Frank Purdue, one of the founders of Purdue Chickens, telling the American consumer that his chickens were better than any other chickens. The advertising agency helped to build Frank's case (and mythology) with clever, memorable copy: "It takes a tough man to make a tender chicken." and "My chickens eat better than you do." At the same time, Frank Purdue had an ingenuous quality that seemed to help make his pitch believable. The American consumer took one look at his face (which, with his bald head and peculiar shaped nose, looked like the backside of a freshly plucked chicken), and decided that this was indeed a man who knew chickens. Frank Purdue and his committment to giving America a better chicken became the core executional idea which built the Perdue brand mythology.

The Purdue Poultry brand is an apt example of how an appropriate, appealing brand mythology can be based on the company's heritage and the personal history of its founder. Growing at annual rate of 17 percent, Purdue Inc. has leveraged its founder's commitment to quality to build a brand mythology that has helped it to become the fastest growing poultry business.

• • •
Conclusion

This chapter supplemented the knowledge you acquired about building a brand mythology in Chapter 6 with the practical aspects of properly positioning and executing the brand mythology for your advertising campaigns. The final chapter of this book explores how to help guarantee the continued success of your brand's mythology—how to keep it flexible in these changing times and how to deal with threats to your brand's existing mythology.

Chapter 8

• • • • • • • • • • •

Maintaining Your Brand's Mythology

Maintaining your brand's mythology is a three-step process:

1. Uncover and understand your brand's existing mythology.
2. Evaluate and assess your brand mythology—you must decide whether or not it represents the best mythology for your brand.
3 Decide what changes (if any) should be made in your brand's mythology. For example, you may decide that the brand mythology is still working well but the user imagery communicated through advertising needs to be updated and contemporized.

In any case, you will be using the tools and techniques outlined in Chapter 6 to uncover, understand, and evaluate your brand's existing mythology. Because each brand is unique, the process must be done on a case-by-case basis. Thus, a case study approach is the only viable way to illustrate maintenance techniques. The first case study, Campbell's Soup, will be covered in more detail to give you a clear understanding of the maintenance process and how to use the various tools and techniques. However, in the interest of brevity, and to avoid redundancy, the other two case studies (Harley-Davidson and Budweiser) will be covered in a more summary fashion.

• • •
Case Study 1: Campbell's Soup (Balancing Physical and Emotional Benefits)

Campbell's Soup is a great example of a familiar brand with a strong, enduring brand mythology that works to communicate a balance of product benefits and emotional/psychological benefits. At the product level, its mythology communicates the idea that Campbell's Soup is a delicious, quality product and a trusted brand name that has become a cultural fixture in most households. On a more emotional/psychological level, the brand mythology works to associate the Campbell's Soup brand with goodness, mother love, children, nurturing feelings, and a wholesome image.

Step 1: Uncovering and Understanding the Brand Mythology

Brand Identity Profile

The brand identity profile (BIP) technique introduced previously in Chapter 6 is the primary tool used to uncover and understand your brand's mythology. The BIP technique helps to reveal Campbell's Soup's unique perceptual inventory—the imagery, feelings, symbolism, and associations connected with Campbell's Soup in the consumer's mind. You need to collect a complete perceptual inventory all of the images, feelings, symbolism, and associations for Campbell's Soup. Again, this is best handled qualitatively, in a series of in-depth interviews or focus groups. You ask consumers everything they associate with Campbell's Soup, using questions such as these:

- "When you think of Campbell's Soup, what comes to mind?"
- "What images, associations, and feelings do you connect with Campbell's Soup?"

You would most likely get responses like this:

It's a quality product, a familiar product. . . . A product I grew up with. When I think of Campbell's Soup I think of children.

I picture a mom serving a warm bowl of Campbell's Soup to her children on a cold, rainy day.

I think of the Campbell's Soup kids: wholesome and healthy.

I think of goodness. Campbell's Soup gives me a warm, fuzzy feeling. I associate it with mother love, with nurturing.

Your consumers should generate an exhaustive list of images, associations, and feelings. In order to facilitate the interviewing process and to make sure the consumer generates an exhaustive list, you can ask consumers to think of images, associations, and feelings in terms of four different areas:

- the product
- product usage
- users/user imagery
- values/benefits

Figure 8.1

Hypothetical Perceptual Inventory: Campbell's Soup

Value/Benefits

Warm feeling

Nurturance

Mother love

Comforting

Wholesome

Goodness

Caring

Sharing

Usage

Lunch

Snack

Meal accompaniment

When I'm feeling sick

When I'm down

A cold winter day

After school

A rainy damp day

Comfort food

User

Family

Mom

Children

Everybody

Campbell soup kids

Product

Quality

Red and white label

A trusted brand name

A familiar brand

A brand I grew up with

A great American brand

Variety of soups

A part of our culture

Andy Warhol

Americana

The exhaustive list of images, associations, and feelings generated by consumers represents Campbell's Soup's unique perceptual inventory.

Once you have developed an exhaustive list of the brand's images, associations, and feelings, you then ask consumers to rank them in terms of the degree to which each of these various elements connotes "Campbell's Soupness" or somehow captures the essence of the Campbell's Soup brand.

What you ultimately develop is the Campbell's Soup brand identity profile: a rank-ordered short list of the images, attributes, feelings, and associations that are most strongly associated with Campbell's Soup and that best capture and convey the essence of Campbell's Soup.

For example, Campbell's Soup's BIP might look something like this:

Mom

Kids

Campbell's Soup kids

Warm feelings

Nurturing feelings

Secure feelings

Feelings of being taken care of

Americana—Norman Rockwell

Wholesome

Quality

You then take those elements from the rank-ordered list that most connote "Campbell's Soupness" (such as mom, children, and nurturing) and qualitatively probe them for insights and a deeper understanding of what these elements mean in the consumer's psyche. Through interpretation and interpolation, this should lead you to an understanding of the brand's core image and/or values—its essence or soul. For example, in examining Campbell's Soup's BIP you would find that the spiritual center, the soul of the Campbell's Soup Brand, is "mother love or a feeling of nurturance."

Brand Snapshot

In addition to the BIP, you can use another complementary research technique called the "brand snapshot." The brand snapshot is particularly useful for uncovering the core image, which is at the center of the brand mythology and which also generally defines the brand's soul or essence. The brand snapshot is the single image that best conveys the essence of a brand and its brand mythology—what the brand stands for in the consumer's mind. This is how it works. You ask consumers: "Describe the one image that best portrays what Campbell's Soup means to you—the one image that captures the Campbell's Soup moment, the essence of Campbell's Soup. What do you see? Describe the picture."

For most well-established brands, consumers can readily identify the single image or snapshot that seems to capture the essence of the brand and its mythology. For example, the image or brand snapshot that consumers play back for Bailey's Irish Cream Liquor is generally something like: "I see a Christmas holiday setting: people wearing sweaters, relaxing in front of a roaring fire, sipping Bailey's Irish Cream." For Campbell's Soup, consumers generally play back something like: "I see a mother giving her child a bowl of warm soup on a cold, dreary winter's day." If the consumer cannot come up with a brand snapshot or core image, it usually means that your brand mythology is unclear or not well established in the consumer's mind.

The BIP combined with the brand snapshot usually reveal the brand's core image/values around which the brand mythology is built. Once you have identified the dominant images, values, and symbols for the brand, you can generally piece together the brand mythology. The core image and brand identity profile for Campbell's Soup clearly reveal a brand mythology based on nurturance, mother love, children, and Americana.

• • • • •

Maintenance Tip:

It is also interesting to compare your brand's profile and snapshot with those for competitive brands. How does your brand stack up against the competition in terms of rich imagery, feelings, and associations? Contrast how your BIP and brand snapshot varies among different consumer groups.

• • • • •

Step 2: Revealing the Brand Personality

In order to further understand your brand's overall mythology and image, you must also uncover and understand the brand's personality. Some of the projective techniques outlined in Chapter 6 can help you flesh out Campbell's Soup's brand personality (what Campbell's Soup would be like if it were a person). Generally, the most straightforward way to understand the brand personality is to simply ask the consumer: What would Campbell's Soup be like if it was a person? Most consumers would probably offer a response like one of these:

It's a she . . . a mom with two or three children. . . . She's a Den Mother for the Scouts, involved in school functions.

She drives a station wagon or a minivan . . . and she and the kids are on their way to a Little League game.

In short, consumers perceive Campbell's Soup as "the all-American Mom—warm, caring, and nurturing." The brand personality also helps to give you a feeling for the brand's spiritual center or soul.

To sum up, the BIP, brand snapshot, and brand personality can help you to further dimensionalize Campbell's Soup's brand mythology, image and essence/soul. The brand's overall image and brand mythology grow out of its core essence or soul. It is clear from the information that you have gathered that Campbell's Soup has built a wonderfully appropriate, appealing brand mythology around mother love and children.

Step 3: Finding the Heart of the Campbell's Soup Brand Mythology

Ultimately, in order to evaluate and assess the brand mythology, the advertiser must also understand the soul of the brand mythology—what gives the brand mythology its power. The advertiser must ask these questions:

- What is the basis for the brand mythology?
- Where does it come from?
- Is the brand mythology rooted in the latent product mythology—the essence of soupness? Or is the brand mythology rooted in some aspect of our cultural mythology?
- Is the brand mythology based on an archetypal, soul-felt image that gives the mythology its power?

An understanding of the soul or core essence that is the basis for the brand mythology will help the advertiser understand what gives the brand mythology its power and what aspects of the brand mythology can and cannot be changed (the soul of a brand mythology cannot be changed without essentially changing the brand). The advertising team must understand which elements of the brand mythology cannot be changed without changing the brand's overall mythology and identity. This is essential to maintaining brand mythologies.

In any case, you need to understand the basis for the Campbell's Soup brand mythology—a mythology built around nurturance and the mother-child relationship. What gives the core image (nurturance through the mother-child relationship) its power? You know that the mother-child relationship is a powerful, archetypal, soul-felt image that touches us both on the conscious and unconscious levels. But is there a basis for associating this image with soup?

Step 4: Exploring the Brand Category's Latent Product Mythology

The latent product mythology often holds the key to understanding the brand mythology. If you delve into the latent product mythology of soup—its history, facts, and folklore—you find that there seems to be something very basic and primal about soup. There is something intrinsically comforting about a warm fluid. A warm bowl of soup seems to comfort both the body and the soul. In many cultures, soups and broths are also perceived as having restorative, almost magical powers. The image of a sick person being nursed back to health is archetypal, a universally recognizable image that can ultimately be traced to the image of a mother nursing her child.

Historically, soup seems to be as old as human culture. The first evidence of soup making occurred in the remnants of a simple grain soup used in prehistoric times (7000 to 8000 BC). The word soup was probably derived from the German word *sop*, which referred to the bread used to soak up the broth. Soup has always held wide appeal. It is tasty, easy to prepare, and it has traditionally been a mainstay for the poor (from the Middle Ages to modern times, as persists in today's soup kitchens).

In the Middle Ages, the soup pot or cauldron was a fixture in most homes. In the larger homes it was a large cauldron, generally located in the center of the room. The notion of a stockpot or pot-au-feu probably came out of the image of the cauldron with its ever-changing broth enriched daily with whatever happened to be available.

And soup is most often associated with women, with the image of the bonne femme ladling soup from her kitchen kettle, and the image of the mother lovingly serving soup to her child. These images are consistent with Campbell's Soup's brand essence and core image (mother love/nurturing). Consumer research and the history and folklore of soup both point to the fact that one of the most pervasive and enduring images of soup is a mother lovingly serving warm soup to her children. The more recent mother-soup association that comes out of the consumer research has undoubtedly been influenced and reinforced by Campbell Soup's advertising. Starting in the 1930s, mothers and children have been a central theme in Campbell's advertising. However, it is also clear that this image predates Campbell's Soup's advertising—it originates in the history, folklore, and imagery surrounding soup.

The Historical Connection Between Women and Soup

The historical connection between women and soup seems simple enough: It is undoubtedly related to the fact that traditionally, the primary role of women was the care and feeding of children. And soup is a warm, tasty, nourishing food that was particularly appealing to poor families, because with a few meager ingredients, a mother could feed a brood of hungry

Figure 8.2

Campbell's Soup Ad

Courtesy of Campbell Soup Company and D'Arcy Collection of The Communication Library of the University of Illinois at Urbana-Champaign

children. But the connections among women, children, and soup are more than historical. There is something immediately recognizable about a mother feeding her child a bowl of soup: The image resonates in our unconscious psyches because it is a soul image—an image that touches something primal and instinctive in all of us.

The Symbolic Connections Between Women and Soup

You must seek to understand the soul of a generic product by examining the canon of mytho-symbolic images that surround that product. Each image helps to illuminate some aspect of the product and, when taken as a whole, the mytho-symbolic images can bring a depth of understanding that otherwise would be impossible. Understanding the symbolism that surrounds the Campbell's Soup image (mother-child-soup) will help to maintain its brand mythology over the long term.

You can use the analogical approach (mythological amplification) to further your understanding of the symbolic connections among women, children, and soup. At the most basic level, there is a connection between women and fluids. Citing Freud (*The Interpretation of Dreams*) and Abraham (*Dreams and Myths*), Carl Jung says that "the maternal significance of water is one of the clearest symbols in all of mythology" (Jung, 1990, p. 218). In mythology and the psychoanalytic literature, deep water symbolizes the womb and the unconscious. And in some sense the two are really one and the same, because our life begins in the unconscious watery realm of our mother's womb.

In *Sexual Personnae*, Camille Paglia describes the connections among women, fluids, and the force of nature:

> Woman's body is a sea acted upon by the month's lunar wave-
> motion. Sluggish and dormant, her fatty tissues are gorged with
> water, then suddenly cleansed at hormonal high tide. Edema is our
> mammalian relapse into the vegetable. Pregnancy demonstrates the
> deterministic character of woman's sexuality. Every pregnant
> woman has her body taken over by chthonian force beyond her
> control (Paglia, 1990, p. 11).

The first living creatures emerged from the "primordial soup." This primal moment is re-created in the woman's womb—when we emerge from the amniotic waters of our mother. The ritual of baptism recognizes the connection between water and birth: the person is either submerged or doused with water to signify the rebirth into Christianity.

There is also a connection between a woman's menstrual fluids—a kind of life soup—and the primordial soup from which all life sprang. Paglia, in her inimitable, provocative style, makes the connection between a woman's menstrual fluids and this "primordial soup":

Women have borne the symbolic burden of man's imperfections, his grounding in nature. Menstrual blood is the stain, the birthmark of original sin, the filth that transcendental religion must wash from man. Is this identification merely phobic, merely misogynistic? Or is it possible there is something uncanny about menstrual blood, justifying its attachment to taboo? I will argue that it is not menstrual blood per se which disturbs the imagination—unstanchable as that red flood may be—but rather the albumen in the blood, the uterine shreds, placental jellyfish of the female sea. This is the chthonian matrix from which we rose. We have an evolutionary revulsion from slime, our site of biologic origins. Every month, it is woman's fate to face the abyss from which we rose" (Paglia, 1990, p. 11).

On another level, soup also symbolizes mother's milk. Gaston Bachelard, the philosopher-psychoanalyst, traces the unconscious, symbolic connections between fluids—water and milk:

All liquid is a kind of water for material imagination. . . from a psychoanalytic point of view, we must say that all water is a kind of milk. More precisely, every joyful drink is mother's milk. Here we have an example of an explanation at two levels of material imagination, at two successive degrees of unconscious depth: first, all liquid is a kind of water; then all water is a kind of milk" (Bachelard, 1983, p. 117).

Since the dawn of creation and across all cultures, humankind has conceived of a Great Mother archetype—the universal giver of life and nourishment. Neumann notes, "The clearest expression of this giving outward is the breasts, which typify woman as giver of nourishment" (Neumann, 1991, p. 123). Neumann makes reference to Briffault (*The Mothers*), who points out that "the Greeks believed that the first patera, or bowl, was molded from Helen's breast" (Neumann, 1991, p. 123). Symbols of the breast are generally open, wide-mouthed vessels (such as a bowl, goblet, or chalice), whereas symbols of the belly are closed (pot, egg, oven, or cave) (Hall, 1980, p. 53).

Jung makes mention of the fact that the root word for mother's breasts, mama, is found in all languages (Jung, 1990, p. 251). And one of the earliest images of feminine idolatry was the Cow Goddess. Mesopotamian Egyptians worshipped the Heavenly Cow. During droughts the Egyptians would milk their cows and let the milk run onto the parched earth in the hopes of appeasing the Cow Goddess so that she might bring rain.

There is, then, a symbolic connection between a bowl of soup and mother's milk. Both are warm, nourishing fluids given by a mother to her child. Both are served from containers that have similar shapes.

In *The Hidden Persuaders*, Vance Packard cites a quote from *Advertising Agency* magazine: "Soup is unconsciously associated with man's deepest need for nourishment and reassurance. It takes us back to our earliest sensations of warmth, protection, and feeding. Its deepest roots may lie in prenatal sensations being surrounded by the amniotic fluid in our mother's womb" (Packard, 1957, p. 102). Packard's insights were influenced by the work of Ernest Dichter and the school of motivational research. Unfortunately, Packard's work was later sensationalized and to some extent discredited by people looking for "hidden, subliminal images of breasts in ice cubes." But Vance Packard was essentially right—advertising contains hidden persuaders, hidden emotional benefits that motivate consumers to choose one brand over another.

The nurturing quality of soup is confirmed by consumer research. Consumers often admit that they derive both physical and emotional satisfaction from eating a bowl of soup. Many people turn to soup when they are feeling depressed and overwhelmed by the demands of life. When probed further, these same people explain that soup is also a comfort food that not only nourishes and warms their insides but also makes them feel safe and loved.

There is also a connection between the woman's belly/womb and the soup kettle. Again, Neumann describes the "elementary character" of the feminine archetype as "containing." He states that the central feminine symbol is "the vessel." "The basic symbolic equation: Woman = body = vessel corresponds to what is perhaps mankind's—man's as well as woman's—most elemental experience of the feminine" (Neumann, 1991, p. 39).

For early cultures, the containing, vessel aspect of women often took expression in pottery that featured symbolic breasts. The Zuni women made breast-shaped pitchers. They left the nipple open until the pitcher was finished, then ritualistically sealed it off. The Zuni women believed that unless they performed this ritual, they would be barren or their children would die (Neumann, 1991, p. 123).

The Virgin Mother Mary was sometimes referred to as the "Holy Vase" (Harding, 1990, p. 136). Ships as vessels are therefore symbolically feminine. The ancient Greeks not only referred to a ship as *she* but also often used carved female figureheads on the bow. The captain was also referred to as the ship's husband and was expected to go down with the ship.

Jung touches on some of the feminine images and symbols in a summary description of the Great Mother:

> The mother symbol is archetypal and refers to a place of origin, to
> nature, that which passively creates, hence to substance and matter,
> to material nature, the lower body (womb) and the vegetative
> functions. It connotes also the unconscious, natural and instinctive

life, the physiological realm, the body in which we dwell or are contained, for the "mother" is also a vessel, the hollow form (uterus) foundations of consciousness (Jung, 1933, p. 24).

The containing, vessel aspect of the feminine character is in turn connected once again with water and life:

The natural elements that are essentially connected with vessel symbolism include both earth and water. This containing water is the primordial womb of life, from which in innumerable myths life is born. . . . But the maternal water not only contains; it also nourishes and transforms, since all living things build up and preserve their existence with water or milk of the earth (Neumann, 1991, pp. 47-48).

There is yet another mytho-symbolic connection between the transformative power of the cauldron or kettle and the transformative power of a woman's body. The Great Mother is also the "Great Container." Her body is both an extension and instrument of nature, the cauldron containing the amniotic soup wherein we are first stirred to life. The creation of life in a woman's body is a reenactment of the primordial moment when life was created in nature—an example of ontogeny literally recapitulating phylogeny.

In *The Moon and the Virgin*, Nor Hall refers to the primary work of woman as "transforming":

The work of woman is transformation: making something out of nothing: giving form to formless energy. Her instruments in this work are tripod and cauldron, her elements blood and milk. . . . She is both container and contained. . . . She transforms matter and is herself transformed (Hall, 1980, p. 169).

Hall cites Neumann, who outlines the three blood transformation mysteries of woman. The first is menstruation, wherein the girl is transformed into a woman. The second is pregnancy—the transformation of a lifeless biomass into a new human life. At the same time pregnancy brings with it an archetypal transformation of the woman from maiden to mother. And finally, there is a transformation of blood into milk.

Menstrual blood was also believed to have transformative powers—both good and bad—outside the womb. The blood of virgins, especially the first flow of a young girl, was considered especially potent (Hall, 1980, p. 173).

The cauldron, like the woman's belly/womb, was believed to be an instrument of transformation and regeneration. It was a central element in alchemy as well as many religions. "The cauldron is believed to have the power to change base material into spiritual, the mortal into immortal" (Harding, 1990, p. 140). Soup is also thought to have magical, transformative powers. In pretechnological societies, medicine men and witch doctors often "heal" the sick (who are frequently malnourished) with a cooked chicken, sometimes in the form of chicken soup.

Worshippers of the ancient Moon Goddess used a silver cauldron to collect animal and human blood, which they believed had restorative powers. Esther Harding makes reference to the fact that Vestal Virgins and priestesses used a silver cauldron, The Cauldron of Regeneration, to collect the blood of first-born children, prisoners, and animals that were beheaded at the alter of the Moon Goddess (Harding, 1990, p. 138). The blood was offered up to the Moon Goddess and was believed to have regenerative powers.

In exploring the latent mythology of soup, we have examined some of the mytho-symbolic imagery surrounding soup in order to understand the soul of soup, and at the same time understand the basis for the nurturing mother-child imagery that is the basis for the Campbell's Soup brand mythology. Through mythological amplification, you have come to understand what gives the image of a mother giving her child a bowl of soup its recognizable, archetypal power.

• • • • •

> **Maintenance Tip:**
> Periodically ask yourself this question: If my brand could "own" one image or one idea, what would it be?
>
> In this case, Campbell's Soup owns the image of a mother giving her child a bowl of soup. The Campbell's client and advertising team most likely arrived at this image intuitively, but by continually testing what your brand's level of ownership is for the brand's mythology, you can help keep advertising on track in furthering the brand's ownership of its image.

• • • • •

As you have seen in this exploration of the latent product mythology, the image of a mother giving a child a bowl of soup is a powerful, archetypal image that captures and conveys the essence of soup's appeal: a feeling of being loved and nurtured. It is an image that strikes the consumer not only on a conscious level but also on an unconscious/instinctive level.

Step 5: Guarding a Successful Brand Mythology

Campbell's Soup has used the image of a mother giving soup to her child, an image that stems from the category's existing, latent mythology, to build a brand mythology. This brand mythology has helped to create an enduring brand identity and personality for Campbell's Soup, which has, in turn, worked successfully to create an emotional bond between the brand and the consumer. Campbell's Soup has built one of America's favorite brands not simply by selling soup but also by selling mother love and goodness.

This may raise a question in your mind: Does this preclude the idea of Campbell's Soup having advertising that shows a father serving soup to his children? Of course not. Men also have a nurturing side, which may hold different kind of appeal. In other words, although the image of a man serving soup to his children may not have the same archetypal power, it may work because it is less expected. Moreover, the nurturing male image may also be appealing because it is consistent with the social changes occurring in our society, and it can help to keep Campbell's Soup's brand mythology contemporary and in step with the times. The nurturing male image puts a more contemporary spin on the core idea of nurturance, but it is still consistent with the brand's core values. Recall the advertising campaign for a "hearty" soup featuring Jimmy Stewart's voice—the all-American guy who appeals to us as a Superdad.

• • •
Evaluating a Successful Brand Mythology

Before you delve into Case Study 2, take a moment to address a series of questions that pertain to assessing how well your brand mythology is working in the marketplace. After all, Campbell's success doesn't ensure yours or help you determine how successful your competitors have become at owning their brand's mythology.

Once you have developed a thorough understanding of your brand mythology, you need to evaluate it—to understand whether it represents the best mythology for your brand. This is a complex question, and there are no easy, formulaic answers. However, there are some guidelines that can help you to evaluate existing brand mythologies. The first order of business is to determine whether the brand mythology is working, both in the marketplace and in the consumer's mind. Ideally, a successful, enduring brand mythology should work in both.

Testing Whether the Brand Mythology Works in the Marketplace

Longevity

The first way the brand success is measured is simple: longevity. Take a look at how long the brand has been around. Is it a well-established brand with a long history of advertising, or is it a relatively new brand that is just beginning to advertise? Obviously, if the brand has not been around long enough to develop and establish a brand mythology, it is impossible to determine whether the brand mythology is working. On the other hand, if the brand is well established, with a history of advertising, you should be able to learn whether the brand mythology is working in the marketplace.

Market Share

The key to determining how well the brand mythology is working in the marketplace is market share. Tracking studies, which collect and correlate market share data, advertising/media spending, and the consumer's attitudes and perceptions of your brand contrasted to competitive brands, are invaluable in assessing how well your brand mythology is working in the marketplace. Tracking studies enable you to determine what, if anything, your advertising (the brand mythology is communicated through advertising) is communicating and how well the advertising is working to maintain your brand's market share.

● ●

"The key to determining how well the brand mythology is working in the marketplace is market share."

● ●

For example, the study may tell you that your advertising is not working to communicate your brand positioning and/or the brand's attributes or benefits. This is a clear indication that you need to change your advertising. Or you may learn that your advertising is working to communicate your brand positioning, attributes, or benefits, but it is not helping to maintain market share. This would suggest that your brand positioning or the attributes and benefits communicated in your advertising are not compelling enough to get the consumer to use your brand. You then would need to rethink your brand positioning, attributes, and benefits in terms of what you wish to communicate.

Look to your competitors for insights by asking yourself:

- Which of the competitive brands seems to be doing the best job of building or maintaining market share?
- What kind of positioning is that brand using?
- What kind of benefits is that brand promising?
- What kind of brand mythology has its advertisers created through the advertising?

You can choose to use the same brand positioning and even the same benefits as the more successful brands—but not the same brand mythology. For example, if you create a brand mythology for a brand of cigarettes, it would not be a good idea to try to create a brand mythology around the American cowboy. You must develop your own unique brand mythology; otherwise, the consumer will perceive your brand as a copycat brand (not to mention the fact that your competitor will probably bring legal action against you).

• • • • •

> ## Maintenance Tip:
> It may be stating the obvious, but if you are dealing with a stable brand with a large, growing, or stable market share, chances are the brand mythology is working reasonably well in the marketplace. If, on the other hand, you're dealing with an unstable brand that is losing market share in a stable or growing market, you must determine if the reason for losing market share is due to an inappropriate, obsolete, or ineffective brand mythology, or to changing market conditions.
>
> Unfortunately, advertisers with brands that are losing market share all too often make the mistake of changing their advertising and/or overall brand mythologies, when the problem is due to changing market conditions. For example, you may be losing market share because you are in a category that is changing—where, for example, consumers are switching to low-fat brands. In this kind of situation, changing the advertising and the brand mythology will only exacerbate the situation by creating a confused brand mythology and blurring the brand's image.
>
> If you have an ailing brand, discern whether market conditions— which have nothing to do with the brand mythology—are affecting the brand's market share.

• • • • •

If you are fortunate enough to have a profitable brand with dominant market share, you still need to understand whether the brand mythology is the best that it could be. In order to do this, you must also determine how well the brand is working in the consumer's mind.

Testing Whether the Brand Mythology Works in the Consumer's Mind

In order to determine whether the brand mythology is working in the consumer's mind, you learn to what extent the brand mythology is communicating a brand positioning and benefits that are relevant, motivating, and compelling. Once again you must turn to consumer research: the who, why, and how. You must come away with an understanding of the perceived brand user; the consumer's motivations for using the brand (product-level motivations as well as emotional/psychological motivations); and how the brand is used.

For Campbell's Soup you would most likely glean the following:

- Who: The heavy Campbell's Soup user is perceived as a mother with young children.

- Why: The motivations for using soup are these:

- Product-level motivations
    —Trusted brand name/brand I grew up with
    —Quality product
    —Taste/kids love the taste
    —Nourishing and easy to prepare

- Emotional/psychological-level motivations
    —It's a comfort food
    —It makes the consumer feel safe and secure
    —It makes the consumer feel loved
    —It gives the consumer a nurtured feeling

- How: Soup is generally perceived as an accompaniment to other foods (such as soup and sandwich) or a quick and easy meal or snack. It is used most often for lunch, and soup consumption is higher in winter and in colder regions of the country.

An understanding of the brand's who, why, and how for consumers together with an understanding of the brand (using the BIP, brand snapshot, brand personality, and brand essence) should help you determine whether the brand mythology is working in the consumer's mind. There are a number of key issues that can help you in assessing your brand mythology.

Awareness

Ask whether the target consumer is adequately aware of the brand mythology. Obviously, in order for a brand mythology to work, it must be well established in the consumer's mind. You must examine the brand's perceptual inventory and BIP. If the consumer has no perceptions of the brand or vague, unclear ones, if they are not sure what the brand stands for, you have an awareness problem. You need to make sure that your communications (brand advertising) are consistent and are reaching your target audience with enough frequency to make the consumer aware of your brand mythology.

Appropriateness/Appeal/Relevance

Ask whether the target consumer buys into the brand mythology. Is the brand mythology appropriate given the intended consumer? Does the brand mythology's soul or core values, personality, user imagery, and overall identity appeal to the target consumer?

This is a difficult but critical issue. If the brand mythology or some aspect of the brand mythology (personality, user imagery, and so on) is not appropriate for or does not appeal to the target consumer, the brand mythology will not be as effective as it could be, or it will be rejected entirely. The same is true with relevance. You may have a terrific brand mythology, but if the message it communicates is not relevant to the target consumer, it will not work. If the brand positioning and benefits communicated by the brand mythology do not mesh with the consumer's motivations for using the product, the mythology will not be relevant or motivating.

• • • • •

> **Maintenance Tip:**
> Sometimes a brand mythology that is not working can be easily fixed, and sometimes it is difficult if not impossible to fix. Once established, the core image/value or soul of a brand is difficult and expensive to change. It requires "major surgery." Marlboro, which early in its life cycle was more well known abroad, was able to successfully change its core brand image/value and identity from a brand that was originally an elegant woman's cigarette to a rugged man's cigarette. It was done when Marlboro was not well known in this country (which no doubt made the changeover easier)—but it was still a "sex change." In most cases, you should change a brand's soul or core values only as a last resort.

• • • • •

More typically, you are dealing with other elements of the brand, such as "tweaking" or updating its personality and user imagery. You must continually reassess your brand mythology to ensure that it remains viable. Brand mythologies need to be continually contemporized and rejuvenated/revitalized in order to continue to appeal to consumers. This is especially true of brand mythologies that are "borrowed mythologies," ones that are essentially a reflection of our cultural mythologies.

The question of obsolescence comes up with many well-established brands. Their core values are usually still relevant and viable, but the brand's imagery, personalties, and sensibilities often become out of synch with the times, and they need to be rejuvenated and contemporized.

You can also change the brand positioning and benefits communicated by the brand mythology, but this is more difficult, because it is closer to the brand's core. For example, you might decide to reposition a brand of dishwashing detergent from a positioning focused on the brand's efficacy (cleans better than other detergents) to a positioning that focuses on the brand's environmentally safe formula (will not pollute the environment). The brand's efficacy would most likely still be communicated in the advertising but the primary focus would be on the environmental advantages of its formula. The key point is that you would still use the same brand mythology. For example, if you had used advertising to create a brand mythology around a mythical character, Harry—a new age husband who pitches in at home and regularly does the dishes—you could continue to show Harry to maintain that same brand mythology, but use him to communicate the environmental benefits of your brand.

Credibility

The overall brand mythology must be believable—otherwise, the consumer will reject it. The credibility issue typically comes up when the advertising/brand mythology overpromises, making product claims that the product simply cannot deliver. Consumers will tolerate some overpromise or hype—they understand that advertising is a form of selling. If you tell consumers that your packaged cakes taste as good as bakery cakes and in fact the packaged cakes taste almost as good, consumers will generally go along with some exaggeration. But if your packaged cakes taste awful (not even as good as other packaged cakes) consumers will feel that you are trying to pull the wool over their eyes and will understandably reject your brand.

The other area where the issue of credibility comes up is when the brand tries to radically alter its image. For example, if your brand is perceived as a value or budget brand and you try to create a brand mythology to reposition the brand as an upscale, top-shelf brand, you will generally encounter credibility problems. Any time a brand mythology flies in the face of existing consumer perceptions and beliefs about a brand, you will probably have a problem with credibility. Sometimes you can overcome the credibility problem by delivering in terms of the product. In other words, time the advertising change with changes in the product so that it is indeed a high quality, top-shelf product.

• • •

Case 2: Harley-Davidson Motorcycles   (Managing a Brand Mythology with a Powerful Underground Element)

The Harley-Davidson motorcycle provides an interesting example of a product with a powerful, appealing brand mythology, which, for a while the company lost sight of, then rediscovered. Harley-Davidson's mythology seems to be partly derived from the latent product mythology and partly borrowed from an aspect or our cultural mythology. The Harley-Davidson product line features a fascinating brand mythology because it also has a powerful underground element which, although it contributes to the brand's mystique, also has a negative aspect that must be managed and kept under control to avoid undermining the appealing aspects of the Harley mythology.

Harley-Davidson is more than a motorcycle company; it's a part of our cultural history—an American legend and tribute to Yankee ingenuity. The Milwaukee company was started in 1901 on a "shoestring and a prayer" by William Harley and Arthur Davidson—in a 10-by-15-foot wooden shed. The prototype Harley, which was essentially a motorized bicycle, used a carburetor that was fashioned from a tomato juice can. Through the years Harley-Davidson grew and prospered and went on to establish a highly successful racing heritage that helped to build its reputation.

Harley-Davidson motorcycles saw combat in two world wars and was one of two American motorcycle companies (the other was Indian Motorcycles) that survived the Great Depression. It remained family owned until 1965, when it was taken over by AMF.

Despite its relatively small size, Harley-Davidson is ranked high on *Fortune* magazine's list of most-admired corporations (Caminiti, 1992, p. 74). For many years, Harley-Davidson built a high-quality, uniquely appealing American motorcycle. At the same time, Harley-Davidson also built a uniquely appealing brand mythology. It is a brand mythology that has worked to build a strong, enduring brand, mystique, and cult following that made Harley-Davidson the envy of other motorcycle manufacturers.

In *Quintessence*, Betty Cornfeld and Owen Edwards list the Harley-Davidson FLH Electroglide Classic, also known as the "Hallelujah Machine," as the quintessence of motorcycleness (Cornfeld and Edwards, 1983).

For years, Harley-Davidson could do no wrong. But then in the 1970s, the company began to falter—to the point where it was on the verge of bankruptcy. Japanese companies had flooded the market with sleeker, more modern looking motorcycles that offered better quality and lower price tags. Badly shaken and vulnerable, Harley-Davidson made a desperate attempt to copy the Japanese by introducing smaller, sleeker motorcycles, but the company couldn't beat the Japanese at their own game.

Like American auto makers, Harley-Davidson had become complacent and lost its competitive edge. The company had lost sight of the commitment to quality that had built the company. To compete against the Japanese, they had to get back to basics—they had to build a motorcycle that was second to none. But Harley-Davidson had not only lost its sense of commitment to quality but also its identity. The company had to get back in touch with its spiritual center—its brand essence and identity. Harley-Davidson had to rediscover its brand mythology.

Richard Teerlink (CEO of Harley-Davidson) and his top executives went riding with Harley riders to become reacquainted with what consumers wanted. The group came away convinced that they needed not only to focus on making "quality improvements" but also to stick to making the kind of "macho bikes" that had built the Harley legend (Caminiti, February 10, 1992, p. 77). By focusing on the big, macho bikes (hogs) that built the Harley-Davidson brand, Harley's CEO was instinctively getting back to the company's original mythology.

Step 1: Uncovering and Understanding the Brand Mythology

Again, the first step in understanding the brand mythology is to examine the brand's overall perceptual inventory (the images, values, feelings, and symbols associated with the brand) and draw from the perceptual inventory those images that best capture and convey what the Harley-Davidson brand means to the consumer. Using the BIP technique, you would find that the images, feelings, symbols, and associations that compose the Harley-Davidson BIP would probably look something like this:

Male

Macho

Excitement

Freedom

American

Power

Rebel

Marlon Brando

The Wild One

Bikers

Hell's Angels

Using the brand snapshot technique, you might find that the core image that captures the essence of Harley-Davidson and the image around which its brand mythology is built would be something like this:

I picture Marlon Brando wearing a black leather jacket, aviator sunglasses, and heavy boots, riding on a Harley.

I see Peter Fonda and Dennis Hopper roaring down the highway on their Harleys to the tune of "Born to be Wild."

Step 2: Reveal the Brand Personality

The brand personality (what the brand would be like if it were a person) would also undoubtedly be masculine and rebellious—a young, male rebel in black leather roaring down the highway.

Step 3: Finding the Heart of the Harley-Davidson Brand Mythology

In order to understand the Harley-Davidson brand mythology, you must once again understand its basis. What is behind the brand mythology? Where does its power come from? Is the brand mythology rooted in the latent product mythology—in the essence or soul of "motorcycleness?" Or is the brand mythology rooted in some aspect of America's cultural mythology?

Step 4: Exploring the Latent Product Mythology

The Harley-Davidson brand mythology has its roots both in the latent product mythology (macho motorcycles), and in an aspect of America's cultural mythology. During the years following World War II, there were thousands of restless, unemployed veterans. Disengaged, disenchanted, and unable to settle down to a "normal" life, some of the veterans began traveling the California highways on motorcycles—big, macho, road bikes—Harley-Davidsons.

Living on the fringe of American society, they began to band together to form packs or gangs, of which Hell's Angels is perhaps the most famous. The original founders of Hell's Angels were World War II aviators who called themselves Hell's Angels during the war years. These former aviators were outsiders with nothing to tie them down: no commitments, no responsibilities—postmodern man on a motorcycle.

The postwar California motorcycle gangs represented a new cultural phenomenon in America—a subculture with its own mythology and ethos. And in the 1950s, Hollywood tried to capture and convey this motorcycle subculture in the film, *The Wild One* (a case of Hollywood mythologizing a mythology—as is often the case). The movie was based on a little known incident that occurred in the small town of Hollister, a farming community at the foothills of the Diablo mountains. Drawn by a motorcycle rally and Fourth of July celebration, a number of motorcycle gangs got into a drunken brawl. The incident was reported in *Life* magazine and happened to catch the eye of an obscure movie producer named Stanley Kramer. The rest is history.

The film, now a classic, created a sensation and catapulted Marlon Brando to stardom. A brooding Brando seemed to embody all of the qualities of the nomadic rebel bikers: their wildness and rebelliousness, their aimlessness, and their existential angst.

In some sense, *The Wild One* was not only a movie, it was a visual trope. The image of a pouty, truculent Marlon Brando, wearing a black leather motorcycle jacket, standing alongside his big macho motorcycle, roared into America's psyche. The film was a terrific, two-hour commercial for big macho motorcycles like the Harley-Davidson. In one fell swoop, Hollywood not only mythologized the postwar motorcycle subculture, it also established the big macho motorcycle and black leather motorcycle jacket as their symbols. Even today, Hell's Angels requires all of its members to own a big (1200cc or more) Harley-Davidson motorcycle. And Hell's Angels marriage ceremonies use the Harley-Davidson Motorcycle Manual as their "bible" (Lavigne, 1987, p. 121).

The imagery and symbolism established in *The Wild One* was reinforced during the psychedelic years of the 1960s, when Peter Fonda and Dennis Hopper rode their Harley-Davidsons across the screen in *Easy Rider*. The spirit of the film and the essence of Harley-Davidson seemed to be captured in that one scene where Fonda and Hopper are roaring down an open highway on their Harleys—to the tune of "Born to Be Wild." The feeling captured in this image and music—a feeling of wildness, power, and freedom—is the brand essence or spiritual center of the Harley-Davidson brand mythology.

Motorcycle Symbolism

To further understand the latent product mythology of motorcycles, you need to look at some of the symbolism surrounding motorcycles. What is the symbolic connection between men and motorcycles? However, because motorcycles have only been around for a hundred years or so, you must look to the motorcycle's counterpart in pretechnological times: the horse. The similarity between a motorcycle and a horse is obvious. Both are straddled and ridden. And a man on a motorcycle is archetypically akin to a man on a horse. In fact, a popular motorcycle magazine is called Iron Horse. Understanding the symbolic, psychic significance of horses, and the image of a man on a horse, is the key to further understanding the motorcycle's latent mythology.

Jung stated that the horse is "a symbol of the animal component in man" (Jung, 1990, p. 277), and "it represents the nonhuman psyche, the subhuman, animal side, the unconscious. . . . The horse is a dynamic and vehicular power: It carries one away like a surge of instinct. . . . It is subject to panic like all instinctive creatures who lack higher consciousness" (Jung, 1990, p. 107). Pegasus, the mythical winged horse, was said to have sprung from the decapitated head of Medusa, who was beheaded by Perseus. Medusa represents the Great Mother (the primordial womb from which all life springs and the primordial tomb to which all life must someday return). And Poseidon, the monster God of the sea, was Medusa's "invincible phallic consort" and Pegasus' father (Neumann, 1973, p. 216). "The horse belongs to the chthonic-phallic world; he represents nature and instinct, which are all-powerful in half-human creatures like the Centaurs" (Neumann, 1973, p. 217). Centaurs (half men and half horse) also represented the dual spiritual and animal nature of man.

Because of its speed, the horse also signifies the wind. In German legend, the wind is known as the "wild huntsman in lustful pursuit of the maiden" (Jung, 1990, p. 278), which again cycles back to the connection between horses and the wild, instinctive libido.

On some level, the motorcycle, like the horse, is a symbol of all that is wild and instinctive. This wild, libidinal instinct is often manifested as feelings of sexuality and power. For example, pubescent girls often dream of wild horses, which in the psychoanalytic literature is interpreted as an awakening of their sexuality.

A man on a motorcycle is archetypically similar to a man on a horse. Historically, men on horseback are associated with the Warrior archetype. The use of horses in warfare can be traced back to the Middle East at about 4000 B.C. Empires were won and lost on the strength of the cavalry soldier. In the thirteenth century, Genghis Khan and his mongol hordes used horse-mounted archers to conquer Russia, China, Central Asia, Burma, Vietnam, India, and Persia, Syria, and Palestine (Windrow and Hook, 1989, p. 31).

It is sometimes erroneously believed that Genghis Khan's army won so many victories because of their great numbers, but in fact he was often outnumbered. His victories were due to the grit and determination of his mongol soldiers and his cavalry—his "invincible horse-archers" (Windrow and Hook, 1989, p. 32). Genghis Khan's armies were ruthless; they ravaged the countries they conquered, blazing a trail of killing, plunder, and rape. They unleashed a demonic male energy that terrorized the world. War is the ultimate expression of the what Hill calls the "negative, dynamic masculine." In the writings of his time, Genghis Khan's armies were described as "a force more supernatural than human"—as "demons loosed from Tartarus" (Windrow and Hook, 1989, p. 32).

Motorcycles and Masculinity

Men and motorcycles seem to go together. Right from their inception, motorcycles have been almost exclusively a male phenomenon. The motorcycle has a definite male character. In contrast to the elemental feminine character that was described earlier as "containing" and represented by the uterus and vessel, the elemental male character is projecting/penetrating and represented by the projecting/penetrating penis. Gareth Hill, a clinical social worker and Jungian analyst, describes the "dynamic masculine," as represented by "the image of the penetrating phallus" (Hill, 1992, p. 9).

Women are also excited by motorcycles, but usually from a different perspective. Women are excited by the maleness of it all, by the sight of males full of themselves, high on testosterone—strutting their stuff. And the men are in turn excited by women who get excited. This sexuality is captured and successfully exploited in motorcycle magazines, such as *Iron Horse*, which depict seminaked women on their cover, symbolically stroking or straddling a motorcycle.

The Demonic Masculine

Because of its association with motorcycle gangs like Hell's Angels, the big macho motorcycle has also become a negative symbol of the Warrior—his demonic side, which is manifested in unprovoked hostility, violence, killing, rape, and war. The negative aspect of the Warrior is what Hill calls the "negative dynamic masculine, whereby the creative male thrust is perverted into destructiveness, as expressed in the images of rape, directed violence, paranoia, life-taking technologies, and disregard for nature and the ecological consequences of one's actions" (Hill, 1992, p. 12).

The image of a motorcycle gang like Hell's Angels swooping down to terrorize an unsuspecting town is reminiscent of Genghis Khan's mongol hordes—a demonic force—malevolent marauders (there is actually a California motorcycle gang that calls itself the Mongols).

The horse is also a symbol of the demonic. Because it represents the instinctive, unconscious, animal nature in humans, horses mythologically symbolize the antichrist (devil) and the demonic:

> The devil has a horse's hoof and sometimes a horse's form. At critical moments he shows the proverbial cloven hoof. . . . The devil, like the nightmare, rides the sleeper; hence it is said that those who have nightmares are ridden by the devil. In Persian lore the devil is the steed of God. He represents the sexual instinct; consequently at the Witches' Sabbath he appears in the form of a goat or horse (Jung, 1990, p. 277).

Some notorious motorcycle gangs capitalize on this association by using names and symbols that represent the demonic, such as the Pagans (with their symbol of "a horned fire god who brandishes a sword and sits crosslegged on an arch of flames" (Lavigne, 1987, p. 170).

Cycle "Old Ladies" and Their Demon Lovers

In his harrowing book, *Hell's Angels*, Yves Lavigne gives us a shocking view of life inside the Hell's Angels motorcycle gang. The book gives readers an eye-opening view of a world ruled by unbridled, negative, male energy. Murder, rape, violence, and drug dealing are commonplace. When the male is completely cut off from his feeling, feminine side, women become devalued. Lavigne says that in motorcycle gangs like Hell's Angels, women have no rights; they are regarded as personal property ("old ladies") to be used by any of the club members, or they are used as prostitutes.

Despite this, bikers seem to have no trouble attracting women.

It is against this backdrop of the Warrior archetype run amok that Harley-Davidson sought to revitalize its brand mythology in the 1970s.

Step 5: Walking a Fine Line

Over the years, Harley-Davidson has, for obvious reasons, tried to downplay certain aspects of its brand mythology, primarily its association with outlaw motorcycle gangs like the Hell's Angels. Harley-Davidson's toughest marketing task is keeping the negative aspects of its incredibly powerful brand mythology under control.

This seems to be borne out by its advertising, which generally emphasizes the positive, dynamic masculine and the freedom and excitement that come with owning a Harley. Obviously everyone who rides a Harley is not an outlaw biker. On the other hand, undoubtedly, the negative elements of the Harley-Davidson brand mythology have contributed to the Harley mystique. The rebel/bad boy image and outlaw biker mythology may operate on a fantasy level. Men like to see themselves as exhibiting a little of the negative, dynamic masculine. And many women seem to like it, too.

• • •
Evaluating a Revamped Brand Mythology

Consumers who buy Harley-Davidson motorcycles aren't buying just a motorcycle, they are buying a mythology. In fact, Harley-Davidson iron-on decals are sold in malls and on the Home Shopping Network—ostensibly, for people who want to be part of the Harley-Davidson mythology but either can't afford or don't want the motorcycle.

The advertising and marketing people who manage and maintain the Harley-Davidson brand have a unique situation. The brand has an underground mythology that has created a powerful, appealing brand mystique, but that if fully acknowledged could overpower the brand, create a negative brand image, and alienate many potential Harley-Davidson consumers. There are thousands of Harley-Davidson enthusiasts who are not outlaw bikers (Malcolm Forbes was one notable example).

The question remains, how can Harley-Davidson maintain its rebel image, which clearly works to fuel the brand's mystique, without involving some of the strongly negative images and associations of outlaw biker gangs? Harley-Davidson addressed this question by developing an advertising strategy that avoids the image issue altogether, focusing instead on the product's attributes and benefits.

Harley-Davidson's advertising positions the brand as the great American freedom machine. The advertising focuses on the emotional benefits of owning a Harley—the feeling of freedom and excitement. This is a wise emphasis. It would be impossible to employ the rebel image in advertising without also bringing up all of the strong negative biker gang associations.

Besides, Harley's underground mystique is sustained by Hollywood and word of mouth.

In addition to doing a fine job of managing and revamping a difficult brand mythology, Harley-Davidson redoubled its commitment to making a high-quality, uniquely American motorcycle. Harley-Davidson motorcycles are sought the world over today. Because of the company's commitment to quality, its production is limited. If you are looking to purchase a 1993 Harley-Davidson, get in line—there is a waiting list.

• • •

Case 3: Managing Budweiser's Male Identity in a Changing World

Budweiser offers an excellent example of a brand that uses a complex mix of mythical characters, symbols, places, and moments—all of which work on different levels to engage and entertain, and to communicate important product attributes and benefits as well as powerful emotional and psychological benefits. Indeed, Budweiser advertising has created an extraordinarily powerful, compelling brand mythology that has helped to make Budweiser Beer one of the most successful, enduring brands in the world.

As you will learn, the company's primary challenge has been to monitor societal changes and to ensure that Budweiser's brand mythology stays in sync with today's male image.

Step 1: Uncovering and Understanding the Budweiser Brand Mythology

Once again, you begin by uncovering Budweiser's unique perceptual inventory of imagery, symbols, feelings, and associations. You then cull from the perceptual inventory those elements that, in the consumer's mind, most accurately represent the essence of Budweiser. This represents Budweiser's BIP. Budweiser's BIP would look something like this:

Maleness/Machismo/Male Identity

Clydesdales

Eagle

Beechwood Aging

Red-and-White can

Blue-collar Male

Ed McMahon

Crisp, Clean Taste

Spotted Dog

Budweiser's Use of Symbolism

Budweiser's use of symbols, both to enhance and communicate the Budweiser brand mythology, is exemplary. The Budweiser brand has a rich array of symbols and imagery that have become part of the brand's unique perceptual inventory.

A symbol works to break through our conscious psyche and evoke imagery and feelings that touch our soul.

The Clydesdales

The Budweiser Clydesdales are a superb example of a symbol that has become an enduring brand icon. They are one of the strongest associations consumers have with the Budweiser brand. The Clydesdales are an appropriate, complex advertising symbol; one that seems to capture both the rich, quality heritage of Budweiser, and the dignity and pride of the working-class male.

The Clydesdales were introduced in 1933 when August A. Busch, Sr., sent an eight-horse hitch of Clydesdales to New York and selected areas of the country. In one highly publicized incident, the Clydesdales strode down New York's Fifth Avenue to deliver a case of Budweiser to Governor Al Smith. Newspapers reported that the Clydesdales drew such huge crowds that traffic came to a halt, and extra police had to be brought in. When people see the Clydesdales for the first time, they are truly astonished by their size and magnificence. The average weight of a Clydesdale is about 2,000 pounds, and their average height is about 17 hands (one = 4 inches). The horses were originally bred in Scotland and are all direct descendants of Baron Buchlyvie, a champion Clydesdale that was foaled in 1900.

The power of a complex advertising symbol like the Clydesdales stems from its appeal, appropriateness, immediate recognition, and immediate evocation of the brand's mythology with all of its rich imagery and feelings. Budweiser drinkers wax poetic when you mention the Clydesdales:

I love the Clydesdales . . . they're really beautiful.

I like the way they walk . . . like they're real proud.

> Those Clydesdales are really something. . . . I went to see them at Busch Gardens. You can't believe how big they really are; they're majestic.

When you push blue-collar beer drinkers to understand the significance of the Clydesdales, you find that on some level the blue-collar beer drinker not only admires the majestic Clydesdales but he also identifies with them:

> They're big and strong . . . they're masculine . . . they're workhorses . . . they work hard, but they have a lot of pride and dignity. They carry themselves like royalty.

Anheuser-Busch Eagle

The Anheuser Busch eagle is second only to the Clydesdales in terms of the images beer drinkers associate with Budweiser beer. This is hardly surprising, because the eagle has been around since the 1870s and has been a corporate symbol of Anheuser Busch. To their credit, the Anheuser-Busch people recognized early on the importance of creating and registering trademarks. "The first trademark adopted by the E. Anheuser Co.'s Brewing Association comprised the representation of an eagle with raised wings, in association with a capital A, and a shield constituting a perch for the eagle" (Krebs, 1953, p. 408).

The letter A has some positive symbolic associations. A or alpha is the first letter in the alphabet. Alpha represents the highest; A is the highest grade. But the eagle is clearly the more powerful element. Beer drinkers love the Anheuser-Busch eagle. When asked to free-associate, consumers respond with two dominant associations:

- America—The package's eagle reminds beer drinkers of the bald eagle—the symbol of America. Indeed, the Anheuser-Busch A and eagle has helped to give Budweiser a uniquely American character. Through the years, Budweiser's perceived American character has been further reinforced by other symbols like Lady Liberty, its red, white, and blue packaging, and its advertising that has always been patriotic and supportive of American ideals.

- Power—The other most common association that beer drinkers make with eagles is a sense of their power.

The eagle is indeed powerful and awesome. It is a bird of prey, with a unique ability to spot its prey from high in the sky, and swoop down to kill it with its powerful talons. The eagle is beautiful and majestic, but also ruthless and unfeeling. The notion of an "eagle eye" has some physiological basis. The eyes of eagles, hawks, and other birds of prey have evolved so that they have two or more deep recesses (foveal pits) in the back of their retinas that enables them to focus on a small object such as a rabbit from distances of as much as five miles.

In mythology, the eagle is clearly masculine, solar, celestial—a symbol of the sky-god. The eagle, hawk, and other birds of prey are symbolically different than other birds that symbolize the soul and are often associated with goddesses and other feminine imagery. Athena, the Greek Goddess who sprang from Zeus's head, often took the form of a bird. The eagle also stands apart from other powerful animals such as the lion, in that there is no ambivalence about its gender symbolism. The lion, which is both a masculine and feminine symbol, is often an escort of the early God-desses. The Roman goddess Cybele has a chariot that is drawn by lions.

The eagle symbolizes the ascendance of the masculine spirit. It soars above the earth, flying, unblinking toward the sun and the heavens; the eagle is associated with Zeus, the masculine principle, and the penetrating power of the intellect. The Egyptian God Horus was born to his mother Isis as the sun and is depicted with the head of a hawk (the hawk has essentially the same significance as the eagle). American Indians wore headdresses made of eagle feathers as a symbol of the Thunderbird, the Great Spirit.

The eagle is a symbol of power, strength, courage, fearlessness, and pride. But unlike other powerful animals, which only represent physical power, the eagle also represents the power of the unique human intellect and spirit. In mythology, the eagle is often pitted against the bull, lion, or serpent, and the eagle always emerges victorious. The bird symbolizes the victory of human intellect and higher spiritual nature over the lower, instinctive, animal nature (Jung, 1990, p. 59).

The eagle is also a symbol of war and the warrior. It is depicted holding Zeus/Jupiter's lightning bolt in its talons. Eagles are widely used as military symbols and insignias. The bald eagle, the symbol of America, carries an olive branch, which is a symbol of peace, but it also carries a talon full of arrows (a symbol of war)—just in case. The eagle's association with war and warriors can be traced back to the Babylonian culture, in which an eagle is depicted as the escort of the god Marduk, who overthrew his goddess grandmother and who represents the emergence of a Warrior sensibility and culture.

The final step toward understanding Budweiser's brand mythology, soul, and overall identity is to take those elements from the rank-ordered list that most connote "Budweiserness" and qualitatively probe them for insights and a deeper understanding of what these elements mean in the consumer's psyche.

Step 2: Revealing the Brand Personality

Maleness and male identity together with a sense of patriotism are at the core of the Budweiser brand mythology. Budweiser has always had one of the strongest male identities in the beer category. If you ask male beer drinkers to rank beer brands in terms of which ones are most masculine or macho, Budweiser is consistently perceived as the beer with the strongest male identity. On some level, beer drinkers recognize that a beer's image is important because it says something about the beer drinker—after all, it is your choice. A beer with a strong, even tough, masculine personality is often preferable in the male world where there is an adversarial, confrontational aspect that underlies most male interactions.

• • • • •

> **Maintenance Tip:**
> One of the questions I used to ask beer drinkers to assess a beer's machismo was: You walk into a strange bar full of tough, working-class guys. When you walk into the bar, there is a hush and the guys turn to look at you. The bartender asks: "What'll ya have?" In this situation, which beer would you feel most comfortable ordering?
>
> Because of its strong male identity, Budweiser was invariably the beer drinker's first choice.

• • • • •

Step 3: Finding the Heart of the Budweiser Brand Mythology

Budweiser has created a powerful, compelling, essentially male brand mythology, a mythical male world that celebrates maleness, traditional male values (such Warrior values as independence, strength, and courage). The male identity that is at the heart of the Budweiser brand mythology is based on the Warrior-Hero archetype. The Bud Man is everyman, every guy who has had to go out and do battle in the world—to prove that he has what it takes to make it in a man's world. The Budweiser brand mythology is a paean to "the average Joe;" at the same time, it also celebrates the work ethic and America. The Budweiser brand mythology connects with male beer drinkers on an emotional level by providing inherently compelling emotional/psychological benefits: a sense of masculinity/male identity, recognition, feelings of patriotism, and self-esteem.

At the same time, Budweiser's brand mythology also works at the product level to communicate Budweiser's commitment to quality and compelling product attributes/benefits (great taste supported by beechwood aging) and to continually assert Budweiser's leadership: "The King of Beers."

The Budweiser brand mythology is a complex mythology that comes out of the brand's heritage, the latent product mythology, and American culture. The brand's rich heritage as a quality beer manufacturer is reflected in its imagery (Clydesdales, Anheuser-Busch eagle, the red and white label, "The King of Beers" slogan, and so on). The Budweiser brand mythology also has at its core the male beer drinker. The idea of building a brand mythology and brand identity around maleness or a sense of masculine identity and patriotism comes out of the product's latent mythology as well as some aspects of America's cultural mythology.

Step 4: Exploring the Latent Product Mythology

Like soup, beer has been around as long as humankind. There is evidence of beer drinking dating back to a Babylonian clay tablet that depicts a scene showing the preparation of beer in 6000 BC. And the cuneiform tablets of the ancient Sumerians depict people sitting around a large vessel drinking beer from straws. People, gods, and goddesses were given a daily allotment of beer, and judging by some of the remaining records, some of those early goddesses could really put it away.

In the pre-Hellenic matriarchal cultures, women were generally in charge of watching over the food supply (such as grains)—and the beer. The Babylonians had two goddesses to watch over their beer: Ninkasi and Siris. Women were also in charge of serving beer. In the Epic of Gilgamesh, the earliest recorded hero-myth, Gilgamesh mourns the loss of his comrade-in-arms, Enkidu, by drinking beer and recounting his sorrows to the old ale-woman. Sumerian Babylonian taverns were maintained exclusively by women (apparently the world's first barmaids), with charges and payments recorded on wet clay tablets . . . a young woman named Ku-bau, the forerunner of all barmaids who married well, founded a royal dynasty at Kish in 3100 BC (Waldo, 1958, p. 12).

The Egyptians undoubtedly learned how to make beer from the Sumerians, and they passed it along to the Greeks, who in turn passed it along to the Romans; and the Romans introduced beer to the Saxons and northern races, for whom it became a dietary mainstay. Early on the Germans developed a beer heritage and a reputation for brewing great beers. In AD 99, the Roman historian Tacitus reported that beer drinking had already established itself in the Teutonic culture.

The Scandinavian, Germanic, and Celtic tribes all brewed a beer-like beverage—either from grains (ale) or from honey and water (mead). By the writing of Beowulf, the beer hall and mead hall were already an established part of the culture. Ancient Norse legends feature the mythical Valhalla, the safe haven to which the Valkyries, Odin's warrior maidens, carried heroic men who were slain in battle—and where the heroes were greeted with horns brimming with ale.

The alchemists dubbed alcohol the *aqua vitae* ("water of life"). In classical mythology, alcoholic drinks (especially wine) are associated with

Dionysus/Bacchus. There is an ambivalence attached to both the god and the festivals in his honor. On the one hand, Dionysus (and his Roman counterpart, Bacchus) is described in an early Greek poem as the "joy-god":

> He whose locks are bound with gold,
> Ruddy Bacchus, Comrade of the Maenads, whose
> Blithe torch blazes.

On the other hand, Dionysus is also perceived as the "heartless god, savage, brutal":

> He who with a mocking laugh
> Hunts his prey,
> Snares and drags him to his death
> With his Bacchanals (Hamilton, 1969, p. 59).

In a similar manner, the Dionysian/Bacchanalian festival has both an uplifting, joyful aspect and a darker, orgiastic one. On the positive side, the Dionysian festival celebrates spring, the first appearance of new vines and nature's continuing cycles of renewal. This takes expression in a joyous outdoor ceremony that has elements of both theater and religion. However, the worship of Dionysus also has a scary, negative aspect that is represented by the drunken maenads who in their orgiastic frenzy tear apart living creatures and smear themselves with their blood.

The ambivalent mythological images reflect alcohol's ambivalent effects on the human psyche. On the one hand, alcohol can cheer the spirit and help the weak take heart. On the other hand, alcohol can also unleash the murderous, instinctive, unfeeling aspect of the human psyche. Alcohol works on the higher centers of the brain. It numbs the conscious part of our brain and brings us in touch with the unconscious psyche—our instinctive, feminine nature that we share with other animals.

The popularity of alcohol lies in its ability to help us "forget our troubles" or at least not care about them. But, as William James has pointed out, the other reason for alcohol's popularity is that it provides a quick-and-easy vehicle for entering the unconscious and nonordinary states of consciousness—states of ecstasy. Ecstasy can be associated with divinity and higher states of consciousness. However, it is not without its dangers. Ecstasy and states of intoxication are also associated with the Terrible Mother "madness," and the "dissolution of the ego":

> The negative intoxicant and poison—in contrast to medicine—and everything which leads to stupor, enchantment, helplessness, and dissolution, belong to this sphere of seduction by the "young witch." In the negative mysteries of drunkenness and stupor, the

personality and consciousness are "regressively dissolved"; poisoned by negative orgiastic sexuality, narcotics, or magic potions, they succumb to extinction and madness" (Neumann, 1991, p. 74).

Before the Middle Ages, the brewing of beer was left to women. Women would brew simple beer from a grain mash that they fermented in their cauldron (again, note the transformative powers of woman at work!). Beer-making recipes were handed down from mother to daughter, and a young woman's ability to brew a good beer was an important virtue that added to her appeal among would-be suitors. When the young girl married, she and her mother brewed a big batch of "bride ale" for the wedding feast. However, in Medieval times, monks and monasteries became famous for producing higher-quality beers, and beer making gradually became less the responsibility of women.

Although women have been drinking beer as long as men, beer drinking gradually came to be more closely associated with men and Warrior cultures. That perception still exists among beer drinkers. Beer drinking conjures up images of German beer halls and Vikings celebrating their latest victory. In modern times the predominant user imagery is still masculine and generally working class. Around the turn of the century, beer was the beverage of choice for most of the working-class male immigrants who worked long hours to serve America's industrial machine. Beer was either a blessing or a curse, depending on your perspective, of the working-class male.

As America prospered and struggled through two world wars, beer-drinking became an accepted part of our culture. Over the years, Budweiser advertising continued to reinforce and perpetuate the masculine identity and user imagery of beer.

Right from the beginning Adolphus Busch seemed to have a genius for advertising and promotion. He intuitively understood the power of associating appropriate symbols and imagery with the Anheuser-Busch Brewery and the Budweiser Brand. Three major themes underlie most of the advertising and symbolism:

- quality heritage
- a sense of male identity
- patriotism

One of the most famous early Anheuser-Busch advertisements was "Custer's Last Fight." The advertisement was based on a painting commissioned by Adolphus Busch, and "it depicted the last few moments of the savage battle between the doomed fire snorting cavalry general and the Indians in the valley of the Little Big Horn River" (Krebs, 1953, p. 329). The picture, often displayed in tavern windows, was said to have almost a magnetic effect on people. This advertisement was based on the Warrior archetype, one of the earliest successful uses of the Warrior archetype in beer advertising.

Through the years, Budweiser advertising increasingly made use of appealing male imagery based on the Warrior, which as Chapter 4 explained, is the dominant male archetype in most cultures. One of the most memorable Budweiser campaigns was the "This Bud's for You" campaign (launched in 1979), which recognized and celebrated the heretofore unsung efforts of the blue-collar/working-class Warrior—the guy who struggles every day to put food on his family's table. This campaign was Anheuser-Busch's response to the Miller's "Welcome to Miller Time" campaign, which together with Philip Morris's marketing clout, had increased Miller Beer's market share to the point of threatening to overtake Budweiser. The campaign successfully beat back Miller's challenge, and it endured well into the 1980s. Many memorable commercials came out of this campaign, but one especially outstanding example was entitled "Cvolski."

Cvolski Commercial

The Cvolski commercial is a mythological gem (mythologem). It opens in a dark, forboding union hall, where some official is calling out the names of men who are being assigned to a construction job. The union official calls out "Cvolski," but he has trouble pronouncing it. Young Cvolski steps forward and respectfully, but proudly, corrects the pronunciation. The commercial then cuts to the young man on the job. We see that he is determined to do his best, but he is a little nervous. We see him drop his toolbox while his fellow workers look on disapprovingly, wondering if this guy is going to make it. Then we see him meticulously finishing off a staircase. He has proven himself. He has proven that he really is up to the job, and at the end of the commercial the guys acknowledge that he has passed muster by inviting him to join them in having a beer.

The Cvolski commercial is typical of the kind of advertising that helped to build the Budweiser brand mythology. It is a complex commercial that reaches viewers on a number of different levels. On one level, the advertisement represents a distinctly male sensibility: A guy has to prove that he has what it takes to make it in a man's world. Again, acceptance into the male world is an important aspect of maleness, a male ritual and rite of passage.

On another level the Cvolski commercial celebrates the blue-collar worker (Warrior), the unsung hero who "makes America work." The commercial provides some sorely needed recognition for all those nameless guys out there doing the thankless jobs that keep our country running. At the same time the commercial reminds us of Budweiser's quality heritage and its "crisp, clean taste" supported by its unique "beechwood aging process."

On yet another level, the commercial celebrates America. Cvolski reenacts the mythology that built America, a mythology that said "Give me your tired, your hungry, and your poor." This blue-collar American mythology promises working-class people that America is the land of opportunity, a place where everyone who is willing to work hard has a chance to succeed. The United States is a nation of immigrants, and there is a little bit of Cvolski in every one of us.

Step 5: Keeping a Successful Brand Mythology in Sync with Its Consumers

The core values (Budweiser's quality heritage, a sense of male identity, and patriotism) and the images and symbols (the Clydesdales, eagle, and so on) that convey the Budweiser brand mythology continue to make Budweiser a powerful, enduring brand. Budweiser has built a powerful brand mythology that has worked to provide male beer drinkers with a badge, a sense of masculinity created around the Warrior archetype. However, like everything else in our complex, modern world, male mythologies are becoming more diverse and more complex. A male mythology based single-mindedly on the Warrior archetype is just too stereotypical for today's males. Consequently, Budweiser has evolved its brand mythology to reflect the changes occurring among today's males. To be sure, the core of the Budweiser brand mythology is still based on the Warrior, but it is a more complex image.

Budweiser commercials now acknowledge other aspects of masculinity, focusing on the joys of becoming a new father and the tender side of the father-son relationship. We also see women in beer commercials being portrayed with much more respect and recognition. This, too, is a reflection of the new sensitivity among today's males as exemplified by their willingness to be more involved with their children and in their increased recognition and respect for women. Beginning in the 1980s, advertising researchers began to hear more beer drinkers complain about advertising that was demeaning to women or portrayed women as "bimbos." The challenge for the 1990s and beyond will be to continue to help the Budweiser brand mythology evolve, to keep it contemporary and in synch with changing male values and sensibilities.

• • •
Advertising: Still the Most Powerful Tool for Building and Maintaining Strong, Enduring Brands

There has been a lot of press lately about the "decline of advertising," but advertising is still the most powerful tool advertisers have for building and maintaining brands.

Advertising can persuade and increase short-term sales, but that is only half of its power. The other factor in advertising's clout lies in its unique ability to build and maintain strong, enduring brands. Remember, a brand is a perceptual entity that exists in the consumer's mind. Advertising provides a powerful vehicle for accessing the consumer's mind to create an appropriate perceptual inventory of imagery, associations, and feelings for a brand.

Advertising builds brands by wrapping products in our dreams and fantasies, by mythologizing them. Advertising builds brands by humanizing products and personifying them with distinct identities, personalities, and sensibilities that reflect our own. In this way, advertising makes it possible for the consumer to form an emotional bond with your brand.

Work wisely with the power that mythology in advertising affords your products.

References
• • • • • • • • • • •

Anderson, Sherwood, 1992. "The Night I Became the Son of My Father," in *Fathers, Sons & Daughters*, Los Angeles: Jeremy P. Tarcher, Inc.

Bachelard, Gaston, 1983. *Water and Dreams,* Trans. Edith Farrell, Dallas: The Pegasus Foundation.

Bachofen, J.J., 1992. *Myth, Religion and Mother Right, Selected Writings of J.J. Bachofen*, Trans. Ralph Manheim, Preface by George Boas and Introduction by Joseph Campbell, Princeton, New Jersey: Princeton University Press.

Baring, Anne and Jules Cashford, 1991. *The Myth of The Goddess*, New York & London: Arkana Viking.

Barthes, Roland, 1957. *Mythologies*, New York: The Noonday Press.

Berendt, John, Feb. 1993. "A Few Words About Balls," Esquire Magazine.

Bloom, Allan, 1987. *The Closing of The American Mind*, New York: Simon and Schuster.

Bly, Robert, 1990. "The Hunger for the King in a Time with No Father," in *Fathers and Mothers*, Dallas, Texas: Spring Publications, Inc. 1992. *Iron John*, New York: Vintage Books.

Bovee, Cortland L. and William F. Arens, 1986. *Contemporary Advertising*, 2nd ed., Homewood, Illinois: Irwin.

Burton, Richard F., 1987. *The Book of The Sword*, New York: Dover Publications.

Caminiti, Susan, 1992. "The Payoff From A Good Reputation," Fortune Magazine, Feb. 10.

Campbell, Joseph, 1968. *The Hero With A Thousand Faces,* Princeton, New Jersey: Princeton University Press.

_____ 1988. *The Power Of Myth,* New York: Doubleday.

Carter, Betty, 1992. "Fathers and Daughters," in *Fathers, Sons & Daughters*, Los Angeles: Jeremy P. Tarcher, Inc.

Cellini, Benevenuto, 1927. The *Autobiography of Benevenuto Cellini*, Trans. John Addington Symonds, New York: Garden City Publishing Co.

Cornfeld, Betty, and Owen Edwards, 1983. *Quintessence*, New York: Crown Publishers, Inc.

Dichter, Ernest, 1960. *The Strategy Of Desire*, New York: Doubleday & Co.

Dowd, Maureen, Oct. 10, 1992. "Of Knights and Presidents: Race of Mythic Proportions," *New York Times*, Downing, Christine, Editor, 1991. *Mirrors of The Self*, Los Angeles: Jeremy P. Tarcher, Inc.

Eisler, Riane, 1988. *The Chalice and the Blade*, Harper: Francisco.

Emerson, Ralph Waldo, 1955. *The Oxford Dictionary of Quotations*, 2nd Edition, London: Oxford University Press.

Erikson, Erik H., 1968. Identity Youth and Crisis, New York: W.W. Norton & Co.

Estes, Clarissa Pinkola, 1992.*Women Who Run with the Wolves*, New York: Ballantine Books.

Feig, Barry, Jan. 27, 1986. "Products Need Share of Heart," *Advertising Age*.

Festinger, Leon, 1957. *A Theory of Cognitive Dissonance*, Evanston, Ill.: Row Peterson.

Fields, Rick, 1991. *The Code of the Warrior*, New York: Harper Perrenial.

Flint, Peter B., May 7, 1992, Pg. A1. "Marlene Dietrich, 90, Symbol of Glamour, Dies," *New York Times*.

Frymer-Kensky, Tikva, 1992. *In the Wake of the Goddesses*, New York: The Free Press.

Gilligan, Carol, 1982. *In a Different Voice*, Cambridge, Massachusetts and London, England: Harvard University Press.

Gimbutas, Marija, 1989. *The Language of the Goddess*, San Francisco: Harper & Row.

Grof, Stanisloav, and Joan Halifax, 1977. *The Human Encounter with Death*, New York: E..P. Dutton.

Grof, Stanislav, with Hal Zina Bennet, 1992. *The Holotropic Mind*, San Francisco: Harper.

Haber, R.N., and R.B. Haber, 1964. "Eidetic Imagery: I. Frequency," *Perceptual and Motor Skills*, 19.

Haley, Russel I., 1984. "Benefit Segmentation—20 Years Later," *The Journal of Consumer Marketing*, Vol. I.

Hall, Nor, 1980. *The Moon and the Virgin*, New York: Harper and Row.

Hamilton, Edith, 1969. *Mythology*, New York: Mentor Book.

Harding, M. Esther, 1971. *Woman's Mysteries*, Boston & Shaftesbury: Shambhala Publications, Inc.

Hawthorne, Nathaniel, 1937. "The Snow-Image," *The Complete Novels and Selected Tales of Nathaniel Hawthorne*, New York: Random House, Inc.

Heisig, James W., 1989. "The Mystique of the Nonrational," *Archetypal Process*, Ed. David Ray Griffin, Evanston, Ill.: Northwestern University Press.

Hill, Gareth S., 1992. *Masculine and Feminine*, Boston & London: Shambhala Publications, Inc.

Hillman, James, 1990. "On Senex Consciousness," in *Fathers and Mothers*, Dallas, Texas: Spring Publications, Inc.

_____ 1990. "The Great Mother's Son, Her Hero, and Puer," in *Fathers and Mothers*, Ed. Patricia Berry, Dallas,Texas: Spring Publications, Inc.

Holmes, Richard, 1990. *Coleridge: Early Visions*, New York: Viking.

Homer, 1962. *The Odyssey*, Trans. George Herbert, Ed. Howard Porter, New York: Bantam Books.

Jamieson, Kathleen, 1992. *Packaging The Presidency*, 2nd Ed., New York and Oxford: Oxford University Press.

Jung, C. G., 1933. *Modern Man in Search of a Soul*, San Diego, New York, London: HBJ Book, Harcourt Brace Jovanovich.

Jung, C. G., 1964. *Man and His Symbols*, New York: Doubleday.

_____ 1968. *The Archetypes and the Collective Unconscious*, Princeton, New Jersey: Princeton University Press, Bollingen Series, XX.

_____ 1983. *Alchemical Studies,* Trans. R. F. C. Hull,Princeton, New Jersey: Princeton University Press, Bollingen Series XX.

_____ 1985. *Practice of Psychotherapy*, Trans. R. F. C. Hull, Princeton, New Jersey: Princeton University Press.

_____ 1989. edited and recorded by Aniela Jaffe, *Memoires, Dreams, Reflections*, New York Vintage Books.

_____ 1990. *Dreams,* Trans. R.F.C. Hull, Princeton, New Jersey: Princeton University Press.

_____ 1990. *Symbols of Transformation*, 2nd Ed., Princeton, New Jersey: Princeton University Press, Bolligen Series, XX.

Jung, C. G., and C. Kerenyi, 1949. *Essays on a Science of Mythology*, Princeton, New Jersey: Princeton University Press, Bollingen Series XXII.

Jung, Emma, 1957. *Animus and Anima,* Dallas, Texas: Spring Publications, Inc.

Keen, Sam, 1991. *Fire In The Belly*, New York: Bantam Books.

Kiley, Dan, 1983. *Peter Pan Syndrome,* New York: Dodd Mead & Co.

Kors, Alan C., & Edward Peters, 1976. *Witchcraft in Europe*, Philadelphia: University of Pennsylvania Press.

Krebs, Roland, in collaboration with Percy J. Orthwein, 1953. *Making Friends in Our Business*, USA: Anheuser Busch/Cunio Press, Inc.

Larsen, Stephen, 1990. *The Mythic Imagination*, New York: Bantam Books.

Lavigne, Yves Lavigne, 1987. *Hell's Angels*, New York: Carol Publishing Group.

Ledbetter, T. Mark, 1991. "Sons and Fathers: Or Why Son Is a Verb," in *Mirrors of the Self*, Ed. Christine Downing, Los Angeles: Jeremy P. Tarcher, Inc.

Luke, Helen M., 1991. "Mothers and Daughters: A Mythological Perspective," in *Mirrors of the Self*, Los Angeles: Jeremy P. Tarcher, Inc.

Manchester, William, 1979. *American Caesar*, New York: Dell Publishing, Inc.

———— 1980. *Goodbye Darkness*, Boston, Toronto: Little, Brown & Co.

Manning, Aubrey, 1989. "The Genetic Bases of Agression," *Aggression and War: Their Biological and Social Basis*, Eds. Jo Groebel and Robert A. Hinde, Cambridge: Cambridge University Press.

Martineau, Pierre, 1957. *Motivation In Advertising*, New York: McGraw Hill.

Matarasso, P.M., 1969. Trans., *The Quest of the Holy Grail*, London: Penguin Books.

May, Rollo, 1991. *The Cry for Myth*, New York: W.W. Norton & Co.

Melville, Herman, 1986. *Moby Dick*, Ed. Harold Beaver, London: Penguin Books.

Miedzian, Myriam, 1991. Boys *Will Be Boys*, New York: Doubleday.

Miles, Michael, 1992. 4 A's Advertisement, *New York Times,* Nov. 24, A 16.

Moore, Robert L., 1989. "Psychocosmetics: A Jungian Response," *Archetypal Process*, Ed. David Ray Griffin, Evanston, Ill.: Northwestern University Press.

Morgan, Robin, 1989. *The Demon Lover*, New York and London: W.W. Norton & Co.

Murdoch, Maureen, 1990. *The Heroine's Journey*, Boston & London: Shambhala Publications, Inc.

Neumann, Erich, 1991. *The Great Mother*, Trans. Ralph Manheim, Princeton, New Jersey: Princeton University Press.

———— 1970. *The Origins and History of Consciousness*, Trans. R. F. C. Hull, Foreward by C.G. Jung, Princeton, New Jersey: Princeton University Press.

———— 1990. "On the Moon and Matriarchal Consciousness," *Fathers and Mothers*, Ed. Patricia Berry, Dallas, Texas: Spring Publications, Inc.

Nichols, Sallie, 1991. *Jung and Tarot: An Archetyal Journey*, Intro. Laurens van der Post, York Beach, Maine: Samuel Weiser, Inc.

Nietzche, Friedrich, "Human, All-Too-Human," Ed. Walther Kaumann, *The Portable Nietzsche*, New York: The Viking Press.

Norris, E.E., Mar. 17, 1975. "Your Surefire Clue to Ad Success; Seek Out the Consumer's Problem," *Advertising Age*.

Ogilvy, David, 1966. *Confessions of an Advertising Man,* New York: Atheneum Publishers.

Packard, Vance, 1957. *The Hidden Persuaders,* New York: David McKay Co., Inc.

Paglia, Camille, 1990. *Sexual Personae*, London & New Haven: Yale University Press.

———— 1992. *Sex, Art, and American Culture*, New York: Vintage Books.

Pearson, Carol S., 1989. *The Hero Within*, San Francisco: Harper San Francisco.

———— 1991. *Awakening The Heroes Within*, San Francisco: Harper San Francisco.

Peterson, Richard F., 1982. *William Butler Yeats*, Boston: Twayne Publishers.

Printer's Ink, January 31, 1918.

Reeves, Rosser, 1961. *Reality in Advertising*, New York: Alfred A. Knopf, Inc.

Rice, Edward, 1991. *Captain Sir Richard Francis Burton*, New York: Harper Perennial.

Rotundo, E. Anthony, 1985. "American Fatherhood," *American Behavioral Scientist*, Vol. 29, No. 1, September/October.

Sacharow, Stanley, 1982. *Symbols of Trade,* New York: Art Direction Book Company.

Sandage, C. H., and Vernon Fryburger, 1975. *Advertising Theory* and Practice, 9th Ed., Homewood: Ill.: Richard D. Irwin, Inc.

Sellery, J'Nan Morse, 1989. "The Necessity for Symbol and Myth," *Archetypal Process*, Ed., David Ray Griffin, Evanston, Ill.: Northwestern University Press.

Shelly, Mary, 1991. *Frankenstein*, New York: Bantam Books.

Slotnick, Richard, 1992. *Gunfighter Nation*, New York:Atheneum.

Solomon, Jolie, Aug. 16, 1985. "Want Mr. Right? He's in Aisle Two with the Other Cleaning Products," *The Wall Street Journal*.

Trout, Jack, and Al Ries, 1972. "The Positioning Era Cometh," *Advertising Age*, April 24.

Trout, Jack, and Al Ries, 1981. *Positioning: the Battle for your Mind*, New York: McGraw-Hill.

Vamos, Mark N., Apr. 1, 1985. "New Life For Madison Avenue's Old Time Stars," *Business Week*.

Vitale, Augusto, 1990. "The Archetype of Saturn or the Transformation of the Father," in *Fathers and Mothers,* Dallas, Texas: Spring Publications, Inc.

Von Franz, Marie-Louise, 1981. *Puer Aeternus*, Santa Monica, Calif.: Sigo Press.

Von Goethe, Johann Wolfgang, 1952. *Faust*, Chicago, London, Toronto, Geneva: William Benton Publisher.

Waldo, Myra, 1958. *Beer and Good Food,* Garden City New York: Doubleday.

Warner, Marina, 1983. *Alone of All Her Sex,* New York: Vintage Books.

Weilbacher, William M., 1979. *Advertising*, New York: MacMillan Publishing Co., Inc.

Windrow, Martin, and Richard Hook, 1989. *The Horse Soldier,* Oxford University Press.

Wyly, John, 1989. *The Phallic Quest*, Toronto, Canada: Inner City Books.

Zweig, Connie, 1991. "The Conscious Feminine: Birth of a New Archetype," in *Mirrors of the Self*, Ed. Christine Downing, Los Angeles: Jeremy P. Tarcher, Inc.

Index

A

Abraham, 235
Absentee parent, 91
Achievers, 172
Actualizers, 172
Ad hoc product/service attributes, 14
Adam, 72, 105
Adam and Eve, 64
  see Eve
Advertising
  see Brand-building, Gender-specific,
    Image
  archetype, 161
  brand, 5
  budget, 197
  cost, 25
  execution, 160, 217-225
    center, 212-214
    steps, 212-218
  message, 55, 159, 160, 163
    conveying factors, 199
  mythmaking, 49-51
  mythology, 50, 55, 59, 160, 217
    building brand mythology, 208-217
  positioning
    examples, 221-226
    role, 198-202
  power, 1
  role, 24-25, 50
  storied form, 31
  strategy, 163
    see Individual
  unique power, 207-208
Affiliative feeling, 126

Alchemy, 57
Amazon archetype, 133
Amazonian character, 113
Amazonism, 77-78
American
  Express Traveler's checks, 141
  psyche, 157
Analogic approach, 53, 57-59
Anderson, Sherwood, 93-95
Androcentric values, 131
Anheuser Busch, 195, 207
  Eagle, 260-263
Anima, *see* Jung
Anthropology, 1
Apparitions, 40, 42
Appeal, 243-245
Approach/avoidance situation, 179
Appropriateness, 248-250
Archaic
  foundations, 41
  remnants, 36
Archetypal
  dream, 38
  Feminine, 67
  figures, 42
  image, 28, 35, 37-39, 54
  imagery, 37, 40, 121
    origin, 122
  journey, 75-78
  level, 66
  Lilith character, 72
  patterns, 48
    see Human experience
  stages, 37

symbols, 36
values, 76
Warrior-Hero, 76
Archetypes, 35-38, 41, 42, 54, 59, 61,
    113, 224
    see Advertising, Amazon, Bipolar, Bi-
        valent, Caregiving, Child, Cow-
        boy-Hero, Dynamic, Feminine,
        Great Father, Great Mother,
        Maiden, Maiden/Seductress,
        Maiden/Virgin, Mother, Peter
        Pan, Puer, Senex, Transcen-
        dent, Virgin/Harlot, Vir-
        gin/Maiden, Warrior,
        Warrior-Hero
    power, 160
Arens, William F., 195
Art, 58
Arthurian mythology, 139
Assets, see Tangible
Associations, 8, 10, 20, 27, 163
    see Latent
Associative learning, 16
Attributes, 6, 11, 23
    see Ad hoc, Brand, Generic, Mytholo-
        gized, Physical product, Prod-
        uct, Product/service
Audience share, 25
Aunt Jemima, 124, 126-128
Automatic writing, 47
Avis, 215
Awareness, 243
    see Consumer

B
Bachelard, Gaston, 236
Bachofen, Johann Jakob, 34, 57, 58,
    60, 61, 77, 81, 86, 87, 103, 104,
    225
Backer, Bill, 172
Backer & Spielvogel Advertising, 172
Bailey's Irish Cream, 231
Barbie, 69
Baring, Ann, 32-33, 105, 106

Barthes, Roland, 30
Bates (Ted) Advertising, 15
BBD&O, 157, 209
Beaver, Harold, 33, 44
Behavioral
    reality, 15
    sciences, 1
Belief(s), 19, 20, 47, 152
    dynamics, 174-175
    map, 174
    structure, 174
Believers, 172
Ben & Jerry's Homemade, Inc., 152-
    154
Benefits
    see Brand, Emotional/psychological,
        Physical product, Product, Prod-
        uct/service, Spiritual
    approach, 204
Bennigan's, 182
Berbach, Bill, 19
Berendt, John, 116
Beserkis, 111
Big dreams, 40
BIP, see Brand Identity Profile
Bipolar archetype, 92
Bivalent archetype, 92
Bloom, Allan, 83
Bly, Robert, 91, 96, 117
BMW, 174
Bond, 66, 90
    see Emotional
Bounty Candy Bars, see M&M
Bovee, Cortland L., 195
Brand, 3, 5-27, 49
    see Advertising, Marines, Navy, New
        brand
    attributes, 10, 122
    benefits, 122
    character, 68
    concept, 11-25
    definition, 6-10
    development, 23
    essence, 17

execution, 189-226
heritage, 216-217
identity/image, 18
image, 11, 18-22
    strategy, user image comparison,
        207-208
latent product mythology compari-
    son, 10
loyalty, 18, 27
managers, 27
message, 189-226
personality, 11, 17-20, 27
positioning, 11, 23-25, 163, 189-232
product aspect, 6-8
snapshot, 235-236
soul, 11, 17
space, 49
understanding, 186-188
Brand identity, 18-22, 17
    profile (BIP), 160, 186-188, 233-235
    worth, 21-22
Brand mythology, 4, 8-10, 16, 23, 24,
    27, 50, 52, 54, 84, 121-158
    see Advertising mythology, Danger-
        ous, Marlboro, Revamped
    analysis, 121-123
    broader scale, 152-158
    building, 159-263
        information/insight/ideas, 163-187
    evaluating, 245-250
    guarding, 244-245
    level functioning, 122-123
    maintaining, 159-263
    typology, 123
    uncovering/understanding, 234-237,
        247, 254-257
Brand-building advertising, 27, 159
Branding, 20-21
Brandness, 5
Breck Girl(s), 124, 128-129
Bud Man, 54, 56, 124, 176, 207
Budweiser, 15, 20, 30, 176, 187, 197,
    198, 201, 233, 258-269
    see Clydesdales

male identity, managing, 258-269
Budweiser Man, 124
Burnett, Leo, 6
    Agency, 205
Burton, Richard F., 65, 139, 141
Burnett, Leo, 143
Buyout, see Leveraged

C
Calkens, Ernest, 205
Calvin Klein, 201
    Jeans, 131-132
Campbell, Joseph, 31-34, 38, 44, 48,
    49, 57, 58, 96, 97, 109
Campbell's Soup, 16-19, 126, n214,
    229-245
    see Soup
Carasso, Isaac, 223
Caregiving archetype, 76
Carter, Betty, 99
Cashford, Jules, 32-33, 105, 106
Catch-22, 119
Catherine the Great, 76
Cellini, Benevenuto, 40
Challenge, 97
Child archetype, 75
Charlie Perfume, 132, 206
Clairol, 74
Classical mythology, 57
Clean, Mr., 141-143, 214
Clinton campaign, 158
Clydesdales, 254-255
Coca-Cola, 50, 51, 117, 256
    Girl, 129
Cognitive
    dissonance, 19
    framework, 193
    functioning, 19
    structure, 19
Cohen, Ben, 153
Coke, 217
Coleridge, Samuel Taylor, 46
Colgate, 197
Collective unconscious, 35

Communal society, 87
Communicating arts, 1
Communication
  storied form, 31
Company mythology, 152, 153
Competition, 21, 26
Component, see Conscious, Percep-
    tual, Product, Unconscious
Concept, see Brand
Conscious, 59
  component, 34
  psyche, 57
Consciousness, 35, 41, 59, 61
    see Ego-consciousness, Human,
      Inner, Matriarchal, Nonordin-
      ary, Patriarchal
Consistency, 203-204, 225-226
Consonance, 19
Consumer, 3, 15, 18, 50, 74, 153
  see Target
  attention, 123
  awareness threshold, 6
  desires, 165
  identity needs, 56
  insight, 163, 223-225
  mind, 5, 8, 10, 16, 21, 23-25, 50,
      164, 190-191, 193, 197-202,
      247-248
  motivation, 17, 242
  need, 14, 165
  psyche, 49
  research, 160, 214-215
  understanding, 167-185
    examples, 176-178, 180-183
  values, 1, 8
  wants, 165
Consumerism, 48, 49
Content analysis, 183-184
Copernicus, 35
Core values, 17
Corporate
  identity, 206
  mythology, 152
Corporation, mythologization, 152-154

Couponing, 27
Cowboy, see Gunslinger, Warrior-Cow-
    boy
Cowboy-Hero archetype, 76
Crazy Horse, 112
Creation myth, 105
Creative
  force, see Unconscious psyche
  platform, development, 212
  power, 80
Credibility, 245
Crest, 197
Crocker, Betty, 68, 69, 124, 126
Crocker, William G., 124
Cross-dressing, 72
Crystal Light, 133
Cultural
  identities, 8
  myth(s), shaping, 59-60
  mythology, 52, 54, 122, 154, 178,
    217
  stereotype, 75
  values, 50
Culture
  see Male, Matriarchal, Patriarchal,
    Primitive, Warrior
  value, 47
Cvolski commercial, 262-263

D
Dangerous brand mythology, 252
Dannon Yogurt, 10, 221-223
D'Arcy, Maisius, Benton & Bowles, 174
Darwin, 35
Daughter, see Father, Mother
Davidson, Arthur, 246
Davis, R.T., 128
Davis Milling Company, 128
Dawn, 197
Daydream(s), 44, 45
Della Femina Travisano, 157
Demographics, 167-168
Demonic masculine, 250
Dichter, Ernest, 17, 173

Dietrich, Marlene, 72
Dionysian
  Great Mother, 102
  rites, 113
Dissonance, *see* Cognitive
Divine, 46, 47
Don Juanism, 92
Doyle Dane Bernbach, 156
Dream(s), 1, 41, 42, 44, 50
  see Archetypal, Big, Daydream, Idio-
    syncratic, Night
  imagery, 39
Dundes, Alan, 155
Dusenbery, Phil, 157
Dynamic feminine, 69-70
  maiden archetype, 70-74
  negative aspects, 70-74
Dynamic masculine, 100-107

E
Earth, *see* Mother
Earth Mother, 82
  Goddess, 66
Earth Spirit, 42
Eidetic image, 41, 45
Ego, 35, 55
Ego-consciousness, 85
Eisler, Riane, 118
Electronic
  media, 49
  space, 49
Emerson, Ralph Waldo, 5
Emotion(s), 24
Emotional
  benefits, 23
    see Physical/emotional
  bond, 21, 27, 50, 51, 161
  positioning, 25
Emotional/psycholgical
  benefits, 11, 16-17, 25, 123, 191,
    198, 202
  strategy, 208-209
  level, 25, 174
  motivation, 179

positioning, 24, 198
Enjoli, 132-133
Enlightenment, 34
Entrepreneurs, 5
Erikson, Erik, 167
Essences, 35
  see Soul
Estes, Clarissa Pinkola, 65
Ethnographic approach/ethnography,
  170-171
Eurocentrism, 29
Eve, 65, 105
  see Adam
Evil spirit, 63
Ewing, Abby, 69
Experience, *see* Human, Mythological,
  Mythopoeic, Psychological, Spiri-
  tual, Visionary
Experiencers, 172
Explanation, storied form, 31

F
Fantasy, 1, 8, 50
  see Symbolic
Farm mythology, 147
Father
  see Great Father, Terrible
  daughter, 98-99
  figures, *see* Media
    absence, 91-92
  Heaven, 87, 88
  Nature, 143-146
  quest, 97-99
Fathers and sons, 92-93
Fatherhood, 86, 88
  see Modern, Patriarchal
Father-son relationship, 90
Feelings, 3, 8, 10, 16, 20, 24, 27, 159,
  163
  see Affiliative
Feig, Barry, 208
Female
  see Male
  character, 129

imagery, 133
mythology, 52, 53, 55-84, 85, 124
  newly emerging, 83-84
sexuality, 64, 65, 81, 131
Warrior, 77, 110
Femaleness, 78, 103
Feminine
  see Archetypal, Dynamic, Static
  archetype, 75-76, 82
  embracing, 78, 80
  images/symbols, 242
  mythology, 81, 82, 84
  side, 119
  space, 83
  stereotype, 133
  values, 78
Femininity, 59, 69, 83, 133
  aspects, 59-60
Femme fatale, 72, 74
Festinger, Leon, 19
Fiction, see Narrative, Symbolic
Folger's Coffee, 11, 14
Foote, Cone, and Belding, 74
Ford (Motor Company), 22
Form, 23, 189
Formal mythology, 31
Fragmentation, see Media
Freud, Sigmund, 35, 36, 38, 47, 103,
    104, 235
Fryburger, Vernon, 23, 189, 194
Frymer-Kensky, Tikva, 63
Fulfillers, 172
Fundamental male role, 100-105

G
Gaia, 61, 66, 87
Gender, 113
  identity, 53, 55-57, 59
  specific, 53, 55
    advertisement, 56
General Mills, 68, 124
Generic product attributes, 11, 14
Ghosts, 47
Gilligan, Carol, 103

God, see Male, Patriarchal, Senex,
    Sky, Warrior-Hero
Goddess, 68, 87, 106
  see Great, Great Mother, Irrepress-
      ible, Matriarchal, Moon,
      Mother, Paleolithic
  mythology, 106
Goethe, 42, 45
Goodwrench, Mr., 134, 136
Great Container, 67
Great Depression, 246
Great Father, 86-88, 122, 155
  archetype, 90, 133-134, 136
Great Goddess, 113
Great Mother, 38, 60, 61, 66-68, 74,
    85, 92, 103, 113, 122, 124, 126,
    132, 145, 155, 231, 242
  see Dionysian
  archetype, 59-66, 69, 241
  Goddess, 136
Great Mother/Aunt, 128
Great Spirit, 88
Green, Nancy, 128
Greenfield, Jerry, 153
Grof, Stanislav, 42, 45
Gunslinger, 136
  see Warrior-Gunslinger
  Cowboy, 137

H
Haber and Haber, 41
Haeterism, 81
Haley, Russell, 211, 213
Hall, Nor, 238
Hallett, Jeff, 21, 184
Hallmark, 122, 215
  Cards, 151
Hamilton, Edith, 29, 30, 87
Hara Kiri, 112
Harding, M. Esther, 34, 63, 68, 82,
    243, 244
Hari, Mata, 72
Harley, William, 251
Harley-Davidson, 233, 250-257

Harlot, 131-132
  see Virgin/Harlot
Hathaway Shirt Man, 140, 141
Heart, see Share
Heineken, 20
Heisig, James, 30, 43
Heritage, 11, 231-232
  see Brand
Hero
  see Cowboy-Hero, Warrior-Hero
Hero-Warrior, 106
Heston, William, 134
Hidden Valley salad dressing, 122, 147-
  148
Hill, Gareth, 60
Hillman, James, 86, 92
Hoka Hey, 112-115
Holmes, Richard, 46
Holotropic breathing, 42, 45
Homer, 107
Hook, Richard, 255
Horney, Karen, 104
Human
  consciousness, 36
  experience, archetypal patterns, 34
  psyche, 29, 34, 110
  soul, 28, 29
  species, 35
  spirit, 58
  unconscious, 4
Hypnagogic fragment, 45

I

Identity
  see Corporate, Gender, Male, Mascu-
    line
  confusion, 168
Identity/image, see Brand
Idiosyncratic dream, 38
Image, 10, 27, 39, 198
  see Archetypal, Brand, Eidetic, Femi-
    nine, Identity/image, Male,
    Mytho-symbolic, Self-image, Un-
    conscious, Universal, User

advertising, 210-213
Imagery, 3, 8, 19, 20, 28, 57, 163, 201
  see Archetypal, Dream, Female,
    Mytho-symbolic, User, Warrior
Imagination, 45, 58
  see Mythic, Mythopoeic
Individual advertising mythology, 164
Industrial Revolution, 89, 91
Ingredients, 11, 23
Inner consciousness, 44
Insight
  see Brand mythology
  importance, 165-167
Irrepressible goddess, 107

J

Jaffe, Aniela, 39
Jaguar, 22
Jamieson, Kathleen Hall, 156
Jell-O Pudding Pops, 91
Joan of Arc, 76
Jolly Green Giant, 143-146
Jung, Carl, 28, 31, 35-43, 46, 47, 53,
    57, 58, 60, 61, 63, 80, 85, 224,
    225, 240, 242, 255
  anima, 119
Jung, Emma, 80, 82

K

Kant, Immanuel, 30
Keen, Sam, 117
Kennedy, John F., 29
Kentucky Fried Chicken (KFC), 148
Kerenyi, C., 31, 46, 47
Kiley, Dan, 92
Kodak, 122, 150, 151, 215, 220
Kool-Aid, 220
Kosmos, 36

L

Labels, 10
Larsen, Stephen, 45
Larson, Gary, 41
Lasker, Albert, 1

Lasky, Victor, 29
Latent
  association, 16
  mythology, 16
  personal mythology, 154
  product mythology, 6, 221, 222, 227-
      230, 253, 264-267
    brand mythology comparison, 10
    exploring, 238-244
Learning theorists, 16
Ledbetter, T. Mark, 98
Leveraged buyout, 26
Liabilities, 19
Lifestyle, 15, 19, 31, 54, 56
Lilith, see Archetypal
Literature, 58
Little League, 77
Logos, 10
Lone Ranger, 136, 137
  myth, 76
Longevity, 240-241
Louis Rich Cold Cuts, 147
Love, 17
Loyalty, see Brand
LSD, 42
Luke, Helen M., 67
Lunar phase, 86, 87

M
M&M/Mars, 210
  Bounty Candy Bars, 148
MacManus, Theodore F., 211
Macrosegmentation model, 171-172
Madonna, 133, 145
Magician, 141-143
Maiden, 128-129
  see Dynamic, Nymph, Virgin/Maiden
  archetype, 85, 128
Maiden/Seductress archetype, 132
Maiden/Virgin archetype, 69
Male, 64, 75
  character, 114
  god, 107
  identity, 118

  see Budweiser
mythology, 52, 53, 85-120
  projective character, 103
  rites/rituals, disappearance, 95-97
  role, see Fundamental
  sexuality, 114
  Warrior, 64, 78
    culture, emergence, 105-107
    image, 110-112
Male/female
  psyche, 56
  soul, 56
Male-female differences, 81
Maleness, 78, 103, 119
Management, see Women
Managers, see Brand
Manchester, William, 59, 60, 156
Manhood, 96
Manning, Aubrey, 115
Manufacturers, 5, 6, 23, 183, 190
Manufacturing plant, 11
Marines, 25, 60
  see U.S. Marine Corps
  brand, 25
Market, 123
  research, 170
  share, 6, 21, 163, 247-248
Marketers, 21, 183, 212
Marketplace, 23, 246-251
  positioning, 23, 189-190
Marlboro, 211
  brand mythology, 10
  Man, 8, 21, 54, 136-137, 211, 220
Martineau, Pierre, 20
Masculine
  see Demonic, Dynamic, Static
  embracing, 78, 80
  identity, 103
  space, 83
Masculinity, 59, 78, 83, 103, 222
  see Motorcycle
Maslow, Abraham, 171
  Hierarchy of Human Needs, 172
Mass communication, 6

Materialism, 48, 83
Matriarchal
  consciousness, 93
  goddess cultures, 64
  phase, 86
  realm, 61
  societies, 62
Maxwell House 1892 Coffee, 146-147
May, Rollo, 48
Maytag Repairman, 136
McCann Erickson Advertising Agency, 1
McDonald's, 50, 51, 148, 151-152, 198, 199, 211, 212, 223, 226
MCI, 133
Media, 55
  see Electronic
  father figures, 90-97
  fragmentation, 25
  proliferation, 25
Megamergers, 22
Melville, Herman, 33, 44
Merger, 26
Message
  see Advertising
  strategy, 160, 203
Miles, Michael, 27
Military Warrior, 138-141
Miller
  Brewing Company, 5
  Genuine Draft, 16, 197
  Lite, 5, 209
Miller, Arthur, 48
Mills, Donna, 69
Modern fatherhoood, 88-90
Monroe, Marilyn, 69
Moon goddess, 68
Moore, Colin, 148
Morgan, Robin, 112, 118
Morris, Philip, 21, 27
  Companies, 27
Motel 6, 228-230
Mother
  see Earth, Terrible

archetype, 75
daughter, 66-67
Earth, 87, 88
love, 61
Nature, 64, 104, 114, 145
Motherhood, 87
Motivation, see Consumer, Emotional/psychological, Negative, Product, Rational
Motivational research, 172-174
Motivators, 17
Motorcycle
  masculinity, 250-251
  symbolism, 249-250
Mousetrap, 5, 204
  myopia, 6
Mozart, 45
Murdoch, Maureen, 69, 80, 98, 99
Mysterium tremendum et fascinans, 43
Mystical
  force, 28
  states, 35
Mysticism, 47
Myth, 1, 27, 29, 30, 32, 47, 59
  see Creation, Cultural, Lone Ranger, Solar, Vegetative, Warrior, Warrior-Hero
  power, 27
  responsibility, 48-49
Mythic
  event, 38
  imagination, 41
Mythical
  characters, 121-123, 123-146
  moments/situations/themes, 121-123, 150-152
  places, 121-123, 146-149
Mythlessness, 48
Mythmaking, 49, 60
  see Advertising
Mythological
  experience, 28, 31-33, 46-47
  source, 33-34
  figures, 45

realm, 28-51
Mythologization, 14, 30, 49, 152, 207
  see Corporation, Reagan
Mythologized
  attributes, 14
  user image, 15
Mythology, 3, 4, 6, 25, 28, 44, 52-158
  see Advertising, Arthurian, Brand,
      Classical, Company, Corporate,
      Cultural, Farm, Female, Femi-
      nine, Formal, Goddess, Latent,
      Male, Marlboro, Navy, Per-
      sonal, Product, Pure, Warrior,
      Women, World
  definition, 29-34
  importance, 31
  language, 28
  need, 47-48
Mythopoeic
  experience, 32, 33
  imagination, 39, 44
  sources, 57
  visions, 47
Mytho-symbolic
  connection, 238
  icon, 201
  image, 218
  imagery, 3, 4, 121
    origin, 122
  worlds, 49, 50

N
Naisbitt, John, 183, 184
Narcissus, 44
Narrative fiction, see Symbolic
Nature, see Father, Mother
Navy
  see U.S.
  brand, 25
Negative
  motivation, example, 178-179
  perception, 182

Neumann, Erich, 37, 38, 58, 60, 67,
    68, 72, 85, 86, 104, 241, 242,
    243
New brand
  introduction-existing product cate-
      gory, 195-197
  introduction-new product category,
      191-195
  examples, 195-197
New York Telephone, 51
Ney, Ed, 157
Night dream, 45
Nightmares, 39, 44, 45
Nonordinary consciousness, 45
Norris, E.E., 209-211
Numen/numinous, 42
Nymph/Water Maiden, 129, 131

O
Occultism, 47
O'Doul's, 195
Odysseus, 107-115
Ogilvy, David, 18, 140, 211
Ogilvy and Mather, 140, 157
O'Hara, Maureen, 60
Oil of Olay, 56
Olive Garden, 182
Oscar Mayer, 198, 199, 207, 224
Ovid, 97

P
Packaging, 3, 11, 23, 24
Packard, Vance, 237
Paglia, Camille, 46, 69, 74, 81, 82,
    102, 114, 235, 236
Paleolithic
  goddess, 66
  sensibility, 32
Paracelsus, 41
Parent, see Absentee
Passisivity, 70
Paternal love, 61
Paternity, 87
Patriarchal

consciousness, 86, 87, 93
culture, 90, 102
fatherhood, 88
God images, 134
phase, 87
society, 78
Patriarchy, 104
Pearson, Carol S., 75
Penn, Willliam, 134
Pepsi, 217
Perception(s), 15, 16, 19, 159
see Negative, Personality
Perceptual
components, 15-17
entity, 23
inventory, 20
positioning, 23, 194
Personal mythology, 152, 154
see Latent
Personality, 10, 163, 165, 198, 199
see Brand
inventory, 20
perception, 18
Personification, see Product
Perspective, 3-51
Peter Pan syndrome, 92
Peterson, Richard F., 47
Phase, see Lunar, Matriarchal, Patriar-
chal, Solar, Tellurian
Philosopher, 236
Physical
attributes, 21
dimension, 5
product, 5, 10, 16, 24
attributes, 191
benefits, 198
Physical/emotional benefits, balancing,
227-240
Physiological realm, 61
Plato, 35
Poe, Edgar Allen, 46
Polaroid, 209
Polykoff, Shirley, 74
Positioning

see Advertising, Brand, Emotional,
Emotional/psychological, Marketplace, Perceptual
strategy, 214
tools, 224-227
Power, 17, 74, 261
see Advertising, Archetype, Creative
symbol, 181
Presidential candidate, 154-158
Pretechnological Warrior, 110
Pricing, 11, 24
Prima materia, 41
Primitive culture(s), 63, 82
Prizm, 172
Problem-Solution strategy, 215-217
Proctor and Gamble, 141, 197, 220
Product, 3
see Generic, Latent, New brand,
Physical
aspect, see Brand
attributes, 11, 14, 209
benefits, 11, 14-15, 17, 209
strategy, 209-210
choosing, 173
components, 11-15
example, see Consumer
level, 174
motivation, 174
mythology, 6
parity, 5, 25
personification, 17, 18
popularity, 184
proliferation, 25
trends, 184-185
usage, 16, 179-180
Product/service
attributes, 11-15
see Ad hoc
benefit, 11, 14-15
Proliferation, see Media, Product
Promotions, 24, 27
Psyche, see American, Consumer, Conscious, Human, Male/female, Unconscious

Psychic
  content, 17
    see Product
  cosmos, 85
  dimension, 5
  force, 28, 34, 35
  projections, 33
  response, 30
  truth, 41
Psychoanalysis, 58
Psychoanalyst, 66, 80, 92, 103, 241
Psychoanalytic approach, 173
Psychographics, 168-170
Psychological
  benefits, 23
    see Emotional/psychological
  experience, 48
  space, 23, 49
Psychology, 1
Psychosis, 39
Puccini, Giacomo, 45
Puer (aeternus) archetype, 92
Purdue, Frank, 230
Purdue Chickens, 230-231
Pure mythology, 207

Q

Quaker Mill, 134
Quaker Oats
  Company, 128
  Man, 133-134

R

R&C, *see* Rejuvenation
Rational product level motivation, 179
Reagan, Ronald
  mythologization, 154-158
Realized user image, 15
Realm, *see* Matriarchal, Mythological,
    Physiological
Reebok Tennis shoes, 133
Reed, Donna, 59
Reeves, Rosser, 15, 209
Reis, Al, 192

Rejuvenation & contemporization
    (R&C), 214
Relevance, 248-250
Repetition, 225-226
Research, *see* Market
Revamped brand mythology, evaluat-
    ing, 252-253
Rice, Edward, 65
Richardson Group, 228
Riney, Hal, 157
Rites/rituals, *see* Male
Road warrior, 228
Role, *see* Women
Role model, *see* Warrior-Hero
Rolex, 20
Roman, Kenneth, 157
Rotundo, E. Anthony, 88
Rutt, Chris L., 128

S

7-Up Uncola, 215
Saint Paul, 40
Sales, 27, 190
Samurai, 112, 139
Sandage, C.H., 23, 189, 194
Sanka Coffee, 91
Schubert, Franz, 45
Schwartz, Tony, 156
Scope Mouthwash, 165
Scott, Randolph, 60
Seattle (tribal chief), 32
Seductress, *see* Maiden/Seductress
Self, 55
Self-concept, 55
Self-discovery, 109
Self-esteem, 17
Self-image, 15
Self-worth, 69
Sellery, J'Nan Morse, 44
Senex
  archetype, 86, 134
  god, 134
Sensibility, 1, 31, 53, 54, 56, 123,
    131, 152

see Paleolithic
Service(s), 11, 51
  see Product/service
Sexuality, 63, 64, 69
  see Female, Male
  sexism comparison, 74-75
Seymour, Henry, 134
Share, *see* Audience, Market
Share of heart, 161
Shelley, Mary, 45, 46
Showdown, 115-117
Size, 23, 189
Sky cult, 102
Sky god, 64, 105
Social
  trends, 183-184
  value system, 17
Society, *see* Communal, Matriarchal, Patriarchal
Sociology, 1
Soft sell, 205
Solar
  myth, 106
  phase, 86
Son, *see* Father
Soul, 30, 47, 51, 53
  see Brand, Human, Male/female
Soul/essence, 199
Soup, *see* Campbell's, Women
Space, *see* Electronic, Feminine, Masculine, Psychological
Spirit, 43, 51
  see Earth, Evil, Great, Human
Spiritual
  benefits, 48
  experience, 46-47
Spock, Dr., 76-77
Stanford Research Institute, 171
  VALS model, 171-172
Static
  feminine, 60-66
  masculine, 86-88
Stereotype, 124
  see Cultural, Feminine

Storied form, *see* Advertising, Communication, Explanation
Strivers, 172
Stroh's Brewery, 14
Strugglers, 172
Subspecie aeternitatis, 32
Superbowl, 116
Superman, 76, 137
Superwoman, 80, 132
Sword symbolism, 138-140
Swordness, 36
Symbol(s), 5, 8, 10, 27, 47, 58, 155, 218-219
  see Archetypal, Feminine, Power
  canon, 38
  group, 38, 59
Symbolic
  fantasy, 49
  narrative fiction, 30
Symbolism, 3, 28, 57, 58, 207, 263
  see Motorcycle, Sword

T
Takeovers, 22
Tangible assets, 21
Tao, 40
Target consumer, 19, 31, 244
  defining, 167-168
Technology, 54
Teerlink, Richard, 246
Tellurian phase, 86
Terrible
  father, 99
  mother, 66-69, 72, 110
Thomas, Evans, 116
Time (magazine), 177-178
Timex, 20
Transcendent
  archetypes, 36
  ideals, 36
Travisano, Ron, 157
Trend, 183
  see Product, Social
Trout, Jack, 192

Trout and Reis, 192, 210, 215
Tuesday Team, 157

U
Unconscious, 28, 35, 38, 40, 58, 85
  see Collective
  component, 34, 38
  confrontation, 39-43
  image, 46
  psyche, 3, 4, 28, 34-47, 50, 53, 54,
      57, 59
    creative force, 43-46
Unconsciousness, 41-45, 61, 68
Underwood, Charles G., 128
Unique selling proposition (USP), 15,
    203-205
Universal
  event, 38
  forms, 35
  image, 35, 47, 54
  patterns, 48, 54
Universality, 53
U.S. Air Force, 25
U.S. Marine Corps, 138-141
  see Marines
U.S. Navy, 25
Usage, 6, 11
  see Product
User image, 11, 15-16
  see Mythologized, Realized
  brand image strategy comparison,
      207-208
User imagery, 56, 244
USP, see Unique selling proposition

V
VALS, see Stanford
Values, 1, 15, 19, 20, 31, 47, 54, 56,
    123, 152
  see Androcentric, Archetypal, Con-
      sumer, Core, Cultural, Culture,
      Feminine, Social, Warrior-Hero
Vegetative myth, 145
Venus of Willendorf, 66

Virgin
  see Maiden/Virgin
  Mary, 70, 107
  Mother Mary, 237
Virgin/Harlot
  archetype, 70
  dichotomy, 131
Virginia Slims, 123, 132-133
Virgin/Maiden, 69-70
  archetype, 70
Vision(s), 40, 42
  see Mythopoeic
Visionary experience, 40
Vitale, Augusto, 99
Viva Towel, 217
Volkswagon
  Beetle, 19
  Rabbit, 19
Von Franz, Marie Louise, 92

W
Wall Street Warrior, 141
Warner, Marina, 70, 107
Warrior
  see Female, Hero-Warrior, Male, Mili-
      tary, Pretechnological, Road,
      Wall Street, Western, Wild West
  archetype, 36, 59, 75, 84, 110, 117,
      122, 132, 218
  culture, 81, 115, 155
  epic, 108
  imagery, 133
  myth, 109
  mythology, 25
  outmoded, 117-120
  skills, 116
  virtues, 75
  world, 115
  worship, 118
Warrior-Cowboy mentality, 76
Warrior-Gunslinger, 137
Warrior-Hero, 100-107, 136
  see Archetypal
  archetype, 76, 137

amplification, 107-115
god, 88
myth, 108
women, 76
role models, 76
values, 76
Wayne, John, 59
Weilbacher, William M., 165
Weller, Jim, 157
Wells, William, 123
Werthmueler, Lina, 103
Western Warrior, 136-137
White Rock
Girl, 129, 131
Mineral Springs Company, 131
Wild West Warrior, 136
Williams, Marco, 96
Windrow, Martin, 255
Windrow and Hook, 255
Women
changing role, 78-83
management, 133
new mythology search, 80-83

soup
historical connection, 238-240
symbolic connection, 240-241
Wonder Bread, 204
Woodman, Marion, 83
World mythology, 53
World War II, 89-90
Wranglers, 20
Wyly, James, 117, 118

X
Xerox, 216

Y
Yankelovich, 183
Yeats, William Butler, 47
Yin/yang, 52
Young & Rubicam, 157
Advertising, 180

Z
Zweig, Connie, 82, 83

About the Publisher

PROBUS PUBLISHING COMPANY

Probus Publishing Company fills the informational needs of today's business professional by publishing authoritative, quality books on timely and relevant topics, including:

- Investing
- Futures/Options Trading
- Banking
- Finance
- Marketing and Sales
- Manufacturing and Project Management
- Personal Finance, Real Estate, Insurance and Estate Planning
- Entrepreneurship
- Management

Probus books are available at quantity discounts when purchased for business, educational or sales promotional use. For more information, please call the Director, Corporate/Institutional Sales at 1-800-998-4644, or write:

Director, Corporate/Institutional Sales
Probus Publishing Company
1925 N. Clybourn Avenue
Chicago, Illinois 60614
FAX (312) 868-6250